STUDIES IN THE AṢṬASĀHASRIKĀ PRAJÑĀPĀRAMITĀ AND OTHER ESSAYS

STUDIES IN THE AṢṬASĀHASRIKĀ PRAJÑĀPĀRAMITĀ AND OTHER ESSAYS

LINNART MÄLL

MOTILAL BANARSIDASS PUBLISHERS
PRIVATE LIMITED • DELHI

First Indian Edition: Delhi, 2005
First Edition: Tartu, 2003

ISBN: 81-208-2747-3

MOTILAL BANARSIDASS
41 U.A. Bungalow Road, Jawahar Nagar, Delhi 110 007
8 Mahalaxmi Chamber, 22 Bhulabhai Desai Road, Mumbai 400 026
236, 9th Main III Block, Jayanagar, Bangalore 560 011
203 Royapettah High Road, Mylapore, Chennai 600 004
Sanas Plaza, 1302 Baji Rao Road, Pune 411 002
8 Camac Street, Kolkata 700 017
Ashok Rajpath, Patna 800 004
Chowk, Varanasi 221 001

Printed in India
BY JAINENDRA PRAKASH JAIN AT SHRI JAINENDRA PRESS,
A-45 NARAINA, PHASE-I, NEW DELHI 110 028
AND PUBLISHED BY NARENDRA PRAKASH JAIN FOR
MOTILAL BANARSIDASS PUBLISHERS PRIVATE LIMITED,
BUNGALOW ROAD, DELHI 110 007

Contents

Preface

I am honored to be asked, ten time-zones removed, for a prefatory assessment of the author whose thought-world the reader is about to enter. The task is eased by forty years of personal and scholarly interaction, ever since a first communication found its way between Tashkent and Los Angeles, way before cyberspace, when distances were compounded by the gulfs and curtains of the Cold War. Soon I was able to hail in print the advent and ascent of a young scholar who bade fair to shoulder the mantle of the distinguished Sanskritists of the University of Tartu in the 19th century, culminating in Leopold von Schroeder (1851-1920). Neither the latter nor his latter-day comparand Linnart Mäll had it easy in the clutches of ever-looming Russian imperial oppression. It had led Schroeder first to consider a call as Professor of Sanskrit to the newly founded University of Chicago, subsequently to throw in his lot with Austrian academia (first Innsbruck, then permanently Vienna). Mäll had even deeper trouble with the colonial overlords of Estonia, and by the early 1970's was in acute jeopardy of life and liberty for his courageous opposition to the suppression of Buddhism in Buryatia. In those days his western friends did what we could to help via the mass media, including a clandestinely edited extensive spread on the Buryats' plight in the Los Angeles Times, while hiding the "Estonian connection" behind several layers of conspiracy, lest it aggravate Linnart's own predicament. Even when the crudest threats eased, the dilatory consequences for Mäll's academic career were severe enough to discourage lesser spirits. But he persevered, and with changing times never wavered in his defense of unrepresented and downtrodden minorities, rising with the onset of Estonian liberty to their leading advocate on an international level.

All this while Linnart Mäll still managed to operate in the more liberal academic catacombs of Russia, attain an increasing reputation in the West, and resurrect indology, buddhology, tibetology, and sinology as reputable fields of academic endeavour and high culture in Estonia. His translations of key works such as "Bhagavadgītā",

"Dhammapada", and "Daodejing" were disseminated in vast editions. On my occasional forays into Estonia I witnessed how his dynamic lectures on winter nights attracted packed and rapt audiences eager for some kind of satori in the red darkness.

Leopold von Schroeder did his part for native Estonian culture, with his participation in the Estonian Learned Society and his monograph on Estonian wedding customs compared with Indo-European ones ("Die Hochzeitsbräuche der Esten", Berlin 1888). The good Estonian Linnart Mäll has been and is a full participant in the cultural and political life of his liberated land, now an unfettered member of the European Union.

Maybe this juxtaposition of two giants born in Estonia a lincolnesque four score and seven years apart helps anchor the author in time and space. The fine postface by Märt Läänemets fills in further facets about this remarkable scholar.

Jaan Puhvel

Introductory Remarks

Most of the articles in this book were first published in Russian, some in my native language, Estonian; only two recent articles have been published in English. The circumstances related to the emergence and development of my ideas are described in the article "Semiotics as a Possibility for the Study of Religious Texts Under Communist Dictatorship." I hope that the rest of the articles provide a clear understanding of these ideas.

These articles have been written in a certain time and space. In the period since I wrote the earlier articles, Buddhist studies have undergone substantial development. Although now, on some issues I have a different opinion, I have decided not to make any changes or additions in this collection.

However, there is something I would like to add. I wrote my first article, "The Zero Way," on the basis of a report that I delivered at the Kääriku Summer School organized by the Tartu-Moscow school of semiotics in 1964. I further developed these ideas in my next article on *Śūnyavāda*. Since then I've considered analysis of terminology the most important aspect of Buddhist studies. On one hand, it involves investigation of inner links – related to both content and form – within particular texts and, on the other hand, consideration of the level of modern science in the process of creating meta-terminology. I am still convinced that semiotic methods and terms are well suited for such analysis.

I had studied the Mahāyāna texts for a long time and, after a break, I have again returned to this research. My favourite text has been the *Aṣṭasāhasrikā Prajñāpāramitā*. Here I would like to pay homage to Edward Conze whose works have inspired me enormously. Naturally I cannot agree with him on every point but I have never forgotten that he is the founder of modern *Prajñāpāramitā* studies.

What concerns *Aṣṭasāhasrikā*, I believe that this text marks a breakthrough in Buddhism, since it provides an explanation for the emergence of written texts, which gradually replaced the previously predominant oral tradition. In this context I would like to point out that the authors of the *Aṣṭasāhasrikā* developed interesting ideas that have so far received little notice. For example, the term *dharmakāya* does not refer to the Buddha's cosmic body, but as *corpus scriptorum* in Western culture it refers instead to a written text. *Prajñāpāramitā* refers both to *a text* and to a specific state of mind that, in fact, can also be regarded as *a text*.

Dharma, in my opinion, is both a *text* and an *element of a text* that, in its turn, is also an element of the mind - since the mind only manifests itself through an act of text-generation. I believe this can be taken even further: *dharma* can be considered a *text of any length*, anything from a sound or a letter ("a" for instance), a pause, major sūtras like the *Avataṃsaka* or the *Śatasāhasrikā Prajñāpāramitā*, to the whole body of Buddhist literature (Buddha's Teaching).

However, the definition of *dharma* as *a text* should not necessarily have strict limitations. Consequently, *dharma* can also be regarded as a text that generates other texts, i.e. as a *text generating mechanism*. Buddha's first sermon is called the *Dharmacakrapravartana* ("Setting in Motion of the Wheel of Dharma"), which can almost literally be translated as *starting up the mechanism of dharma*. Indeed, it seems to me that in Buddha's sermons there were not only instructions for achieving highest states of mind but also rules for generating texts which, for centuries, have regulated further text-generation.

Consequently, every Buddhist text is programmed, as it were, to generate new texts. (Consider, for instance, the large body of the *Prajñāpāramitā* sūtras). We should not forget that the main aim of Buddhist texts is to generate positive changes in the Buddhist's mind, for it to gradually reach its highest state (*nirvāṇa, anuttarā samyaksaṃbodhi, prajñāpāramitā, sarvajñatā*, etc.). Since Buddhism considers the mind also *a text, an inner text*, then the generation of a new state of mind is considered the creation of a new *inner text*, which is started up by an impulse from the *outer text*. Sometimes *the inner text* has been preserved (either by memorising it, or by writing it down), which means the emergence of a new *outer text*.

It is the interpretation of *dharma* as a *text* and as a *text generating mechanism* that enables us to integrate all the meanings of *dharma* that, until now, have been viewed separately (an element of existence – *nirvāṇa* – Buddha, etc.).

However, I have recently become inclined to believe that the interpretation of *dharma* could be still broader - that, in brief, the basic meaning of *dharma* is *culture*. This does not mean that I have withdrawn from my earlier interpretation because *culture* can also be considered as *a text* in its broadest sense. To follow are some examples to illustrate the advantages of this approach. *Buddhadharma* would, according to this interpretation, refer to the Buddhist culture as opposed to the Brahmanist-Hinduist (*sanātana-*)*dharma*, which in essence is the traditional Indian culture. *Dharma* in such a meaning is represented in the article "The Concept of Humanistic Base Texts".

Everything that I had earlier interpreted as the smallest element of a text, and that most Buddhist scholars after Stcherbatsky still interpret as an element of existence, can now also be seen, to put it simply, as an element of culture. Modern psychology has widely established that a person's outer shape (*rūpa*), feelings (*vedanā*) and the consciousness (*vijñāna*), are partly dependent on a specific state of culture. When influenced by Buddhist culture (*buddhadharma*) these features appear somewhat different from when influenced by some other culture (*dharma*); if a human being grows up in an environment completely void of any culture (*adharmika*), i.e. among wild animals, it is not logical (*yukti*) to refer to his *rūpa*, *vedanā* etc. as *dharmas*, i.e. elements of culture.

Dharma is closely related to the concept of *śūnyatā*. I continue to believe that this term could be translated as 'emptiness' or 'zero'; it should never be interpreted as 'nothingness'. In brief, *śūnyatā* does not mean an absolute non-existence, it rather refers to an infinite number of possibilities to fill what we consider as empty. An empty bottle can be filled with water, milk, sand, etc.; a word, a concept or a text – in brief *dharma* – can be filled with different meanings or assessments, and as a result both negativism and absolute positivism can be avoided, since this approach allows the *text* remain alive. Naturally, emptiness is also associated with the idea of dependent origination.

I found three substructures in the *Aṣṭasāhasrikā Prajñāpāramitā* guided by three concepts. I already mentioned the first concept, *dharma*. The main concept of the second substructure is *bodhisattva*. I find descriptions of *bodhisattvas* who have reached different levels to be quite interesting. However, the principal concept of the *Aṣṭa-sāhasrikā* is, without a doubt, *prajñāpāramitā* – a word that refers both to a text created according to certain rules and to an aspect of the highest state of mind. I would stress that the substructure guided by *prajñāpāramitā* makes the object of our study truly alive – the *Aṣṭasāhasrikā* becomes a text that functions as a Teacher: on one hand it teaches the reader and, on the other hand, it warns him against possible mental disorders that may arise in association with certain textual situations.

I am convinced that, as in any other Mahāyāna sūtras, the structural semiotic approach would enable us to see aspects that until now have remained hidden. When studying a *sūtra*, its own specific structure should be followed; what has been found in the *Aṣṭasāhasrikā* should not be transferred to other sūtras. I am deeply convinced that the Mahāyāna is not a uniform teaching, that there are many texts in the Mahāyāna that are relatively independent. The reader – wanting to understand these texts – should follow specific procedures described in a particular text. So there certainly exist Mahāyāna sūtras that are not guided by the concept of *prajñāpāramitā*, and not even by the concepts of *dharma* and *bodhisattva*.

As far as Mahāyāna and Buddhist terminology generally, it has certainly not remained unchanged throughout time; during the course of history, it has been changing and modifying according to the rules of *dharmacakra* – the process of text-generation. This is why the definitions given by the authors of Mahāyāna śāstras and, in particular, those given by later commentators should not be considered as the only ones valid – a tendency that, unfortunately, has occurred.

In Buddhism, there has been a continuous process of text-generation that has manifested itself in every area of Buddhism, including mythology – a topic described in a few of my articles.

Since I have also translated other classical Oriental texts into Estonian, it has inspired me to write some articles that are not directly related to Buddhism. As I found the *Daodejing* to be a so-called schematic text, conveying this idiosyncracy in the translation brought about ideas that I have expressed in the article "The Course of Translation." My thoughts on comparing the *Bhagavadgītā* – which I have also translated into Estonian – and the *Daodejing* are represented in the article "The Light Path and the Dark Path".

In 1961, one of my teachers – Nikolai Konrad, a scholar of Japanese and Chinese studies – presented an idea that the ever increasing spread of humanistic ideas has been the determining tendency in the history of mankind and that the foundation for this had been laid by Confucius, the Buddha and Jesus Christ. This idea gave me the first impulse to create a concept of humanistic base texts – an issue that I have been studying recently. Although different religions and schools of philosophy – all of which have developed according to their own logic – have emerged on the basis of these base texts, they all have a strong humanistic orientation.

***

Finally, I would like to thank everybody who has helped me to prepare this book. Let this modest book be an expression of gratitude and respect to all my teachers, friends and students too.

The Zero Way

sarvaṃ tathyaṃ na vā tathyaṃ
tathyaṃ ca-atathyam-eva ca
na-eva-atathyaṃ na-eva tathyam
etad Buddha-anuśāsanaṃ

("All is real or without reality
or is real and without reality
or is neither without reality nor real
– this is the teaching of the Buddha")

Nāgārjuna.
Mūlamadhyamakakārikās, XVIII, 8.

There are some technical terms in modern Buddhist studies that seem to be quite definite and established. One of these is 'early Buddhism' (EB) as opposed to 'late Buddhism' (LB). So-called canonical Buddhism is considered as, but not normally termed 'middle Buddhism' (MB) (in terms of time). In recent years it has become common to consider EB as the purest and most authentic representation of Buddhism (B). However, it is MB or LB that is more or less well known to scholars studying Buddhism. They try to reconstruct EB in one of the following possible ways:

1. EB =: MB
2. EB =: LB
3. EB =: MB \ x
4. EB =: MB ∪ x
5. EB =: MB \ x ∪ y
6. EB =: LB \ x etc.

Theoretically, there are 17 possible ways of reconstruction which can be summarized in the following formula:

$$EB =: (MB \setminus x) \cup (LB \setminus y) \cup z.$$

The sign =: means similarity; x – something that is in MB but not in EB; y – something that is in LB but not in EB; z – something that is in EB but lost in both MB and LB.

In order for the formula to make sense, it should have at least either MB, LB or z, since x and y can also be left out if respectively MB and LB to which they belong are not there.

The equations would be correct if:

1. MB and LB were known quantities;
2. EB, MB and LB were signs of the same level.

Further, we would ask the following question: what content does the term B have and in what way is B abstracted from EB, MB and LB? It does not seem to be possible to give a final answer to these questions at this stage. We can only refer to some ways of approaching this problem.

1. Not to prefer EB to MB and LB in terms of understanding the actual meaning of B. EB is one of the outer manifestations of B. However, the outer manifestations of B have existed and exist as sign systems have existed and exist.
2. B should hardly be considered as a sign system since a sign system is not the only response of the mind to existing phenomena (see table). Otherwise we would find ourselves in a completely hopeless situation on a tiny island of sign systems amidst the ocean of existence (cf. Gödel's theorem).

Another response is the way that can be seen as an open sign system. In our terms the difference between a system and a way is that in the case of the latter, signs are separate from that which they denote and are used primarily to change people's minds.

The third response is the zero way (Sanskr. *madhyamā pratipad* – 'the middle way'). A certain approximate description of the zero way can be the tetralemma (Sanskr. *catuṣkoṭikā* – "four limits"), according to which each sign (a) has a denotate or (b) has no denotate, (c) has a denotate and no denotate, (d) has neither a denotate nor the absence of a denotate (see the epigraph to this article). The tetralemma can be represented as the following equation where A is a denotate and A_1 is a sign (*dharma*):

$$A_1 = A + (-A) + [A + (-A)] + \{- [A + (-A)]\}.$$

The right side of the equation equals zero, hence $A_1 = 0$, where 0 corresponds to the Sanskrit term *śūnyatā*. Our outcome coincides precisely with one of the most important Buddhist phrases:

sarva-dharma-śūnyatā.

('emptiness of all signs').

At the level of mathematical logic, the tetralemma can be represented by the formula

A ○ B,

where the logical link ○ means the union of different, even opposite concepts not in the sense of synthesis. There are some equivalents of this link in non-Indo-European languages (in Estonian *olgugi et, ometi*, in Tamil *irundum*, etc.). Alternative conjunctions in new Indo-European languages like Russian *хотя* (khotya) or German *obwohl* are similar in meaning.[1]

	Mental response to existential phenomena	Ability to change	Conservativeness	Limitedness	Logicality (i.e. accepted by common sense)	Signs have a certain denotate	The aim is to explain a phenomenon	The aim is to change a person' s mind
1	System	–	+	+	+	+	+	–
2	Way	+	–	–	–	–	–	+
3	Zero way	0	0	0	0	0	0	0

A Possible Approach Towards Understanding *Śūnyavāda*

0. The dialogue between East and West that has reached synthesis makes us try to understand what it is that the Orient can tell us, so that we can use its achievements as an important component of our own culture.

0.1. The researchers of Eastern cultures have so far applied two different concepts (I am not considering the discourses alleging that the achievements of the East are incomprehensible or inferior).

0.1.1. Occidental and Oriental cultures have developed parallel to each other (either affecting or not affecting each other) and in strict compliance with each other. All significant cultural events have taken place in the cultural areas of both of them in the same historical era (whatever this may mean). The proponents of this axiom usually draw such parallels as Buddha – Christ, logic of Aristotle – *nyāya*, Lao-zi – Socrates, etc.[1]

0.1.2. According to the second concept, both East and West have reached the same results but not necessarily at the same time. This hypothesis enables such comparisons as Kant –Śaṅkara, *śūnyavāda* – 20th century relativism, Buddhism – dialectic materialism etc.[2]

0.1.2.1. I think that the second concept has clear advantages over the first one: the recognition of the fact that cultures do not necessarily develop in the same way, already implies the active role of Eastern cultures. However, one can also immediately see the main drawback of the second concept: its proponents believe that achievements of the East necessarily have analogies in the West and that these have emerged, at the latest, during the lifetime of the proponent.[3] The new facts that are discovered about Eastern cultures concern only details since all the main points are seen as the Eastern analogies of Western phenomena.

0.2. It seems that this is also true for the first proposition in the sense that it sees Oriental phenomena as a convenient playground of scientific viewpoints developed in the West. Buddhism is a good example: different scholars call it a religion, atheism, nihilism, materialism, idealism, rationalism or dialectics.[4] Each of these tends to negate the others. This approach, however, seems to have exhausted itself. The term 'paradoxical' used in recent works shows that a new approach to the East has developed.[5]

0.3. This approach is based on the understanding that the world's civilizations have developed relatively independently from each other. Eastern phenomena can no longer be adjusted to Western schemes. This, of course, does not mean that there may not be certain parallels but if they are not constructed artificially, they unexpectedly crop up at new levels. It is also obvious that achievements by the East are unique in many areas of culture.[6]

0.3.1. Oriental studies should therefore attempt to create models enabling a new approach to the understanding of Western phenomena.

0.3.2. At the beginning this seems to be rather difficult since we are immediately faced with complicated methodological problems, where the solution at first glance seems to depend only on intuition. As far as Buddhist studies are concerned, we should first create central meta-concepts which can be used to describe Buddhism in strict compliance with original ideas of the East. The first link of a new string of concepts could be the term **lysiology**.[7]

1. Lysiology is the doctrine of the liberation of a lysiological person (a lysiological person can be both an individual and a group), whereas liberation means reaching a new level which is higher than the initial level. A teaching can be called lysiological if it contains three components.

1.1. The first component is the description of the initial level, the central point of which is the assertion that it should be overcome. The description should not necessarily conform to reality and a lysiological person does not even have to understand it. The main thing is that it should contain negative judgements (but only such negative judgements that imply the existence of a positive opposite), using which lysiological persons can assess their situation.

1.2. The second element is the determination and description of the final level. Since lysiological teachings prefer to use maximally opposite concepts, the definition of the final level tends to be maximally opposed to the initial level.

1.3. The third element of lysiological teaching is a way. By this term I mean consequent methods needed to take a lysiological person from one level to another. A way is normally described as a process that is opposed to synchronous levels. However, a way is normally divided into a finite number of levels.

1.4. There are a number of lysiological teachings both in the East and in the West. Lysiological teachings may include fields such as medicine, psychoanalysis, different social sciences as well as mystical teachings and yoga. As far as lysiological persons are concerned, Easterners often tend to take the role of an individual lysiological person and Westerners become a collective lysiological person. This difference may be explained by the fact that Easterners have better developed aspirations regarding realization. Westerners, on the contrary, are quite happy with a pleasantly presented theory.[8]

1.4.1. Lysiology has developed as a theoretical and practical science only in the East (particularly in India). Thanks to India, we have detailed theories that could become a basis for a European lysiological theory. All six *darśanas*[9] as well as a great number of other teachings, including the teachings of the *śramaṇaṣ*, the contemporary to Gautama Buddha, are lysiological teachings.

1.5. According to the semiotic model given in section 5, a lysiological process can be described as follows (S – systematic semiotics; T – transformative semiotics):

$$S_1 \rightarrow T(t_1, t_2, t_3, ..., t_n) \rightarrow S_2$$

In this way this process is actually a change of systems rather than going beyond the sign system as such.

2. Buddhists following the tradition of *Prajñāpāramitā* understood it very well. Here we can quote a passage from the *Aṣṭasāhasrikā Prajñāpāramitā*:

> "If thoughts move around 'form' (*rūpa*), they move around sign (*nimitta*). If thoughts move around 'sign of the form', they move around sign. If thoughts move around 'form is a sign', they move around sign. If thoughts move around 'emergence of the form', they move around sign. If thoughts move around 'disappearance of the form', they

move around sign. If thoughts move around 'destruction of the form', they move around sign. If thoughts move around 'form is empty', they move around sign. If thoughts move around 'my thoughts move', they move around sign. If thoughts move around 'I am a bodhisattva', they move around sign, since thus you only reach the thought 'I am a bodhisattva'."[10]

2.1. This passage is about overcoming an *Abhidharma* system where a way is understood as the change of so-called *dharmas* as objects of meditation.

It shows that each *dharma* (using the example of the form – *rūpa*) is only a sign and that a way from one level to another (for example, from the 'form' to the thought 'I am a bodhisattva') does not mean that one goes beyond sign systems.

3. Thus Buddhists considered neither a way nor a system as absolute but worked out a new teaching which is so unique that it hardly has an analogy. In Sanskrit this teaching is called *śūnyavāda*, which can be translated as **zerology**. The central idea of *śūnyavāda* is *śūnyatā* (*suññatā* in Pāli) – a term that has created insurmountable difficulties for researchers of Buddhism.[11]

3.1. Although none of these translations of the word *śūnyatā* is wrong as such, we can see their connection with the concepts that are not free from conventional schemes. But even in this way it is possible to convey the meaning of this word more or less accurately using a suitable interpretation.[12]

3.1.1. At the same time it has long been known that *śūnya* (the abstract form of which is *śūnyatā*) means *zero* in Indian mathematics.[13] Betty Heimann is one of the few Indologists who have expanded this semantic field to the other areas of Indian culture.[14] She thinks that zero was discovered by Indian metaphysicians, both Buddhists and Brahmanists. Mathematics started using zero as late as in the 3rd century AD and described it in the same way as Buddhists describe *nirvāṇa*. Due to the Arabs who became mediators between India and Europe, zero finally reached the Western world.[15] Although I appreciate the contribution of Betty Heimann, I cannot agree with her attempt to identify Buddhism with Brahmanism and reduce the concept of zero to the monist absolute.[16]

3.2. There is another term in Buddhist texts to denote zero, which I even think is a much earlier term – *madhya* (*madhyama*). This is usually translated as 'middle'. Th. Stcherbatsky has pointed out that *madhya* and *śūnya* have the same meaning.[17]

3.2.1. Zero in Buddhism does not mean the absence of something or negation of something but overcoming (or, rather, ignoring) the opposition between a positive statement and a negative statement, "+" and "–". It means that all interconnections are seen as indefinable.

This trend can already be seen in the earliest Buddhist texts, e.g. in the *Saṃyuttanikāya*, Vol. II, p. 17:

> "This world, O Kaccāyana, depends on affirmation and negation. /.../; 'Everything exists' is one extreme; 'nothing exists' is the other. Avoiding these extremes, Tathāgata teaches the zero way."

The same can also be found in the Mahāyāna tradition, e.g. in the *Kāśyapaparivarta*, section 60:

> "'Is' is one extreme and 'is not' is the other. What is between the two extremes cannot be examined. It is inexpressible, undisclosed and unachievable and it does not last. This, Kāśyapa, is the zero that is called the realization of the manifestations of existence."

3.3. Because it is not yet (or might never be) possible to define the object of zerology,[18] it is reasonable to approach it using three models.

4. The first model is the **lysiological** model. At first glance the lysiological trend in Buddhism looks so dominant that it seems to be natural to call Buddhism a lysiological teaching. Indeed, some Buddhist schools emphasize this aspect.

4.1. The lysiological model is based on the fact that Buddhism also sees liberation as a goal (whatever word stands for this concept). It means that we can find all components of a lysiological teaching in Buddhist scriptures.

4.2. The description of the initial level is normally based on the concept of *saṃsāra* or *duḥkha* (Pāli *dukkha*). These words are usually translated as the 'phenomenal world' (which is the opposite of the absolute) and 'suffering', respectively. In this case we are not interested in the interpretation of these terms. Their negative orientation is important. The well-known first Buddhist noble truth can be an example here:

> "This, O monks, is the noble truth of suffering: birth is suffering, old age is suffering, sickness is suffering, association with unpleasant conditions is suffering, separation from pleasant conditions is suffering; not getting what one desires is suffering."[19]

4.3. The final level is described using several different terms such as *nirodha, nirmokṣa, nirvṛti, nirveda,* etc., among which the term *nirvāṇa* is particularly emphasized. As a rule, these are also negative terms since they are opposed to the elements of the description of the initial level in negative terms: "There is, O monks, something unborn, ungrown, unconditioned and unshaped."[20]

4.4. The difference between Buddhism and all other lysiological teachings is that Buddhism sees the way as the zero way (*madhyamā pratipad*) that can be described as an eightfold way for an outsider: right understanding, right thought, right speech, right action, right livelihood, right effort, right mindfulness, right concentration.[21]

4.4.1. The zero way means that the opposition between the initial level and the final level is eliminated and they are seen as identical. Nāgārjuna writes about it surprisingly clearly:

> "What is the limit of *nirvāṇa*, is the limit of *saṃsāra* – there is not the slightest difference."[22]

The *Aṣṭasāhasrikā Prajñāpāramitā* expresses the same idea:

> "Here, Subhūti, a Bodhisattva-Mahāsattva thinks: "I must lead an innumerable number of beings to *nirvāṇa.*" But there are none who are to be led to *nirvāṇa*. Therefore he leads these beings to *nirvāṇa*. But there are no beings who would be led to *nirvāṇa* and there is no person who would lead them to *nirvāṇa*."[23]

> "A Bodhisattva-Mahāsattva is going, although he is going nowhere. /.../ Nobody has gone on this "Great Vehicle" (*mahāyāna*), nobody will go or is going."[24]

4.5. The lysiological model is therefore in the background in Buddhist studies. The main emphasis is placed on other models.

5. The second model can be called the **semiotic** one. This model implies that there are three kinds of practical semiotics in all spheres of society.[25] J. Kristeva has very precisely named them systematic, transformative and paragrammatical semiotics. In Sanskrit they can be named as follows: *dṛṣṭi* ('view, theory'), *yoga* ('transformation') and *śūnyatā* ('zeroness'). We can find parallels for them in the lysiological model: way = transformative practical semiotics. The Indian tradition often sees the terms *mārga* (*pratipad, patha*) and *yoga, śūnyatā* and *madhyamā pratipad* as synonymous and interchangeable.

5.1. This model is not hierarchic, i.e. all its components are parallel. Still, Buddhist zerology understands *śūnyatā* as a more real level compared to the two previous ones that are considered to be illusory (*māyā*).

5.2. The semantic aspect of *śūnyatā* turns relations between signs and denotates to zero (*śūnya*):

> "We say 'bodhisattva, bodhisattva'. What *dharma*[26] does a 'bodhisattva' represent? I cannot see such a *dharma* as 'bodhisattva'. I cannot see the *dharma* 'transcending awareness', either. Since I can find neither bodhisattva nor the *dharma* 'bodhisattva', or transcending awareness or *dharma* 'transcending awareness', what bodhisattva in what transcending awareness should I teach?"[27]

5.3. The syntactic aspect means that signs are seen as free from determined links and they can form any interlinks:

> ""The nature of *dharmas* is deep." – "Because they exist independently." – "The nature of transcending awareness is deep." – "Because pure nature." /.../ All *dharmas* exist naturally independently. What is the independent existence of all *dharmas*, is transcending awareness. Why so? Tathāgatas understood all *dharmas* as undoable."[28]

5.4. The pragmatic aspect shows that a zerological person (*bodhisattva*) does not depend on any sign and can freely operate with any sign:

> "But a bodhisattva does not depend on any *dharma*."[29]

6. The third model can provisionally be named the **psychological** one. It is based on the description of mental activities in three stages.

In Buddhist terminology these stages can be denoted by the terms *avidyā* ('ignorance' or conventional mind), *vijñāna* ('discriminative knowledge' or ability to create new signs) and *prajñā* ('awareness, wisdom'), a synonym of which is *sarvajñatā* ('omniscience'). This model is designed as hierarchic, whereas the aim of the development of the mind is seen as reaching the level of *prajñā* through *vijñāna*. The *prajñā* level contrasts with the others in that it is transcending (*pāramitā*).

6.1. At the *prajñā* level there are no logically determined links between concepts, and persons may or may not create sign situations themselves. The observers who are at the *avidyā* or *vijñāna* level cannot define this process (i.e. they can find no logical justification for the behaviour of a person who is at the *prajñā* level). However, since some *prajñā* situations may coincide with the model of an external observer, they are to a certain extent describable.

6.1.1. It means that each level has its own relationship with logic. I think that the *avidyā* level corresponds to prelogical thinking, the *vijñāna* level to logical and the *prajñā* level to supralogical (although it in fact has quite different logic) thinking, which can be denoted with the formula

A ↺ B.[30]

This logic can be illustrated by the tetralemma described in my paper "The Zero Way" and the following passage from "The Diamond Sutra":

> "Tathāgata has talked about beings as non-beings. Therefore we say "beings, beings."""[31]

A is A because it is $\bar{A}$ (non-A).

6.2. The *avidyā* and *vijñāna* levels are constantly interchanging:

> "*Dharmas* exist so as they do not exist. Their non-existence is called ignorance (*avidyā*). Foolish uneducated common people depend on them and create non-existent *dharmas*. Creating *dharmas*, they strive for the two extremes and do not understand or see *dharmas*. That is why they create non-existent *dharmas*. Creating *dharmas*, they depend on the two extremes and therefore create *dharmas* of the past, *dharmas* of the future and

> *dharmas* of the present. Creating them, they depend on the name and form and create non-existent *dharmas*."[32]

6.3. This constant interchanging where *avidyā* becomes *vijñāna* and vice versa is the state that the lysiological model considers as *saṃsāra*. Transition to the *prajñā* level (which should not be considered as *nirvāṇa*) does not take place intentionally, i.e. it is not possible to determine the point in time and space where the mind reaches the *prajñā* level. We can even say that *prajñā* comes by itself.

6.3.1. The intention of Buddhist zerological texts is to teach people how to recognize the *prajñā* state (this state has a parallel in the semiotic model: paragrammatical practical semiotics as *śūnyatā*). Sophisticated methodology has been developed for this purpose, the description of which goes beyond this article.

7. Zero was invented as a concept of zerology and then transferred from zerology to mathematics. Europe accepted zero as a mathematical concept. Is it not now time to find a profounder implementation for it?

7.1. Still:

> "It is not zero that makes *dharmas* empty. *Dharmas* are empty."[33]

Some Aspects of the Emergence of Mahāyāna

It is quite likely that no other problem in modern Buddhist studies is as exciting as the problem of the emergence of Mahāyāna. Although researchers of Buddhism in the late 19th and early 20th centuries were mostly interested in the so-called Southern Buddhism (Hīnayāna), remarkable results were also achieved in studying Mahāyāna. These are associated with such outstanding researchers as Th. Stcherbatsky, O. Rosenberg, M. Walleser, D. T. Suzuki, etc. They provided us with a certain number of highly valuable translations and studies of Mahāyāna texts. Unfortunately, there are still very few such works. A great number of texts in Sanskrit, Chinese and Tibetan are still unknown to researchers. This has resulted in the current primary drawback for Buddhist studies since each researcher has his or her own Mahāyāna model that is not based on a complete analysis of the texts but on partial and prejudiced knowledge which is, in turn, influenced by some later Indian and Tibetan śāstras. At the same time it is impossible to solve the problem if we do not consider Mahāyāna sūtras. So far there have been few academic studies on Mahāyāna sūtras in Western languages (one of the few examples that could be given is the excellent study by Suzuki[1]).

In this article I would like to present some thoughts and ideas that I have formulated whilst working with the *Aṣṭasāhasrikā Prajñāpāramitā*. This text was apparently created and recorded earlier than other *Prajñāpāramitā* sūtras. Scholars are still arguing about the exact time and place of the creation of the *Aṣṭasāhasrikā*. Since there is a Chinese translation from the second century, it is believed that the original in Sanskrit existed as early as the first century BC.[2] However, I think that it could have actually appeared in the first or even second century AD. There are also different assumptions concerning the place where *Prajñāpāramitā* literature emerged. For example, E. Conze, on the basis of a well-known passage in the *Aṣṭasāhasrikā*, believes that it could be South India[3] but he does not refute É. Lamotte's evidence in favour of North-West India. For me, Prof. Lamotte's arguments are more convincing.[4]

I think that two levels should be distinguished in the creation process of the *Aṣṭasāhasrikā*. This also means that both levels should be taken into consideration when we study the text. The ideas that conventionally may be termed the ideas of *Prajñāpāramitā* could and most probably did emerge much earlier than the text as such was written down. If scholars pay more attention to the first level (the level of the formation of ideas or philosophical content of the *Aṣṭasāhasrikā*), they will find themselves in a rather difficult situation from the very beginning. It is not easy to find out what ideas exactly are ideas of *Prajñāpāramitā* and what role they have played in the general development of Buddhist thought. For example, let us pose a question: can *Prajñāpāramitā* be a predecessor of Nāgārjuna philosophy?

Professor Murti writes: "The Mādhyamika system is the systematized form of the *śūnyatā*-doctrine of the *Prajñāpāramitā* treatises: its metaphysics, spiritual path (*ṣaṭ-pāramitā-naya*) and religious ideal are all present there, though in a loose, prolific garb."[5]

However, as Professor Robinson's studies demonstrate,[6] terminological differences between the two systems are too large. On the other hand, what is by no means less important is the fact that there are unarguable coincidences between Pāli texts and the terminology of the *Aṣṭasāhasrikā*. Of course, one can argue that similar ideas can be expressed using different terms. However, it seems to me that truly scientific Buddhist studies should not go this way. How can we talk of similar ideas if the meaning of the most significant Buddhist terms has not yet been clearly defined? Is it possible at all to construct a model of the development of Buddhist thought if we are still arguing about such terms as *dharma, śūnya, prajñā*, etc.?

Therefore I would say that works related to Buddhist studies should place particular emphasis on terminological studies, and studies of the internal structure of individual texts, whereas both aspects are closely connected with each other, since terms can primarily be considered as elements of a given structure. The drawing up of the final text is the second stage of the formation of the *Aṣṭasāhasrikā Prajñāpāramitā*. The analysis of such a text as an integral whole seems to provide the best outcome at the present stage of Buddhist studies. Further, we are going to take a look at some problems that have arisen from this analysis of the *Aṣṭasāhasrikā Prajñāpāramitā*.

Let us first consider the general nature of this text. E. Conze writes: "The teachings of the Prajñāpāramitā have little significance for the present age. To be quite truthful, they are equally irrelevant to any other age. They are meant for people who have withdrawn from society, and who have little, if any, interest in its problems."[7]

Developing this viewpoint further, we can assume the following. Since this text (or collection of texts) is equally foreign to any historical period, including the period when it was created, it turns out that this text opposing itself to something unchangeable in society can play the same role in any historical situation (even if it is not understood).

I think that although this approach has certain advantages, it is generally deeply erroneous. The first thing one notices while reading the *Aṣṭasāhasrikā Prajñāpāramitā* is its authors' passionate desire to prove something to Buddhists (but not to non-Buddhists as in most sūtras), to prove that this and nothing else complies with the requirements of Buddhist lysiology.[8] The *Aṣṭasāhasrikā* apparently is not a text that would proclaim a number of revelations but a text that seems to foresee all the possible counterarguments by its opponents. Therefore it pays a lot of attention to proofs that use all the achievements of Indian logic, ranging from the usual bivalent logic to sophisticated paradoxical logic that had a particularly strong power of proof in ancient India.

All this provides evidence of the existence of so-called Prajñāpāramitism before the *Aṣṭasāhasrikā* was written down. It is even possible that this school was founded by Gautama's disciple Subhūti. The existence of this school is a fact, since the entire text proves it. Whether it was actually established by Subhūti, is a hypothesis, and an unproved one at that, since it is not yet possible to get the entire picture of the development of ideas of *Prajñāpāramitā*. One should also admit that the *Aṣṭasāhasrikā* is a polemical work created for a certain purpose (as the following analysis shows, this is a specific historical goal). I would suggest that the *Aṣṭasāhasrikā* was specially written for the Kaniṣka's Council.

This hypothesis is based on the fact that the *Aṣṭasāhasrikā* puts special emphasis on the issues that should mostly have interested Kaniṣka's Council. As these issues were mainly related to the definition of the terms, one can suppose that the analysis of the terms of the

Aṣṭasāhasrikā might provide much valuable material for Buddhist studies.

Here we could consider one of the most important terms of the *Aṣṭasāhasrikā*: *pūjā* – 'worship' or 'cult'.[9] Quite often this term appears in the the *Aṣṭasāhasrikā* alongside others such as *satkāra, gurukāra, mānana, arcanā* or *apacāyana*.[10] The *Aṣṭasāhasrikā* generally distinguishes between two levels of worship, whereas the first level is considered as already existing, since all proofs are based on it. This is the worship of the Buddha's relics, which spread particularly widely in the post-Aśokan period and survived in India until the second half of the 1st millennium, which is confirmed by Chinese pilgrims.[11] The *Aṣṭasāhasrikā* denotes the relics with the following terms: 'the body of the Tathāgata, Arhat, Perfect Buddha who has reached complete *nirvāṇa*' (*tathāgatasya-arhataḥ samyaksaṃbuddhasya parinirvṛtasya śarīra*[12]), 'the body of the Tathāgata who has reached complete *nirvāṇa*' (*tathāgatasya parinirvṛtasya śarīra*[13]) and 'the body of the Tathāgata' (*tathāgataśarīra*[14]). The *Aṣṭasāhasrikā* does not deny the worship of the relics but contrasts it to another worship – the worship of the *Prajñāpāramitā*. Also, the *Aṣṭasāhasrikā* does not deny the means of the worship of the relics but transfers the same means to the worship of the *Prajñāpāramitā*. However, what does the word *Prajñāpāramitā* mean here? This is a book, a written text, the *Aṣṭasāhasrikā* itself and all possible other *Prajñāpāramitā* texts. The worship of the *Prajñāpāramitā* is not confined just to these means of the worship but involves new and more important means: copying, spreading and explaining the text. Thus, at the level of performance the worship of the *Prajñāpāramitā* is expressed in a greater number of means, whereas the additional means are not in fact means of worship any longer.

The superiority of the worship of the *Prajñāpāramitā* is also proved axiologically and philosophically. Axiologically both levels are united by the term *puṇya* – 'merit', whereas it is argued that the worship of the *Prajñāpāramitā* (particularly its new means) provides much more merit than the worship of relics.[15] However, *puṇya* is not a Prajñāpāramitist term and it is not defined in the *Aṣṭasāhasrikā*. To avoid this term, another one is used – *dṛṣṭadharmika guṇa* – 'visible quality', which compared to abstract *puṇya* has specific manifestations such as 'long life', 'absence of sicknesses', etc., and is associated with the worship of the *Prajñāpāramitā*.[16]

However, the most interesting is a philosophical proof. The extremely widespread worship of relics leads ordinary Buddhists to the identification of the concepts *buddha* and *tathāgataśarīra*. The main Buddhist formula – *buddha – dharma – saṃgha* – could thus be expressed as *tathāgataśarīra – dharma – saṃgha*. Since the meaning of the word *dharma* had at the time become incomprehensible and partly acquired a new meaning as an 'element of something', it is no wonder that the relics acquired the central meaning in this formula. The authors of the *Aṣṭasāhasrikā* tried to restore the original meaning of the formula (where the second member – *dharma* – had to become the most important after the Buddha died). First the word *śarīra* was added to each part of the original formula. Then the formula looked like *buddhaśarīra – dharmaśarīra – saṃghaśarīra*.[17] *Dharmaśarīra* was supposed to be equivalent to the original meaning of *dharma*, i.e. *dharmaśarīra* = the Buddha's teaching, in this context – the *Prajñāpāramitā*. Since *śarīra* might primarily have meant a 'dead body', *dharmaśarīra* was understood as a 'dead text', the worship of which was expressed in the formal worship of the book. Therefore *dharmaśarīra* was replaced by the word *dharmakāya* ('*dharma* body') meaning a 'living text', what must constantly be read, studied, rewritten, disseminated and explained.[18]

Therefore we can say that such an important term of late Buddhism as *dharmakāya* originally denoted a *text* and its emergence was not related to any intellectual speculations but to existing social conditions and the attempt to prevent Buddhism from turning into a dead dogma and trivial cult (*pūjā*).

Studies in the *Aṣṭasāhasrikā Prajñāpāramitā*

1. *Dharma*

1.1 *Dharma* in European Buddhist studies

Dharma (Tib. *chos*) was apparently the central term in Buddhism during a certain period. This period in all probability began at the time when written Buddhist texts appeared, i.e. the first century B.C. The theory of *dharmas* is largely related to the so-called *Abhidharma* – a theory used to classify *dharmas*.[1]

In the *Prajñāpāramitā* texts the term *dharma* may be encountered quite frequently, and not just encountered: the *Prajñāpāramitā* teaching is unthinkable without this concept. *Dharmas*, different operations with *dharmas*, the 'emptiness of *dharmas*' – these are the objects of *Prajñāpāramitā* thought. However, it is quite clear that the theory of *dharmas* was not elaborated by the *Prajñāpāramitā* teaching. *Dharma* is one of the concepts that are not defined in the *Aṣṭasāhasrikā Prajñāpāramitā*. It means that followers of *Prajñāpāramitā* did not consider the concept of *dharma* as the achievement of their lineage alone.

It is obvious that the theory of *dharmas* constitutes the basis for the *Prajñāpāramitā* teaching. Does it mean that this basis was the Buddhist theory of *dharmas*, the *Abhidharma*, that had already been in existence for a long time? E. Conze suggests that the *Prajñāpāramitā* teaching could be divided into two parts: the criticism of the *Abhidharma*, and the Mahāyāna (i.e. *Prajñāpāramitā*) teaching as such.[2]

Such a transition seems to be rather simplified. First, I do not think that we can consider the formula *sarva-dharma-śūnyatā* in the same sense as *abhidharma-abhavatā,* as does Conze; this formula is more likely to reflect the idea that emerged as a result of certain development of theoretical thought: *dharmas* themselves (rather than the teaching about *dharmas*) are considered from the point of view of *śūnyatā*. This means that the *Prajñāpāramitā* teaching can be considered in relation to the *Abhidharma* as a parallel rather than contradictory phenomenon. Since we also find in the *Abhidharma* terms of *Prajñāpāramitā* that are not subject to criticism but are considered as terms of *Abhidharma*, this assumption seems to be quite acceptable.

Thus, *Prajñāpāramitā* and the *Abhidharma* can be considered as parallel phenomena of the same level, i.e. the level of theoretical development of the Buddhist teaching.[3]

The analysis of the concept of *dharma* in comparison with two other concepts – *bodhisattva* and *prajñāpāramitā* which will be analysed in the next two parts of this study, is facilitated by the fact that in European Buddhist studies there are some substantial achievements in the resolution of this problem on the basis of *Abhidharma* texts. These achievements primarily belong to the so-called Leningrad school[4] in Buddhist studies, mainly O. Rosenberg and Th. Stcherbatsky.[5] As we cannot imagine further research without considering the works of these scholars, I would briefly describe their studies.

O. Rosenberg was the first to introduce the *Abhidharma* of Sarvāstivāda in Europe. Before Prof. Rosenberg, the concept of *dharma* was mainly analysed on the basis of Pāli texts: their material was apparently insufficient to solve such a complicated problem as "Buddhist dharma".[6] The few works that have analysed the word *dharma* using Mahāyāna sources have in part come close to the solution of this problem. Thus, D. T. Suzuki suggested the following translations of *dharma*: law, institution, rule, doctrine, duty, justice, virtue, moral, merit, character, attribute, essential quality, substance, that which exists, being.[7]

O. Rosenberg himself described the situation in Buddhist studies as follows: "The notion of 'dharma' in Buddhist philosophy has such an outstanding meaning that the system of Buddhism in a way can be called the theory of dharmas... European literature on Buddhism has analysed the term a lot but we have not yet managed to establish clearly and convincingly what dharmas are."[8]

Although Rosenberg has not managed to complete this task, the seven groups of the main meanings of *dharma* that he outlined are still the basis for appropriate research:[9]

1. Quality, attribute, predicate;

2. Substantial carrier, the transcendental substrate of a single element of conscious life;
3. Element, i.e. a component of conscious life;
4. Nirvāṇa, i.e. Dharma, the object of the Buddha's teaching;
5. Absolute, truly real, etc.;
6. Buddha's teaching, religion;
7. Thing, object or phenomenon.

According to Rosenberg, the second meaning is predominant: "The main and probably primary meaning of the term can be encountered in philosophical works as well as sūtras where dharmas mean 'carriers' or truly real unknowable substrates of the elements, into which the flow of conscious life is divided in abstraction, i.e. the subject and the world perceived by him, both inner and outer."[10]

Rosenberg's definition of *dharma* is as follows: "Dharmas are truly existent transcendental unknowable carriers-substrates of the elements, into which the flow of consciousness with its content is divided."[11]

Unfortunately, Rosenberg died early and never finished his research. Still, I think that what he did is more significant than all that has been done in this area after him.

Western Buddhist scholars know little about Rosenberg's works. However, the works of another outstanding Leningrad scholar, Th. Stcherbatsky, are well known in the West. Stcherbatsky published a study on this problem in 1923.[12]

It is supposed Rosenberg had a substantial influence on Stcherbatsky's conceptions. However, Stcherbatsky interpreted Rosenberg's discoveries in his own way and, it seems to me, simplified them. In his interpretation, the Buddhist theory of *dharma* is transformed into some form of ontological atomism:

"The conception of dharma is the central point of the Buddhist doctrine. In the light of this conception Buddhism discloses itself as a metaphysical theory, developed out of one fundamental principle, viz. the idea, that existence is an interplay of a plurality of a subtle, ultimate, not further analysable elements of Matter, Mind and Forces. These elements are technically called dharmas."[13]

Stcherbatsky developed this idea in his further works: "...every composite thing contains nothing real over and above the parts of which it is composed. Real are only the parts, that is the ultimate parts, the Elements. Element and Reality are synonymous."[14]

But Stcherbatsky did not answer the question: what is the Element, the *dharma*? He ends his work with a rather sad confession:

"What is dharma? It is inconceivable! It is subtle! No one will ever be able to tell what its real nature is! It is transcendental."[15]

Further studies of *dharma* include noteworthy papers by H. Glasenapp and W. Liebenthal. Glasenapp's article[16] is not quite relevant to our purposes but Liebenthal's article[17] can be seen as a continuation of the line of above-mentioned scholars.

Liebenthal sees *dharma* as an "element of image" and finds that the word "position" (*die Position*) would be equivalent to it in European languages: "Eine Position ist also ein Wort in der Schrift (den Bild) eines Lehrers und wurde von anderen Lehrern abgelehnt, weil sie in deren Schrift nicht passte. So lehnte Gotama Buddha die Position Gott (*Īśvara*) ab, weil sie „nicht" zur Befreiung führt."[18]

O. Rosenberg wrote more than 60 years ago that the problem of *dharma* was not solved. This is still true. Apparently, there will be no solution until the basic Buddhist texts, mainly the *Prajñāpāramitā* and the *Abhidharma*, are thoroughly analysed.

1.2 Two meanings of the term *dharma*

In the *Aṣṭasāhasrikā Prajñāpāramitā dharma* has two meanings, the first of which can be conditionally collated with the sixth, and the second with the third meaning on Rosenberg's list.

***Dharma* in the sense of 'teaching'** is used in the *Aṣṭasāhasrikā* quite frequently.

1. The well-known Buddhist formula *buddha – dharma – saṃgha* (Tib. *sangs rgyas – chos – dge 'dun*) is used in the *Aṣṭasāhasrikā* both in its original,[19] and derivative form *tathāgata – dharma – saṃgha* (Tib. *de bzhin gshegs pa – chos – dge 'dun*).[20]

2. The term *dharmavinaya* (Tib. *chos 'dul*) is used once.[21]

3. The *Aṣṭasāhasrikā* also uses the term *saddharma* (Tib. *dam pa'i chos*) but always in relation to the concept of the "disappearance of *dharma*".[22]

4. *Dharma* as 'teaching' is a component of the words 'teacher' – *dharmabhāṇaka* (Tib. *chos smra ba*) – and 'student' – *dharmaśrāvaṇika* (Tib. *chos nyan pa*).[23]

5. The *Aṣṭasāhasrikā* also mentions the term *dharmacakra-pravartana* (Tib. *chos kyi 'khor lo bskor ba*) – 'turning the Wheel of Dharma'. Since this term in the *Aṣṭasāhasrikā* is used in a situation that is particularly important for the history of Buddhism in India, we will consider it in more detailed way. Bhagavat answers to *devaputras*' exclamation:[24]

> *dvitīyaṃ bata-idaṃ dharmacakra-pravartanaṃ jambudvīpe paśyāma iti.*
>
> *na-idam subhūte dvitīyaṃ dharmacakra-pravartanaṃ na-api kasyacid-dharmasya pravartanam.*[25]

Two conclusions can be drawn from this answer:

a) The *Aṣṭasāhasrikā* denies the late emergence of the *Prajñāpāramitā*;

b) *Dharma* is considered as a word having one single meaning (for us it means that the first meaning is subordinate to the second).

6. In many cases *dharma* means the 'teaching of *Prajñāpāramitā*'. Such expressions as *dharmaṃ deśati, dharmaḥ deśitaḥ* or *ayaṃ dharmo deśyate* suggest declaring the teaching of *Prajñāpāramitā*. *Dharma* in this sense (i.e. in the sense of teaching of *Prajñāpāramitā*) is meant not just for the Bodhisattvas-Mahāsattvas but also for those who are in other vehicles:

> *sa-niḥsaraṇaṃ mayā dharmo deśitaḥ śrāvakayānikānāṃ pratyekabuddhayānikānāṃ bodhisattvayānikānāṃ ca pudgalānām.*[26]

However, this may mean different *dharmas*, i.e. different teachings, and the passage probably means that the Buddha intended each vehicle for a special *dharma*, which is said in later sources (in the teaching on the "three turns of the Wheel of Dharma").[27] An answer to this question has been given earlier: the attitude of the *Aṣṭasāhasrikā* to the idea of different turns of the "Wheel of Dharma" is clearly negative. Moreover, in the *Aṣṭasāhasrikā* we find the idea that *Prajñāpāramitā* is a teaching meant for all vehicles:

> *śrāvakabhūmav-api śikṣitukāmena iyam-eva prajñāpāramitā śrotavyā .../ iha-eva prajñāpāramitāyāṃ śikṣitavya yogam-āpattavyam; pratyekabuddhabhūmāv-api śikṣitukāmena iyam-eva prajñāpāramitā śrotavyā .../ iha-eva prajñāpāramitāyāṃ yogam-āpattavyam / bodhisattvabhūmav-api śikṣitukāmena iyam-eva prajñāpāramitā śrotavyā ...*[28]

Can we make a distinction at all between the use of the term *dharma* in the sense of 'Teaching' and *Prajñāpāramitā*? Did the authors of the *Aṣṭasāhasrikā* do this?

I think they did not: this can perhaps be explained by the extremely complicated and unusual circumstances in the Buddhist community of the time. I do not mean the schism that took place in Buddhism much earlier but the emergence of written Buddhist texts. Due to this circumstance the use of the words *dharma* and *prajñāpāramitā* became so complicated that they in fact became difficult to understand.

In the *Aṣṭasāhasrikā* we can find a considerable amount of material on this problem and we will discuss this later. Here I would only dwell on the concept of *dharmakāya* that is directly related to this problem.

The European scholar mostly knows the term *dharmakāya* (Tib. *chos kyi sku*) from the formula *dharmakāya – saṃbhogakāya – nirmāṇakāya*, the meaning of which is well known in later Buddhism.[29] But this formula alone was not enough to reconstruct the way of thinking, on the basis of which the formula and the term *dharmakāya* could emerge. *Dharmakāya* is used not only in this formula. There is another, probably earlier formula – the opposition *dharmakāya – rūpakāya*. The latter is mentioned in the *Aṣṭasāhasrikā*, although only once:

> *na hi tathāgato rūpakāyato draṣṭavyaḥ: dharmakāyās-tathāgatāḥ.*[30]

The construction *dharmakāyas-tathāgatāḥ* is also used elsewhere in Chapter XXXI. In Chapter IV we find the following interesting passage:

> *yathā ca bhagavan rājapuruṣo rāja-anubhāvān-mahato janakāyasya akutobhayaḥ pūjyaḥ, evaṃ sa dharmabhāṇako dharmakāya-anubhāvān-mahato janakāyasya akutobhayaḥ pūjyaḥ.*[31]

It is unlikely that there is something more than just a play on words behind the comparison of *dharmakāya* and *janakāya*. If there is, it is about another meaning of the word *kāya* – totality, aggregate or bulk. In this sense *dharmakāya* is collated with the term *dharmakoṣa* that is also used in the *Aṣṭasāhasrikā Prajñāpāramitā*:

> *eṣa hi ānanda tathāgatānām-arhatāṃ samyaksambuddhānām-akṣayo dharmakoṣaḥ, yaduta prajñāpāramitā.*[32]

Here *dharmakoṣa* = *prajñāpāramitā*, i.e. the written *Prajñāpāramitā* text. It is quite possible that this construction has only appeared due to the polysemy of the word *kāya*: in this case *dharmakoṣa* = *dharmakāya*. However, this does not explain the origin of this term, although it illustrates it.

Now let us dwell on the last example that interests us:

> *uktaṃ hy-etad-bhagavatā – dharmakāyā buddhā bhagavatāḥ / mā khalu punar-imaṃ bhikṣavaḥ satkāyaṃ kāyaṃ manyadhvam / dharmakāya-pariniṣpattito māṃ bhikṣavo drakṣyatha / eṣa ca tathāgatakāyo bhūtakoṭi-prabhāvito draṣṭavyo yaduta prajñāpāramitā / na khalu punar-me bhagavaṃs-teṣu tathāgataśarīreṣv-agauravam / gauravam-eva me bhagavaṃs-teṣu tathāgataśarīreṣu / api tu khalu punar-bhagavan itaḥ prajñāpāramitāto nirjātāni tathāgataśarīrāṇi pūjaṃ labhante.*[33]

The analysis of this passage could be a study in itself. Its meaning becomes clear after reading Chapters III and IV of the *Aṣṭasāhasrikā Prajñāpāramitā* because the main subject of these chapters is the attitude of proponents of *Prajñāpāramitā* towards the cult of relics.

It is well known that the cult of relics developed rapidly among Buddhists in the post-Aśokan period.[34] The material of the *Aṣṭasāhasrikā* enables us to conclude that it really had enormous dimensions. The *Aṣṭasāhasrikā* takes the cult (*pūjā*) of relics (*tathāgataśarīra*,[35] *tathāgatasya arhataḥ samyaksaṃbuddhasya parinirvṛtasya śarīra*,[36] *tathāgatasya parinirvṛtasya śarīra*[37]) as an existing fact: no part of it tries to negate the value of this cult. But this value is proclaimed within an axiological system based on the concept of *puṇya* that compared to another axiological system based on the concept of *dṛṣṭadharmika guṇa* is considered to be less valuable for a Bodhisattva-Mahāsattva. This circumstance alone could cast doubt on the ultimate value of the cult, even if we ignore the fact that in the *puṇya* system, the cult of relics has a lower value than the cult of the *Prajñāpāramitā*.[38] One way or another, the cult of relics was enormously popular and the authors of the *Aṣṭasāhasrikā* could not ignore it.

Here we are approaching the problem that *Prajñāpāramitā* proponents faced at the beginning of our era, the problem that was solved by creating a new term in theoretical Buddhist thought – *dharmakāya*.

The course of their thoughts can be reconstructed using the material of the *Aṣṭasāhasrikā*. Their reasoning was based on the fundamental Buddhist formula:

buddha – dharma – saṃgha.[39] (1)

After Śākyamuni's *parinirvāṇa* the formula looked as follows:

tathāgata – dharma – saṃgha.[40] (2)

For an ordinary Buddhist of the time, an adherent of the cult of relics, formula (2) implicitly looked as follows:

buddhaśarīra – dharma – saṃgha,

or:

tathāgataśarīra – dharma – saṃgha, (3)

where the first component, i.e. the relics was of course predominant. This obviously contradicted the tradition where *dharma* (in the sense of teaching) had to become the main component after the death of Gautama Buddha. For proponents of the *Prajñāpāramitā*, *dharma* = *prajñāpāramitā*. They had to change formula (3) so that the second component had the main meaning (whereas the original components in the formula had to be preserved).

Returning to formula (1) seemed to be considered impossible: the *Aṣṭasāhasrikā* aspires to describing specific and clearly knowable phenomena, truths and values throughout its text. Formula (3) is in this way more specific than formula (1) due to its first component. But while *dharma* knew no clear boundaries over the centuries because it was verbally communicated from generation to generation, the *Prajñāpāramitā* was a specific written text. In this sense it had a 'body' that also had to be reflected in the formula. Therefore the creation of the following formula seems to be entirely justified:

buddhaśarīra – dharmaśarīra – saṃghaśarīra.[41] (4)

Still, the second component in formula (4) had no advantage over the other components. Moreover, *dharmaśarīra*, similarly to *buddhaśarīra*, could be understood as the 'dead body of *dharma*', which might have happened when the 'cult of the book' emerged.[42]

Then we can understand why *dharmaśarīra* was replaced by its synonym *dharmakāya* (incidentally, *kāya* means 'living body' in Buddhism). Now our formula looks as follows:

buddhaśarīra – dharmakāya – saṃghaśarīra.[43] (5)

This formula is not used in the *Aṣṭasāhasrikā*. This is understandable: the logical completion of its development is that only its central component remains:

dharmakāya. (6)

This concludes the consideration of *dharma* in its first meaning, the 'teaching'.

Now we move on to the **second meaning of the term *dharma*** which, according to Rosenberg, can conditionally be denoted by the word 'element'. This translation, as it was mentioned above, says nothing about the actual specific meaning of this very important Buddhist term but it determines the direction where we should look for this meaning. This study only represents one link at the preparatory stage of this work.

The *Aṣṭasāhasrikā*, as well as other *Prajñāpāramitā* sūtras frequently uses the formula *sarva-dharma* (Tib. *chos thams cad*) – 'all *dharmas*'.[44] Buddhists used this formula to express the equality of all *dharma*s in relation to certain characteristics, such as *sarva-dharma-śūnyatā* – the 'emptiness of all *dharmas*'.

Of course, the *Aṣṭasāhasrikā* lists individual *dharmas*. These include certain states of the Buddhist theory of liberation, both high (*śrāvakabhūmi, pratyekabuddhabhūmi, buddhabhūmi,*[45] *arthattva, sarvajñatā,*[46] *bodhisattva*[47]) and low (*ahaṃkāra, mamakāra*[48]). Negative states such as *jāti, jara, śoka, vyādhi, maraṇa, parideva, duḥkha, daurmanasya, upāyāsa* are also considered to be *dharmas.*[49]

It is known that such characteristics of *dharmas* as *śūnya* and *śūnyatā* as well as *akṣaya* and *aprameyatā* can also be individual *dharmas*.[50]

Dharma as an 'element' has a special meaning in some *Abhidharma* texts – as a unit on a certain 'list' (*mātṛka*). Such lists were different in the texts of different schools. List of the Theravāda is known to contain 82 *dharmas* and that of the Sarvāstivāda has 75.[51] The lists of most other schools are unfortunately so far unknown.

We find several such lists in the *Aṣṭasāhasrikā*. They are given in a short but easily reconstructable form in the text.

The first list is in Chapter II:

> *na rūpe sthātavyam / na vedanāyaṃ na saṃjñāyāṃ na saṃskāreṣu; na vijñāne sthātavyam / na cakṣuṣi sthātavyam / na rūpe sthātavyam / na cakṣurvijñāne sthātavyam / na cakṣuḥsaṃsparśe sthātavyam / na cakṣuḥsaṃsparśajāyāṃ vedanāyāṃ sthātavyam / evaṃ na śrotra-ghrāṇa-jihvā-kāya-manaḥsu sthātavyam / na śabda-gandha-rasa-spraṣṭavya-dharmeṣu, na śrotravijñāne, yāvan-na manovijñāne / na manaḥsaṃsparśe, na manaḥsaṃsparśajāyām vedanāyām sthātavyam / na pṛthivīdhātau sthātavyam / na-abdhātau, na tejodhātau, na vāyudhātau na-ākāśa-dhātau, na vijñānadhātau sthātavyam / na smṛtyupasthāneṣu sthātavyam / na samyakprahāṇa-ṛddhipāda-indriya-bala-bodhy-aṅgeṣu, na mārgāṅgeṣu sthātavyam / na srota-āpatti-phale sthātavyam / na sakṛdāgāmiphale, na anāgāmiphale, na-arhattve sthātavyam / na pratyekabuddhatve sthātavyam / na buddhatve sthātavyam.*[52]

The second list is in Chapter VIII:

> *evam caran subhūte bodhisattvo mahāsattvo na rūpe saṅgaṃ janayati, na vedanāyāṃ na saṃjñāyāṃ na saṃskāreṣu / na vijñāne saṅgaṃ janayati / na cakṣuṣi saṅgaṃ janayati / yāvan-na manaḥsaṃsparśajāyāṃ vedanāyaṃ saṅgaṃ janayati / na pṛthivīdhātau saṅgaṃ janayati, yāvan-na vijñānadhātau saṅgaṃ janayati / na dānapāramitāyāṃ saṅgaṃ janayati, na śīlapāramitāyāṃ na kṣāntipāramitāyāṃ na vīryapāramitāyāṃ na dhyānapāramitāyāṃ na prajñāpāramitāyāṃ saṅgaṃ janayati / na bodhipakṣeṣu dharmeṣu, na baleṣu, na vaiśāradyeṣu, na pratisaṃvitsu, na-aṣṭādaśāsv-āveṇikeṣu buddhadharmeṣu, saṅgaṃ janayati, na srota-āpattiphale saṅgaṃ janayati, na pratyekabuddhatve saṅgaṃ janayati na buddhatve saṅgaṃ janayati, na sakṛdāgāmiphale na anāgāmiphale na arhattve saṅgaṃ janayati na-api sarvajñatāyāṃ saṅgaṃ janayati.*[53]

If we assume that similarly to the *Abhidharma* lists there are four *smṛtyupasthānas*, four *samyakprahāṇas*, four *ṛddhipādas*, five *indriyas*, five *balas*, seven *bodhyaṅgas*, and eight *mārgāṅgas*, the reconstructed list from Chapter II contains 84 *dharmas*:

1. *rūpa*
2. *vedanā*
3. *saṃjñā*
4. *saṃskārāḥ*
5. *vijñāna*
6. *cakṣus*

7. *rūpa*
8. *cakṣurvijñāna*
9. *cakṣuḥsaṃsparśa*
10. *cakṣuḥsaṃsparśajā vedanā*
11. *śrotra*
12. *śabda*
13. *śrotravijñāna*
14. *śrotrasaṃsparśa*
15. *śrotrasaṃsparśajā vedanā*
16. *ghrāṇa*
17. *gandha*
18. *ghrāṇavijñāna*
19. *ghrāṇasaṃsparśa*
20. *ghrāṇasaṃsparśajā vedanā*
21. *jihvā*
22. *rasa*
23. *jihvāvijñāna*
24. *jihvāsaṃsparśa*
25. *jihvāsaṃsparśajā vedanā*
26. *kāya*
27. *spraṣṭavya*
28. *kāyavijñāna*
29. *kāyasaṃsparśa*
30. *kāyasaṃsparśajā vedanā*
31. *manas*
32. *dharmāḥ*
33. *manovijñāna*
34. *manaḥsaṃsparśa*
35. *manaḥsaṃsparśajā vedanā*
36. *pṛthivīdhātu*
37. *abdhātu*
38. *tejodhātu*
39. *vāyudhātu*
40. *ākāśadhātu*
41. *vijñānadhātu*
42 – 45. *smṛtyupasthānāni*
46 – 49. *samyakprahāṇāni*

50 – 53. *ṛddhipādāḥ*
54 – 58. *indriyāni*
59 – 63. *balāni*
64 – 70. *bodhyaṅgāni*
71 – 78. *mārgāṅgāni*
79. *srota-āpattiphala*
80. *sakṛdāgāmiphala*
81. *anāgāmiphala*
82. *arhattva*
83. *pratyekabuddhatva*
84. *buddhatva*

The second list adds six *pāramitās, sarvajñatva*, apparently ten *balas*, four *pratisaṃvids*, four *vaiśāradyas*, and four *āvenika buddhadharmas* and so contains 127 *dharmas*:

1. *rūpa*
2. *vedanā*
3. *saṃjñā*
4. *saṃskārāḥ*
5. *vijñāna*
6. *cakṣus*
7. *rūpa*
8. *cakṣurvijñāna*
9. *cakṣuḥsaṃsparśa*
10. *cakṣuḥsaṃsparśajā vedanā*
11. *śrotra*
12. *śabda*
13. *śrotravijñāna*
14. *śrotrasaṃsparśa*
15. *śrotrasaṃsparśajā vedanā*
16. *ghrāṇa*
17. *gandha*
18. *ghrāṇavijñāna*
19. *ghrāṇasaṃsparśa*
20. *ghrāṇasaṃsparśajā vedanā*
21. *jihvā*
22. *rasa*
23. *jihvāvijñāna*

24. *jihvāsaṃsparśa*
25. *jihvāsaṃsparśajā vedanā*
26. *kāya*
27. *spraṣṭavya*
28. *kāyavijñāna*
29. *kāyasaṃsparśa*
30. *kāyasaṃsparśajā vedanā*
31. *manas*
32. *dharmāḥ*
33. *manovijñāna*
34. *manaḥsaṃsparśa*
35. *manaḥsaṃsparśajā vedanā*
36. *pṛthivīdhātu*
37. *abdhātu*
38. *tejodhātu*
39. *vāyudhātu*
40. *ākāśadhātu*
41. *vijñānadhātu*
42. *dānapāramitā*
43. *śīlapāramitā*
44. *kṣāntipāramitā*
45. *vīryapāramitā*
46. *dhyānapāramitā*
47. *prajñāpāramitā*

48 – 51. *smṛtyupasthānāni*

52 – 55. *samyakprahāṇāni*

56 – 59. *ṛddhipādāḥ*

60 – 64. *indriyāni*

65 – 69. *balāni*

70 – 76. *bodhyaṅgāni*

77 – 84. *mārgāṅgāni*

85 - 94. *balāni*

95 - 98. *vaiśāradyāni*

99 - 102. *pratisaṃvidaḥ*

103 - 120. *āveṇikā buddhadharmāḥ*

121. *srota-āpattiphala*
122. *sakṛdāgāmiphala*

123. *anāgāmiphala*
124. *arhattva*
125. *pratyekabuddhatva*
126. *buddhatva*
127. *sarvajñatva*

Although these lists partly coincide with Theravāda and Sarvāstivāda lists, they mostly seem to be quite unique and rather different from the lists of the *Abhidharma* texts we know. Therefore they are very important for Buddhist studies.

If, as E. Conze supposes, these lists are only included in *Prajñāpāramitā* texts as an object of criticism,[54] it seems possible to reconstruct some *Abhidharma* systems that are unknown to us on the basis of this material.

But if the *Prajñāpāramitā* sūtras are a phenomenon that is parallel to *Abhidharma*, these lists can be considered as *Prajñāpāramitā* lists; and in this case they will not necessarily have an analogy in *Abhidharma* texts.

I think that the second point of view has a clear advantage over the first since it contains a natural basis for the internal analysis of *Prajñāpāramitā*. Moreover, this point of view gives us a chance to avoid dividing the *Aṣṭasāhasrikā* text into two levels: the criticism of *Abhidharma* and the *Prajñāpāramitā* teaching as such.

This viewpoint can be confirmed by the following passage from the *Aṣṭasāhasrikā*:

> *āsu hi subhūte ṣaṭsu pāramitāsu saptatriṃśad-bodhipakṣā dharmā antargatāḥ, catvāro brahmavihārāḥ, catvāri saṃgrahavastūni / yāvaṃś-ca kaścid-buddhadharmo buddhajñānaṃ svayambhūjñānam-acintyajñānam-asamasamajñānaṃ sarvajñajñānam, sarvam tat ṣaṭsu pāramitāsv-antargatam.*[55]

Perhaps, we have yet another (third) list of *dharmas* here. Unfortunately, it seems to be impossible to reconstruct it since we have no information about similar lists, on the basis of which we could replace the abbreviation *yāvat* with necessary *dharmas*. Nevertheless, we can come to the very important conclusion that at least 37 *bodhipakṣa dharmas* (that are also used in the previous lists) are included in the *Prajñāpāramitā* system in the *Aṣṭasāhasrikā*: "There are 37 *bodhipakṣa dharmas* in the six pāramitās, etc."

The most widespread list in the *Aṣṭasāhasrikā* is the minimum list containing only five *skandhas* (*rūpa, vedanā, saṃjñā, saṃskārāḥ, vijñāna*).[56] There are more extensive lists in Chapter VII, for example:[57]

I

1. *rūpa*
2. *vedanā*
3. *saṃjñā*
4. *saṃskārāḥ*
5. *vijñāna*
6. *srota-āpattiphala*
7. *sakṛdāgāmiphala*
8. *anāgāmiphala*
9. *arhattva*
10. *buddhatva*

II

1. *rūpa*
2. *vedanā*
3. *saṃjñā*
4. *saṃskārāḥ*
5. *vijñāna*

6 – 15. *tathāgatabalāni*

16. *sarvajñatā*

The first list might be a shortened version of the full list in Chapter II: the first five and the last five *dharmas* are the same. The second list, in its turn, seems to be a short version of the full list in Chapter VIII as it ends in *sarvajñatā* and includes the section *(tathāgata)-balāni*.

1.3 Three operations with *dharmas*

The *Aṣṭasāhasrikā* describes various operations that a person performs with *dharmas* in detail. In order to facilitate further reasoning, we could construct the following model:

1. *Dharmas* are the elements of the inner and outer world.[58]
2. External elements can become internal and vice versa.

3. *Dharmas* are information for the *manas*.[59]
4. The *manas*, in its turn is an organ that processes *dharmas*.[60]

We are going to consider three such operations using this model.

The first operation is denoted by derivatives of the root *gṛhṇāti* (the main meaning is 'to grab' or 'to grasp'). The *Aṣṭasāhasrikā* in most cases uses the verb *parigṛhṇāti* and only in some cases *saṃgṛhṇāti* and *udgṛhṇāti*, where the latter basically means 'to grasp the *Prajñāpāramitā* text'[61] and therefore apparently is not directly related to our task.[62]

The fact that *parigṛhṇāti* (Tib. *yongs su 'dzin pa*) is a term denoting some operation with *dharmas* is clear even from the following phrase:

prajñāpāramitā bhagavan-na kaścid-dharmaṃ parigṛhṇāti.[63]

In this example *prajñāpāramitā* means the ultimate state of mind in which the operation of *parigṛhṇāti* has already been overcome, i.e. where *dharmas* are no longer 'grasped'. In lower states of mind this operation is considered to be a quite normal phenomenon of the mind. However, a person who aspires to the state of *prajñāpāramitā* should consciously choose *dharmas* necessary for this process and only perform this operation with these *dharmas*. Sometimes this operation is seen from the other side, i.e. a person seems to be 'possessed' by a *dharma*.

The *dharmas* that should be grasped in order to attain the state of *prajñāpāramitā* are as follows:

a) *saddharma* (Tib. *dam pa'i chos*)

> *na-ayaṃ kevalam-atītānām-eva buddhānām bhagavatām saddharma-parigrahaḥ, pratyutpannānām-api buddhānām bhagavatām-eṣa saddharma-parigrahaḥ, anāgatānām-api buddhānām bhagavatām-eṣa eva saddharma-parigrahaḥ.*[64]

b) *prajñāpāramitā* (Tib. *shes rab kyi pha rol tu phyin pa*).

c) *upāyakauśalya* (Tib. *thabs la mkhas pa*)

> *sa ca prajñāpāramitāyā upāyakauśalyena ca parigṛhīto bhavati.*[65]

d) *mahākaruṇā* (Tib. *snying rje chen po*)

> *tena tasyāṃ velāyāṃ mahākaruṇā-parigṛhīto bhavati.*[66]

Such *dharmas* as *arhattva, pratyekabodhi*, etc., should remain outside a Bodhisattva-Mahāsattva's sphere of 'grasping' (*parigrahaṇa*).[67]

The operation *parigṛhṇāti* can be understood as inserting by *manas* in the "composition of a person" (i.e. a certain combination of *dharmas*) a number of new *dharmas* that already exist outside this person.

The next operation is denoted by derivatives of the root *kalpayati* (the main meaning is 'to produce' or 'to create'). The *Aṣṭasāhasrikā* uses both *kalpayati* (*kalpa, kalpanā*) and *vikalpayati* (*vikalpa, vikalpanā*). Since these terms have a special meaning in the works of late Buddhist logicians, they are well known in the literature on Buddhism.

In this connection we should refer to the famous work by Th. Stcherbatsky "Buddhist Logic".[68] His interpretation is based on the sources of the period when the word *dharma* almost completely disappeared from texts. Nevertheless, it can be a basis for our interpretation of this operation in spite of the fact that the *Aṣṭasāhasrikā* appeared at the time when the term *dharma* was most widely spread.

Stcherbatsky's conclusions are based on the assumption that all derivatives of *kalpayati* are basically synonyms.[69] I think that we cannot ignore this assumption.

Kalpanā (Tib. *rtog pa*), *vikalpanā* (Tib. *mi rtog pa*), etc., is a special operation of *manas* that consists in constructing new *dharmas* (absent in the outside world) and projecting them onto the outside world (onto the flow of *dharmas*).[70]

Chapter I of the *Aṣṭasāhasrikā* provides an interesting description of this operation:

> *tair-asaṃvidyamānāḥ sarvadharmāḥ kalpitāḥ / te tān kalpayitva dvayor-antayoḥ saktāḥ tān dharmān-na jānanti na paśyanti / tasmāt-te 'saṃvidyamānān sarvadharmān kalpayanti / kalpayitva dvāv-antāv-abhiniviśante / abhiniviśya tan-nidānam-upalambhaṃ niśritya atītān dharmān kalpayanti anāgatān dharmān kalpayanti, pratyutpannān dharmān kalpayanti / te kalpayitva nāma-rūpe 'bhiniviṣṭāḥ / tair-asaṃvidyamānāḥ sarvadharmāḥ kalpitāḥ / te tān-asaṃvidyamānān sarvadharmān kalpayanto yathābhūtaṃ mārgaṃ na jānanti na paśyanti.*[71]

Here the operation of 'constructing' is understood as an uninterrupted, conditioned and infinite process where already created *dharmas* force a person to create new ones again and again. Thus, the *Aṣṭasāhasrikā* only considers *kalpanā* as a process that does not lead to higher states of mind.[72]

But constructing is also an uncontrolled process; according to the *Aṣṭasāhasrikā*, only the Buddhas have the ability to overcome this constructing:

> *sarva-kalpa-vikalpa-prahīṇo hi tathāgataḥ.*[73]

Therefore the fact that the *Aṣṭasāhasrikā* provides no description of instructions on overcoming this operation is particularly interesting. This goal is achieved step by step, apparently using the operation of 'grasping' the *dharmas* that are 'non-constructions' (*avikalpa*) according to the *Aṣṭasāhasrikā*: *tathatā*,[74] *parama*,[75] *anuttarā samyaksaṃbodhi*.[76]

The last operation that interests us is denoted by the verb *sākṣāt-karoti* (Tib. *mngon sum du byed*) which is normally translated as 'make real', 'implement' or 'realize'.[77] The meaning of this word in Buddhist texts is not related to its original meaning: 'look with the eyes' or 'make visible'.

In the context of our model this concept can be understood as the final completion of a *dharma* in the structure of a person's *dharmas*. Since Buddhism does not see the final goal of a human being in the expansion and development of a human personality (*ego*) in the sense of keeping its original structure, the 'realization of *dharma*' is of course seen as an undesirable action.

Abandoning *sākṣāt-kāraṇa* does not necessarily mean abandoning *parigrahaṇa* – the latter may also be a non-final introduction (acceptance) of a *dharma* in the composition of a personality (while it is possible to abandon it at any time). That is why this is related to *Prajñāpāramitā*:

> *prajñāpāramitā ca me parigṛhītā bhaviṣyati, na sā sākṣāt-kṛtā.*[78]

The *Aṣṭasāhasrikā* explains giving up 'realisation' as follows:

> *yathā hi bhagavan sa eva dharmo na-upalabhyate yaḥ sākṣāt-kuryāt so 'pi dharmo na-upalabhyate yaḥ sākṣāt-kriyate so 'pi dharmo na-upalabhyate yena sākṣāt-kriyeta.*[79]

Along with other *dharmas*, the *Aṣṭasāhasrikā* proclaims giving up the realization of *śūnyatā*:

> *bodhisattvo-mahāsattvo śūnyatāṃ na sākṣāt-karoti.*[80]

The *Aṣṭasāhasrikā* has a similar attitude towards the *dharmas* *ānimitta,*[81] *gambhīra,*[82] *dharmatā,*[83] and *arhattva,*[84] that can only be realized at the level of *śrāvakas* and *pratyekabuddhas.*[85]

Bhūtakoṭi (Tib. *yan dag pa'i mtha'*)[86] has a special place among *dharmas* that should be realized. *Bhūtakoṭiṃ sākṣāt-karoti* means 'attaining the final state of a personality', i.e. the state, after which changing a personality in any way is impossible.

Therefore the *Aṣṭasāhasrikā* denies too early performance of this operation:

> *evam-eva subhūte bodhisattvo-mahāsattvaḥ prajñāpāramitāyaṃ caran upāyakauśalya-parigṛhītaḥ tāvat-taṃ paramaṃ bhūtakoṭiṃ na sākṣāt-karoti, yāvan-na tāni kuśalamūlāny-anuttarāyaṃ samyaksambodhau paripakkāni suparipakkāni.*[87]

But as we can see from the example, *bhūtakoṭi* here has the epithet *parama* – the highest, and the realization of *bhūtakoṭi* without this epithet is completely negated in the *Aṣṭasāhasrikā* since this finally means that a bodhisattva is at the level of *śrāvakas* and *pratyekabuddhas.*[88]

Consequently this state means the absolute isolation of the system of *dharmas* that is called the 'inner world' from the system of *dharmas* that is called the 'outer world' as the one who realizes *bhūtakoṭi* is not capable of performing the two previous operations.

1.4 *Śūnyatā*

The concept of *śūnyatā* (Tib. *stong pa nyid*)[89] has an important place in the Mahāyāna theory of *dharmas*. It undoubtedly is the central term of Nāgārjuna's philosophy that Th. Stcherbatsky denoted as the theory *sarva-dharma-śūnyatā.*[90]

Nāgārjuna's philosophy apparently emerged under the influence of the *Prajñāpāramitā* sūtras. Candrakīrti wrote that Nāgārjuna's teaching is the direct continuation of *Prajñāpāramitā*:

> *ācārya-ārya-nāgārjunasyavidita-aviparīta-prajñāpāramitā-nīteḥ karuṇayā para-avabodha-arthaṃ śāstra-praṇayanaṃ.*[91]

Many scholars have said the same in the 20th century. M. Walleser wrote: "The systematic development of the thought of voidness laid down in the *Prajñāpāramitā Sūtras* is brought into junction with the name of a man of whom we cannot even positively say that he has really existed, still less that he is the author of the works ascribed to him: this name is Nāgārjuna."[92]

Prof. Murti agrees: "The Mādhyamika system is the systematized form of the *śūnyatā*-doctrine of the *Prajñāpāramitā* treatises: its metaphysics, spiritual path (*ṣaṭ-pāramitā-naya*) and religious ideal are all present there, though in a loose, prolific garb."[93]

But R. Robinson's studies lead to a revaluation of this viewpoint. It turns out that almost all the main terms of the *Prajñāpāramitā* sūtras are either not mentioned in Nāgārjuna's kārikās (*prajñā, tathatā, bhūtakoṭi, advaya, bodhicitta, bhūmi*), or are mentioned very rarely (*bodhisattva*).[94]

Only one term, *śūnyatā*, is frequently used both in the *Prajñāpāramitā* sūtras and Nāgārjuna's kārikas. But does it mean that *śūnyatā* is also the main term in the *Prajñāpāramitā* sūtras? I think that such a conclusion would be unfounded.[95]

D. T. Suzuki wrote the same in the foreword to his essay "*Prajñāpāramitā* Philosophy and Religion": "The chief defect, however, with the Diamond Cutter is that it emphasizes the *śūnyatā* aspect of the *Prajñāpāramitā* teaching too strongly, giving to the general reader the impression that this is the Alpha and Omega of the Mahāyāna. (…) The object of this essay is to state that the teaching of the *Prajñāpāramitā* consists in defining the essence of Bodhisattvahood."[96]

Nevertheless, the term *śūnyatā* has such an important place in the *Aṣṭasāhasrikā* that any study of this sūtra is unthinkable without analysing it, and any study of this concept is unthinkable without analysing this text. Unfortunately, the *Aṣṭasāhasrikā* has so far been studied too one-sidedly: only the aspects that confirmed the hypothesis about the origin of Nāgārjuna's teaching from the teaching of the *Prajñāpāramitā* sūtras were sought in the *Aṣṭasāhasrikā*'s *śūnyatā*.

In fact, the *Aṣṭasāhasrikā* provides much more versatile material for studying *śūnyatā*. In the *Aṣṭasāhasrikā* this term is not the only word that expresses a Bodhisattva-Mahāsattva's special relation with *dharmas*.[97] Along with *śūnyatā*, there are many others. These other words can in a way be seen as synonymous to *śūnyatā*. Sometimes they overlap only partly and provide valuable material for the analysis of both the theory and concept of *śūnyatā*.

The main synonyms of *śūnyatā* are *ānimitta* (Tib. *mtshan ma med pa*) and *apraṇihita* (Tib. *smon pa med pa*). Together with *śūnyatā* they form a special subsection on some Buddhist lists under the name of *trivimokṣamukha* – 'three doors of liberation'.[98] The *Aṣṭasāhasrikā* uses the term *trivimokṣamukha* and lists its elements.[99]

Ānimitta is usually translated as 'signlessness' and *apraṇihita* as 'wishlessness'. There is an interesting context for these terms in the *Aṣṭasāhasrikā*:[100]

> *kiṃcā-api śāriputra eteṣāṃ bodhisattvānām-asti mārgaḥ śūnyatā vā ānimitta-caryā vā apraṇihita-manasikāratā vā...*[101]

The example allows us to find out how the authors of the *Aṣṭasāhasrikā Prajñāpāramitā* divided the sphere of use of these synonyms: *śūnyatā* describes the way of a bodhisattva; *ānimitta* denotes behaviour at some achieved level of this way and *apraṇihita* means the state of observation. Using just one example, it is difficult to say how universal this distinction was in Buddhist literature. Nevertheless, it has certain significance in the *Aṣṭasāhasrikā*.

There are a large number of synonyms of *śūnyatā* (*śūnya*) in Chapter XVIII of the *Aṣṭasāhasrikā*:[102]

aprameya[103]	*gzhal du med pa*	immeasurable
asaṃkhyeya	*grangs med pa*	incalculable
akṣaya	*mi zad pa*	inextinguishable
anabhisaṃskāra	*mngon par 'du mi byed pa*	uneffected
anutpāda	*mi 'byung ba*	unproduced
ajāti	*mi skye ba*	no-birth
abhāva	*dngos po med pa*	non-existence
virāga	*'dod chags dang bral ba*	dispassion
nirodha	*'gog pa*	stopping
nirvāṇa	*mya ngan las 'das pa*	subsiding

The following synonyms of *śūnyatā* are listed in Chapter VII of the *Aṣṭasāhasrikā*:[104]

vivikta	*bden pa*	separated
śānta	*zhi ba*	quieted
advaya	*gnyis su med*	non-dual
advaidhīkāra	*gnyis su byas med*	not-divided

The synonyms that can be found in Chapter XII are as follows:[105]

ajānaka	*shes pa po med pa*	unknowable
apaśyaka	*mthong pa med pa*	invisible
aniśrita	*mi gnas pa*	independent
akṛta	*ma byas pa*	undone
avikṛta	*'gyur ba med pa*	unchangeable
anabhisaṃskāra	*mngon bar 'dus ma byas pa*	uneffected
acintya	*bsam gyis mi khyab pa*	unthinkable
śānta	*zhi ba*	quieted
vivikta	*dben ba*	separated
viśuddhya	*rnam par dag pa*	purified

The following list is used in Chapter XII:[106]

anabhisaṃskāra[107]	–	uneffected
anutpāda	*skye ba med pa*	unproduced
anirodha	*'gag pa med pa*	non-stopping
asaṃkleśa	*kun.nas nyon mongs pa med pa*	not-polluted
avyavadāna	*rnam par byang ba med pa*	non-purification
abhāva	*dngos po med pa*	non-existence
nirvāṇa	*mya ngan las 'das pa*	subsiding
dharmadhātu	*chos kyi dbyings*	sphere of *dharma*
tathatā	*de bzhin nyid*	suchness

Two synonyms are given in Chapter XIII:[108]

acintya	*bsam gyis mi khyab pa*	unthinkable
atulya	*mtshungs pa med pa*	incomparable

The following synonym can be encountered in Chapter XVIII:[109]

anabhilāpya	*brjod du med pa*	inexpressible

Anabhilāpya as a synonym of *śūnyatā* is described in the *Aṣṭasāhasrikā* as follows:

yā ca subhūte sarvadharmānām śūnyatā, na sā śakya anabhilāpitum.[110]

The *Aṣṭasāhasrikā* also uses the synonym:

gambhīra[111]	*zab po*	deep

The following words can also be considered as figurative synonyms of *śūnyatā*:

pratiśrutkā-upama[112]	*brag cha lta bu*	similar to echo
māyā-upama[113]	*sgyu ma lta bu*	similar to illusion

A very interesting list of synonyms can also be found in Chapter XI of the *Aṣṭasāhasrikā*:

> *sarvaṃ hi saṃskṛtam-anityaṃ sarvaṃ bhaya-avagataṃ duḥkhaṃ, sarvaṃ traidhātukaṃ śūnyaṃ sarvadharmā anātmānaḥ.*[114]

As this passage is clearly a quote from a canonical sūtra,[115] these synonyms expressing an emotional shade of *śūnyatā* should not necessarily be considered as specifically related to the *Prajñāpāramitā*. But at the same time this passage proves the statement of the *Aṣṭasāhasrikā* that the teaching of *śūnyatā* can also be proclaimed in other than *Prajñāpāramitā* sūtras.[116]

What translation is best for *śūnyatā* on the basis of the *Aṣṭasāhasrikā*? Is it 'emptiness' as most of scholars including F. I. Streng,[117] the author of a monograph on this subject, translates it, 'relativity'[118] or 'zero'?[119]

It seems to me that each of these translations reflects a certain facet of this concept.

The *Aṣṭasāhasrikā* also uses the form *śūnyaka* in a situation where it clearly means 'empty'.[120] On the basis of the following example *śūnyatā* can be interpreted as 'relativity':

> *evaṃ yaś-ca-abhisambudhyate anuttarāṃ samyaksaṃbodhiṃ, yañ-ca-abhisaṃbodhavyaṃ, yaś-ca janīyat, yañ-ca jñatavyaṃ, sarvā ete dharmāḥ śūnyāḥ.*[121]

However, I think that the translation 'zero' is the best in the textual situations where the word *śūnyatā* is used in relation to the versatile nature of its synonyms. I would also draw your attention to the fact that many synonyms form opposite pairs (*anutpāda–anirodha*, etc.) and *śūnyatā* means their neutralization.

Śūnyatā in the *Aṣṭasāhasrikā* is not an ontological fact or 'existing state of affairs'. Neither is it the conception of a theory or an idea that should be understood and 'realized'.[122] It most probably means spontaneously giving up any operations, positive and negative, performed by a person with *dharmas* and at the same time giving up such giving up.[123] Perhaps, the authors of the *Aṣṭasāhasrikā* meant such an understanding in the following passage:

> *yaś-ca atyanta-vivikto dharmaḥ, na so 'sti-iti vā na-asti-iti vā upaiti.*[124]

2. Bodhisattva

The bodhisattva has been one of the most important Buddhist concepts throughout the history of Buddhism. But only in Mahāyāna it received such a wide meaning that the term 'bodhisattva vehicle' or 'bodhisattva way' (*bodhisattvayāna*) has become a synonym of Mahāyāna. Later Buddhism developed a sophisticated scholastic theory of bodhisattva, which was described in the works of such great thinkers as Asaṅga, Śāntideva, Candrakīrti and others.

Unfortunately, late Buddhist thought became so influential that modern Buddhist studies also consider all problems related to this concept of bodhisattva from this point of view.[125] In addition, the concept of the bodhisattva was not uniform even in Mahāyāna. The image and ideal of the bodhisattva were considered differently in different schools and texts and the development of it has a long history. Therefore the investigation of such an ancient and significant source as the *Aṣṭasāhasrikā Prajñāpāramitā* is of paramount importance.[126]

The *bodhisattva* is one of the concepts that are clearly defined in the *Aṣṭasāhasrikā Prajñāpāramitā*. In this respect it can be considered as a purely *Prajñāpāramitā* term (unlike *dharma* which is not defined in the *Aṣṭasāhasrikā*). The definition is given in the very first chapter, which may indirectly refer to the primary importance of the term:

> *apadārthaḥ subhūte bodhisattva-padārthaḥ / tatkasya hetoḥ? sarva-dharmāṇām hi subhūte bodhisattvo mahāsattvo 'saktatāyāṃ śikṣate / sarva-dharmāṇāṃ hi subhūte bodhisattvo mahāsattvo anubodhana-arthena asaktatāyām-anuttarāṃ samyaksaṃbodhim-abhisaṃbudhyate / bodhy-arthena hi subhūte bodhisattvo mahāsattvo ity-ucyate.*[127]

We should bear in mind that the definition of the bodhisattva (here we do not focus on the dialectical method of the authors of the *Aṣṭasāhasrikā*: any definition is in itself a non-definition) contains no hint of the compassionate or divine nature of the bodhisattva, which could be expected from the definitions of later Buddhism.

2.1 Bodhisattva and three *yānas*

The concept of bodhisattva has two meanings in the *Aṣṭasāhasrikā Prajñāpāramitā*: wider and narrower. First, the bodhisattva is a being who strives to change his mind. In this sense, he is only opposed to the 'common person' (*pṛthagjana*), meaning those who do not aspire to change their state of mind.

The *Aṣṭasāhasrikā Prajñāpāramitā*, as well as many other Mahāyāna sources, describes three vehicles, three main possibilities to change one's state of mind: 'vehicle of śrāvakas' (*śrāvakayāna*, Tib. *nyan thos kyi theg pa*), 'vehicle of pratyekabuddhas' (*pratyekabuddhayāna*, Tib. *rang sangs rgyas kyi theg pa*) and Mahāyāna – the 'great vehicle' (Tib. *theg pa chen po*).

Parallel hierarchy based on the notion of 'level' (*bhūmi*) is used in the simultaneous presentation of these vehicles (*yānas*): 'level of śrāvakas' (*śrāvakabhūmi*, Tib. *nyan thos kyi sa*), 'level of pratyekabuddhas' (*pratyekabuddhabhūmi*, Tib. *rang sangs rgyas kyi sa*) and 'level of buddhas' (*buddhabhūmi*, Tib. *sangs rgyas kyi sa*).[128] All three levels are opposed to the 'level of common people' (*pṛthagjanabhūmi*, Tib. *so so'i skye bo'i sa*) that has no parallels in the hierarchy of vehicles.[129]

Thus a bodhisattva in the first meaning is a person who is characterized as abiding on one of the three vehicles mentioned above. It means that the personology of the *Aṣṭasāhasrikā* embraces three main types of bodhisattva: 'bodhisattva abiding on the vehicle of śrāvakas' (*śrāvakayānika bodhisattva*, Tib. *nyan thos kyi theg pa'i byang chub sems dpa'*), 'bodhisattva abiding on the vehicle of pratyekabuddhas' (*pratyekabuddhayānika bodhisattva*, Tib. *rang sangs rgyas kyi theg pa'i byang chub sems dpa'*) and 'bodhisattva abiding on the vehicle of Mahāyāna' (*mahāyānika bodhisattva*, Tib. *theg pa chen po'i byang chub sems dpa'*).[130]

In most cases a 'bodhisattva abiding on the vehicle of śrāvakas' is simply denoted by the term *śrāvaka* and the highest state of śrāvaka by the term *arhattva*[131] or *śrāvakatva.*[132] A 'bodhisattva abiding on the vehicle of pratyekabuddhas' is accordingly denoted as a *pratyekabuddha.* The highest state of the pratyekabuddha is *pratyekabodhi*[133] or *pratyekabodhatva.*[134]

Mahāyānika bodhisattva is opposed to the first two. In this way they can be classified under one term – *śrāvakapratyekabuddha.*[135] The *Aṣṭasāhasrikā* describes *mahāyānika bodhisattva* as the main type of bodhisattva (the other meaning of the term bodhisattva). However, this does not mean that *śrāvakayānika bodhisattva* and *pratyekabuddhayānika bodhisattva* are regarded as being something outside Buddhism. On the contrary, as the *Aṣṭasāhasrikā Prajñāpāramitā* states, they have their authoritative teaching that comes from Gautama himself, as does the teaching of *Prajñāpāramitā.*[136]

The feature that is considered to be characteristic for śrāvakas and pratyekabuddhas is that they only aspire to free themselves. The *Aṣṭasāhasrikā* expresses this as follows:

> *na hi subhūte bodhisattvena mahāsattvena-evaṃ śikṣitavyaṃ yathā śrāvakayānikāḥ pratyekabuddhayānikā vā pudgalāḥ śikṣante / kathaṃ ca subhūte śrāvakayānikāḥ pratyekabuddhayānikā vā pudgalāḥ śikṣante? teṣāṃ subhūte evaṃ bhavati – ekam-ātmānam damayiṣyāmaḥ, ekam-ātmānaṃ śamayiṣyāmaḥ, ekam-ātmānaṃ parinirvāpayiṣyāmaḥ, ity-ātma-dama-śamatha-parinirvāṇāya sarvakuśalamūlā-abhisaṃskāra-prayogān-ārabhante.*[137]

The bodhisattva who has chosen the Mahāyāna vehicle should also develop qualities that for an outsider seem to be similar to those of śrāvakas (*śrāvakaguṇa*); apparently to prevent an outsider (non-Buddhist) from being able to draw a line between different types of personalities in Buddhist lysiology.

But even a *mahāyānika bodhisattva* himself cannot be sure that he has completely overcome the level of śrāvakas and pratyekabuddhas. He can only become convinced of it by acquiring 'skill in means' (*upāyakauśalya*, Tib. *thabs la mkhas pa*) and understanding *prajñāpāramitā* step by step.

The term *pratyekabuddha* is used in the *Aṣṭasāhasrikā* quite rarely and does not significantly enrich our knowledge of it. Moreover, this term is scarcely investigated in contemporary Buddhist studies. However, those who are denoted by the term *śrāvaka* have a positive meaning in the *Aṣṭasāhasrikā*. It is manifested in the fact that although *śrāvaka* is not the most important element in the lysiological space of the *Aṣṭasāhasrikā Prajñāpāramitā* (i.e. according to the *Aṣṭasāhasrikā* śrāvakas cannot reach their purpose, which is only to free themselves), persons denoted by this term fulfil a certain function that is to support the aspirations of the Bodhisattva-Mahāsattva. They are to help the Bodhisattva-Mahāsattva in achieving his goal by giving him their knowledge since they are capable of understanding the 'ultimate perfect awakening' (*anuttarā samyaksaṃbodhi*) but not to reach it.[138]

This idea is even expressed in the structure of the text of the *Aṣṭasāhasrikā Prajñāpāramitā*. All main speakers (except Bhagavat, that is the Buddha) are śrāvakas: Subhūti, Śāriputra, Ānanda, Pūrṇa, etc. The analysis of their relations and differences in their views would be extremely interesting for reconstructing the position of Hīnayānists at the beginning of the Christian era.[139]

2.2 Bodhisattva-Mahāsattva

The second major meaning of the concept of bodhisattva is the 'person who has chosen the vehicle of Mahāyāna'. In this sense, there are several subtypes of bodhisattvas: *bodhisattvayānika pudgala*, *bodhisattva* and *bodhisattva-mahāsattva*.

Bodhisattvayānika pudgala and *bodhisattva* only appear in the *Aṣṭasāhasrikā* on a few occasions and even then mainly in the situations where a bodhisattva renounces the *Prajñāpāramitā* and tries to read Hīnayāna texts.[140] Sometimes, indeed, the term *bodhisattva* can also be encountered in a positive sense.[141]

The main term in the conception of the bodhisattva in the *Aṣṭasāhasrikā Prajñāpāramitā* is *bodhisattva-mahāsattva*. In contemporary Buddhist studies *mahāsattva* is normally translated as an epithet to bodhisattva meaning 'great-natured' or 'great being'[142] and the Bodhisattva-Mahāsattva is not considered as a subtype of bodhisattva. However the commentator of the *Aṣṭasāhasrikā* Haribhadra (in the 9th century) explained the terminological nature of the word *mahāsattva*:

> *śrāvakā api syūr-evam ity-āha – mahāsattva iti.*[143]

The *Aṣṭasāhasrikā* gives three definitions of the term *mahāsattva*. The first belongs to Bhagavat (i.e. Śākyamuni), the second to Śāriputra and the third to Subhūti.

1. *mahataḥ sattvarāśer-mahataḥ sattva-nikāyasya agratāṃ kārayiṣyati, tena-arthena bodhisattvo mahāsattva ity-ucyate.*[144]

2. *mahatyā ātmadṛṣṭyāḥ sattvadṛṣṭyāḥ jīvadṛṣṭyāḥ pudgaladṛṣṭyāḥ bhavadṛṣṭyāḥ vibhavadṛṣṭyāḥ ucchedadṛṣṭyāḥ śāśvatadṛṣṭyāḥ svakāyadṛṣṭyāḥ, etāsām-evam-ādyānāṃ dṛṣṭīnāṃ prahāṇāya dharmaṃ deśayiṣyati-iti, tena-arthena bodhisattvo mahāsattva ity-ucyate.*[145]

3. *bodhisattvo mahāsattva iti bhagavann-ucyate / yad-api tad-bhagavan bodhicittaṃ sarvajñatācittaṃ-anāsravaṃ cittam-asamaṃ cittam-asama-samaṃ cittam-asādhāraṇaṃ sarva-śrāvaka-pratyekabuddhaiḥ, tatra-api citte asakto 'paryāpannaḥ / tat-kasya hetoḥ? tathā hi tat-sarvajñatā-cittam-anāsravam-aparyāpannaṃ tat, yad-api tat-sarvajñatā-cittam-anāsravam-aparyāpannam / tatra-api citte asakto 'paryāpannaḥ / tena-arthena bodhisattvo mahāsattva iti saṃkhyāṃ gacchati.*[146]

The differences between the three definitions are clear, which obviously has a deep meaning. Bhagavat's viewpoint can be considered as purely Mahāyānist: it is only about relations between people and the Bodhisattva-Mahāsattva where the Bodhisattva-Mahāsattva is the subject of compassion, and people are objects of compassion. Śāriputra's definition is purely Hīnayānist: destroying different erroneous views (*dṛṣṭi*) has a meaning primarily in the context of Hīnayāna sūtras.[147] The presence of this passage in the *Aṣṭasāhasrikā Prajñāpāramitā* is rather mysterious: it has absolutely no connection with the teaching of *Prajñāpāramitā* and not even with Śāriputra's other statements.

Subhūti's ideas can be considered as belonging purely to the *Prajñāpāramitā* as they reflect the *Prajñāpāramitā* aspect of the zerological Buddhist doctrine.[148] However, Subhūti's definition lacks Mahāyānist understanding in the direct sense (as it was expressed in Bhagavat's passage). This is understandable: in the *Aṣṭasāhasrikā* Subhūti represents śrāvakas who are capable of understanding extremely sophisticated (also those of *Prajñāpāramitā*) logical constructions but cannot grasp the main meaning of the concept of Bodhisattva-Mahāsattva in the context of Mahāyāna that is to help other beings to reach the ultimate state of mind.

Of course, the views of Bhagavat and Subhūti only express different aspects of the Bodhisattva-Mahāsattva concept in the context of *Prajñāpāramitā*. The *Aṣṭasāhasrikā* elucidates this as follows:

> *dvābhyāṃ subhūte dharmābhyāṃ samanvāgato bodhisattvo mahāsattvas–tasmin samaye durdharṣo bhavati māraiḥ pāpiyobhir-mārakāyikābhir-vā devatābhiḥ / katamābhyāṃ dvābhyām? yad-uta sarva-sattvāś-ca-asya aparityaktā bhavanti, sarva-dharmāś-ca anena śūnyatāto vyavalokitā bhavanti / ābhyāṃ subhūte dvābhyāṃ dharmābhyāṃ samanvāgato bodhisattvo mahāsattvo durdharṣo bhavati māraiḥ pāpiyobhir-mārakāyikābhir-vā devatābhiḥ.*[149]

The main epithet of the Bodhisattva-Mahāsattva in the *Aṣṭasāhasrikā* is 'hard-working' (*duṣkara-kāraka*).[150] It can be found in the descriptions of both aspects of the Bodhisattva-Mahāsattva and its meaning needs no special comments: it is hard to understand the *Prajñāpāramitā* teaching and it is hard to become a person who sincerely considers and is worried about the well-being of mankind and does it concretely, not abstractly.[151] However, the *Aṣṭasāhasrikā* describes the possibility of the fulfilment of this wish so paradoxically that to an unprepared reader it inevitably seems to be saying that no progress is possible:

> *iha subhūte bodhisattvasya mahāsattvasya-evaṃ bhavati – aprameyā mayā sattvāḥ parinirvāpayitavyā iti / asaṃkhyeyā mayā sattvāḥ parinirvāpayitavyā iti / na ca te santi yair ye parinirvāpayitavyā iti / sa tāṃs-tāvataḥ sattvān parinirvāpayati / na ca sa kaścid-sattvo yaḥ parinirvṛto yena ca parinirvāpito bhavati.*[152]

Gradations of the level of the Bodhisattva-Mahāsattva are quite significant. Generally, the level of the Bodhisattva-Mahāsattva depends on how fast he understands the teaching of *Prajñāpāramitā*.[153]

It seems that those who do not understand *Prajñāpāramitā* are abiding at the lowest level of Bodhisattva-Mahāsattva. The Bodhisattva-Mahāsattva who is at a higher level should understand *Prajñāpāramitā* immediately on his first contact with the text.[154]

The Bodhisattva-Mahāsattva who abides on a lower level has certain emotions which the *Aṣṭasāhasrikā* sees as negative: pride, arrogance, contempt (*māna, atimāna, mithyāmāna, abhimāna*). These emotions prevent the Bodhisattva-Mahāsattva reaching the ultimate states of mind – 'omniscience' (*sarvajñatā*) and 'ultimate perfect awakening' (*anuttarā samyaksaṃbodhi*).[155]

Pride and other negative emotions or traits form a complex that is denoted by the term 'defilements of the mind' (*kleśa*).[156] In the *Aṣṭasāhasrikā* the attitude towards the Bodhisattvas-Mahāsattvas who have *kleśas* is clearly negative. It is interesting to read the description of such Bodhisattvas-Mahāsattvas that may reflect conflicting opinions in the Buddhist community at the time.[157]

Controversy in the Buddhist community also manifests itself in how the *Aṣṭasāhasrikā* treats the problem of seclusion. The *Aṣṭasāhasrikā* describes those who demand seclusion (*viveka*) in the direct sense of the word (i.e. separating themselves from society) as the assistants of Māra.[158]

Seclusion has not only played a significant role in religion (in the narrow sense of the word) but has been a social regulatory mechanism throughout Indian history. Therefore the *Aṣṭasāhasrikā* does not seem to be directly against seclusion. It does not reject (as it often does in other cases) the word *viveka*. The *Aṣṭasāhasrikā* does not say that seclusion is bad or that it is not good to separate oneself from society. On the contrary, the *Aṣṭasāhasrikā* advocates the idea of seclusion. However, it also says that seclusion should be understood correctly and correct understanding is not separating oneself from society but separation from the so-called 'disposition' (*manasikāra*) of śrāvakas and pratyekabuddhas. Whether a person lives in a city or in the jungle has nothing to do with actual seclusion.[159]

The *Aṣṭasāhasrikā* is also concerned about the relations of the Bodhisattvas-Mahāsattvas with the Buddhas. These are manifested in the term *vyākaraṇa* which is usually translated as 'prediction'.[160] A prediction is made by some Buddha when a Bodhisattva-Mahāsattva has reached a certain state, after which he is called ***vyākṛta bodhisattva-mahāsattva***.

Not all Bodhisattvas-Mahāsattvas reach the state of *vyākṛta* but only those who correctly understand the teaching of *Prajñāpāramitā*. This, in turn, requires that they have been going along the Mahāyāna path for many lifetimes. Such a Bodhisattva-Mahāsattva bears the epithet *cirayāna-saṃprasthita* ('one who set out a long time ago'),[161] the opposite term is *navayāna-saṃprasthita* ('one who set out a short time ago').[162]

The *Aṣṭasāhasrikā* describes the process of *vyākaraṇa* using the example of Gautama Buddha (Bhagavat), whose future was predicted by Buddha Dīpaṅkara:

> *bhaviṣyasi tvam māṇavaka anāgate 'dhvani śākyamunir-nāma tathāgato 'rhan samyaksaṃbuddhaḥ.*[163]

Bhagavat himself does *vyākaraṇa* for Gaṅgadevā Bhaginī who should become Buddha Suvarṇapuṣpa in the future.[164]

Regarding *vyākṛta bodhisattva-mahāsattva* as a subtype of the Bodhisattvas-Mahāsattvas, the *Aṣṭasāhasrikā* does not solve the problem of whether a Bodhisattva-Mahāsattva himself can become aware of being a Bodhisattva-Mahāsattva. This and many other questions remain unanswered in the *Aṣṭasāhasrikā* and this, I think, shows the tendency of the *Aṣṭasāhasrikā* towards *śūnyatā.*[165]

The following subtype of the hierarchy of Bodhisattvas-Mahāsattvas is ***avinivartanīya bodhisattva-mahāsattva*** ('unreturnable Bodhisattva-Mahāsattva'). In a way, *vyākṛta bodhisattva-mahāsattva* and *avinivartanīya bodhisattva-mahāsattva* seem to represent the same type of bodhisattvas: on the one hand, the *Aṣṭasāhasrikā* considers all Bodhisattvas-Mahāsattvas whose names have been mentioned by the Buddhas to have reached the level of *avinivartanīya*. On the other hand, a *vyākṛta bodhisattva-mahāsattva* can also be at a much lower level.

Avinivartanīya bodhisattva-mahāsattva is the highest bodhisattva level before the level of a Buddha. It is interesting to note that in a way it is compared to the level of arhat (i.e. the last stage of the vehicle of śrāvakas'). It is particularly manifested in the fact that both of them understand the Tathāgata in the same way.[166]

As far as the levels of knowledge (*jñāna*) are concerned, it is believed that an unreturnable Bodhisattva-Mahāsattva has reached the level of unlimited (*ananta, aparyanta*) knowledge.[167] But it is also remarkable that omniscience (*sarvajñatā*) is nowhere considered to be one of his properties.

Apparently, an unreturnable Bodhisattva-Mahāsattva is not aware of being in this state. However (and this is a very interesting psychological observation of the authors of the *Aṣṭasāhasrikā*), they have no doubt (*vicikitsa, saṃśaya*) about this.[168] It means that an unreturnable Bodhisattva-Mahāsattva cannot see the difference between bodhisattva levels. According to the *Aṣṭasāhasrikā*, the fact that a bodhisattva has reached the level of an unreturnable Bodhisattva-Mahāsattva does not mean the formation of a highly developed but at the same time narrow-minded personality. On the contrary, the bodhisattva becomes a comprehensive person who represents all personological types of any classification.

Chapter XVII of the *Aṣṭasāhasrikā Prajñāpāramitā* is titled *Avinivartanīya-ākāra-liṅga-nimitta-parivarta* ('Chapter about the Attributes, Properties and Signs of Unreturnability'). At first glance it contradicts my argument that an unreturnable Bodhisattva-Mahāsattva is not interested in his state. However, my argument is confirmed by Subhūti's introductory question at the beginning of the chapter:

> *avinivartanīyasya bhagavan bodhisattvasya mahāsattvasya ke ākāraḥ, kāni liṅgāni, kāni nimittāni? kathaṃ vā bhagavan vayaṃ jānīyāma ayaṃ-avinivartanīyo bodhisattvo mahāsattva iti?*[169]

This question alone shows that these attributes, etc., are only meaningful for an outsider but not for the unreturnable Bodhisattva-Mahāsattva himself.

Their number is quite large. Some of them concern physical properties. He is characterized as a completely healthy person with no illnesses.[170] It is interesting that his ability to have sexual intercourse is mentioned among other things.[171]

The relations of an unreturnable Bodhisattva-Mahāsattva with the surrounding world are extremely interesting and complicated. He can live both as a hermit and a householder.[172] Still, he is not an average person: although he can do what a *pṛthagjana* does, his interests are outside the sphere of interests of the latter. Chapter XVII of the *Aṣṭasāhasrikā* provides a list of phenomena of the outside world that should not interest an unreturnable Bodhisattva-Mahāsattva: king, thief, army, war, village, borough, city, country, empire, capital, self, minister, prime minister, woman, man, hermaphrodite, carriage, park, garden, cloister, palace, bad spirits, food, drink, clothes, jewellery, perfume, wreathes, pomade, road, crossroads, street, market, game, palanquin, family, song, actor, dance, narration, artist, wandering minstrel, sea, river, island etc.[173]

In this article I am not considering the importance of this list for studying the structure of ancient Indian society. We are primarily interested in the fact that the list reflects the objects that were interesting for people of average education in that era (and maybe in other eras as well).

However, an unreturnable Bodhisattva-Mahāsattva is not even interested in 'spiritual' problems: he does not speak about *Prajñāpāramitā*.[174] This is understandable because *Prajñāpāramitā* is only important at a certain level of the bodhisattva vehicle – the level of the Bodhisattva-Mahāsattva.

3. *Prajñāpāramitā*

In this section, terms in the *Aṣṭasāhasrikā Prajñāpāramitā* denoting the ultimate state of mind will be investigated in a more detailed way. If we use the traditional meta-language of Buddhist studies, we may determine our task as the description of *nirvāṇa*.

3.1 *Nirvāṇa*

In Buddhist literature *nirvāṇa* is just one of the terms that denote the ultimate state of mind that is the goal of aspirations of all Buddhists. The Buddhist liberation is generally characterized by a virtually unlimited set of these terms. I think that this is a sign of the extreme complexity of Buddhism compared to other similar teachings. Even for this reason alone we should stop using one term as the predominant one since this would mean excessive simplification of the description of Buddhist teaching. At least we should stop doing this at the current stage of the development of Buddhist studies while most Buddhist sources have still not been studied scientifically.

As far as the *Aṣṭasāhasrikā Prajñāpāramitā* is concerned, the term *nirvāṇa* (Tib. *mya ngan 'das*), although used here, is clearly secondary in significance. In very few cases it means a realistically achievable state as, for example, in the following passage:

> *yadi kaścid-eva kulaputro vā kuladuhitā vā imāṃ gambhīrāṃ prajñāpāramitāṃ śṛṇuyāt, yāvad-asya devaputrāḥ kṣiprataraṃ nirvāṇaṃ pratikāṅkṣitavyam, na tu-eva teṣāṃ śraddhā-anusāri-bhūmau kalpaṃ vā kalpāvaśeṣaṃ vā caratām.*[175]

Another approach to this term is typical of the *Aṣṭasāhasrikā*. Let us give some examples:

> *sa nirvāṇam-api na manyate.*[176]
>
> *nirvāṇam-api māyā-upamaṃ svapna-upamam .*[177]

The authors of the *Aṣṭasāhasrikā* clearly tried to diminish the significance of the term *nirvāṇa*. In Chapter III the wish to attain *nirvāṇa* is assessed as *rāga*, i.e. a certain *kleśa* (emotion), from which one should liberate oneself:

> *prajñāpāramitā hi rāga-ādīnām yāvan-nirvāṇa-grāhasya-upa-śamayitrī, na vivardhikā.*[178]

Generally, the word *nirvāṇa* is used extremely rarely in the *Aṣṭasāhasrikā*. But, what is most important, *nirvāṇa* is not included in the structure of concepts denoting the highest state where it should belong according to the European tradition of Buddhist studies.

Perhaps, one of the reasons for the exclusion of *nirvāṇa* from the set of the most important terms of the *Aṣṭasāhasrikā* was the clearly expressed trend of this work towards psychological analysis. But the main reason was undoubtedly the positive message of the sūtra: according to the *Aṣṭasāhasrikā*, the highest state is not the negation of the existing state that should be overcome but an essentially new state that has no cause and effect relationship with lower states.

The ultimate state of existence of a person is primarily a psychological fact, the highest state of mind. But at the same time it has an ontological aspect, i.e. it exists outside the person's mind.

As I have already noted, Buddhism as an extremely complicated teaching of liberation aspired to an unlimited number of terms denoting the ultimate state. (It is quite possible that here we see an analogy with Hinduism demonstrating the same tendency with regards to the pantheon.[179]) However, in each particular text we can find the main terms. I think that the main terms denoting the ultimate state of mind in the *Aṣṭasāhasrikā Prajñāpāramitā* are as follows: *prajñāpāramitā, anuttarā samyaksaṃbodhi, sarvajñatā, tathatā.*

All these words can in a way be seen as synonymous, i.e. an observer who is at a certain level can construct a convenient model where all these words are equivalent and even interchangeable.[180] Although this is particularly attractive for a sectarian approach, the expedience of this simplification for scientific Buddhist studies is questionable.

The terms quoted in this study are considered not as synonyms but as the basic elements of different sub-structures.

3.2 *Prajñāpāramitā*

The central term of the structure of the description of the ultimate state of mind is undoubtedly *prajñāpāramitā* (Tib. *shes rab kyi pha rol tu phyin pa*). Moreover, *prajñāpāramitā* is the main term of the *Aṣṭasāhasrikā Prajñāpāramitā* and all the *Prajñāpāramitā* literature. Nevertheless, it is one of least investigated concepts in Indian thought.

Although the etymological meaning of this word is well known, there is no more or less reliable interpretation of its content. What E. Conze and J. May wrote about the meaning of *prajñāpāramitā* can be considered as a brief summary of Buddhist studies devoted to this problem:

"The sanskrit word is *pra-JÑĀ-pāram-itā*, literally 'wisdom-gone-beyond', or, as we might say, 'Transcendental Wisdom'. Buddhists at all times have compared this world of suffering, of birth-and-death, with a river in full spate. On the hither shore we are erring about, tormented by all kinds of unease and distress. On the yonder shore lies the *Beyond*, the Paradise, Nirvāṇa, where all ills have, together with separate individuality, come to an end."[181]

"La nature et le rôle de la *prajñā* mettent en pleine lumière ce rapport ambigu de la *saṃvṛti* et du *paramārtha*, ou se conjuguent continuité et transcendence. L' "intuition intellectuelle" du *paramārtha*, qui lui est homogène, s'appelle *prajñāpāramitā*; et on sait asses que dans le term *pāramitā*, les étymologies traditionelles (*pāram itā*) et les traductions (*pha rol tu phyin pa*)."[182]

But one statement from Chapter VIII of the *Aṣṭasāhasrikā* seemingly shows that the authors of this sūtra did not consider etymological interpretation as the best method for establishing the meaning of this term:

> *sa khalu punar-iyaṃ bhagavan prajñāpāramitā na-apare tīre, na pare tīre, na-apy-ubhayam-antareṇa viprakṛtā sthitā.*[183]

All researchers of the *Prajñāpāramitā* without exception believed that it was possible to find adequate equivalents for the word *prajñāpāramitā* in modern European languages.

Some of them, mainly Japanese scholars headed by D. T. Suzuki completely ignored the independent existence of *prajñāpāramitā* as a term and said that its meaning was equivalent to the meaning of the term *prajñā* that according to Suzuki means 'intuition'.[184]

Others, mostly European and American scholars starting with M. Walleser understood *prajñāpāramitā* as the ultimate limit of *prajñā*. Walleser translated it as "die Vollkommenheit des Erkenntnis". In Th. Stcherbatsky's translation it is the "climax of wisdom".[185]

E. Conze at the beginning of his academic career used the translation 'perfection of wisdom'[186] but in the sixties replaced it by 'perfect wisdom'.[187]

I think that the meaning of *prajñāpāramitā* cannot be established through its grammatical or etymological analysis. Replacing the Sanskrit word *prajñāpāramitā* by a word or a combination of words in the researcher's own language does not mean that we have understood the Sanskrit term. Moreover, this technique does not make research of the *Prajñāpāramitā* literature easier as the suggested translation options only approximately express one aspect of the complex Buddhist term.

Here I do not pretend to solve at once this extremely complicated problem. Moreover, I state that it cannot be solved on the analysis of only one sūtra, e.g. the *Aṣṭasāhasrikā*. But by analysing the *Aṣṭasāhasrikā* we are taking some steps towards the solution of this problem.

My conclusions are based on the assumption that *prajñāpāramitā* is a completely independent term, the semantic field of which does not coincide at all or partly coincides with the meaning of its elements *prajñā* and *pāramitā*. However, I quite agree with the viewpoint that *prajñāpāramitā* can replace *prajñā* in some cases.[188] Generally, it is possible to construct a diachronic model of Buddhism where *prajñāpāramitā* gradually replaces *prajñā*.

The authors of the *Aṣṭasāhasrikā* in all probability believed that a definition of *prajñāpāramitā* was unnecessary and even impossible:

> *atha tām-api prajñāpāramitāṃ na saṃjānīte – iyaṃ sā prajñāpāramitā.*[189]

However, they have included in the *Aṣṭasāhasrikā* two sentences that can be seen as some kind of definition.

The first is in Chapter IV:

> *eṣa ca tathāgatakāyo bhūtakoṭi-prabhāvito draṣṭavyo yad-uta prajñāpāramitā.*[190]

The second definition is in Chapter XII:

> *tathāgatānām asaṅga-jñānaṃ yaduta prajñāpāramitā.*[191]

Of course, these definitions do not meet the requirements of modern science. But I could admit that in a way they helped direct the course of my thoughts towards what I believe to be a more or less correct solution to the problem of the concept of *prajñāpāramitā*. Further investigation of the *Aṣṭasāhasrikā* allowed me to understand the meaning of this complex term in the following way.

First, *Prajñāpāramitā* is a text generated by following special rules. This text can appear as inner speech, oral speech or a written text called *Prajñāpāramitā*, the purpose of which is to create the ultimate state of human mind.

Second, *prajñāpāramitā* is one of the names of the ultimate state of mind reflecting the ability of a person to fully understand the *Prajñāpāramitā* text and create new texts of the same type.

Of course, the Buddhist who participated in the creation of the *Prajñāpāramitā* sūtras saw both meanings as equal: the text meant for him the objectivized mind or the objective aspect of the mind, the ultimate state of mind – the subjective aspect of the structure that was meaningful for him in the *Prajñāpāramitā* sūtras.

Later Buddhists in India apparently considered the second aspect as primary: for them, the text was a more or less true reflection of the state of mind that itself was generally indescribable.[192]

I am certainly interested in all meanings of the term *prajñāpāramitā*. But since I only consider one sūtra, the *Aṣṭasāhasrikā*, in its written form and am totally unfamiliar with the tradition of the oral communication of the text, I have to take into account the character of the available text. As there is much more material on the first meaning of *prajñāpāramitā* in the *Aṣṭasāhasrikā*, the description of this meaning will take more space in this study than the description of the second meaning. At the same time, we should bear in mind that in some cases these two meanings appear totally indistinguishable.

Apparently, the authors of the *Aṣṭasāhasrikā* also had in mind that differentiation between the two meanings of *prajñāpāramitā* was merely conditional. Chapter XI of the *Aṣṭasāhasrikā* gives us following description:

> *ye kecit-subhūte prajñāpāramitāṃ lipy-akṣarair-likhitvā prajñāpāramitā likhitā-iti maṃsyante, asatīti vā akṣareṣu prajñāpāramitāṃ-abhiniveksyante, anakṣarā-iti vā, idam-api subhūte teṣāṃ mārakarma veditavyam.*[193]

Nevertheless, in most cases we have no difficulty in seeing whether *prajñāpāramitā* means the text or the ultimate state of mind.

Prajñāpāramitā as a text is primarily the *Aṣṭasāhasrikā Prajñāpāramitā* as well as many other sūtras created by following the same rules:

> *ya enāṃ prajñāpāramitāṃ bodhisattvo mahāsattvo 'nikṣiptadhuro mārgayati ca paryeṣate ca, sa jāti-vyativṛtto 'pi janmāntara-vyativṛtto 'pi enāṃ prajñāpāramitāṃ lapsyate / tato 'nyāni ca sūtrāṇi prajñāpāramitā-pratisamyuktāni tasya svayam-eva-upagamiṣyanti, upapatsyante.*[194]

The *Prajñāpāramitā* texts are opposed to the other sūtras:

> *punar-aparaṃ subhūte bodhisattvayānikāḥ pudgalā imāṃ prajñāpāramitāṃ sarvajña-jñānasya-ahārikāṃ vivarjya utsṛjya ye te sūtrāntā naiva sarvajña-jñānasya-ahārikās-tān paryeṣitavyān maṃsyante.*[195]

The sūtras that are opposed to the *Prajñāpāramitā* apparently belong to Hīnayāna:

> *te prajñāpāramitāṃ vivarjya utsṛjya chorayitvā tato 'nye sūtrāntā ye śrāvakabhūmim-abhivadanti, pratyekabuddha-bhūmim-abhivadanti, tān-adhikataraṃ paryavāptavyān maṃsyante.*[196]

Prajñāpāramitā as a text may have different forms. The following passage mentions the form of a book (a written text) and oral communication:

> *evaṃ tvaṃ kulaputra pratipadyamāno na-cirena prajñāpāramitāṃ śroṣyasi pustaka-gatām vā dharmabhāṇakasya bhikṣoḥ kāyagatām.*[197]

The authors of the *Aṣṭasāhasrikā* believed that the *Prajñāpāramitā* text was an "eternal book" and that all persons interested in the *Prajñāpāramitā*, including the Buddhas, should make any possible effort to preserve the text:

te 'pi sarve imāṃ prajñāpāramitāṃ samanvāharanti, autsukyam-āpadyante – kim-iti-iyaṃ prajñāpāramitā cirasthitikā bhavet, kim-ity-asyāḥ prajñāpāramitāyā nāma aviniṣṭaṃ bhavet, kim-ity-asyāḥ prajñāpāramitāyā bhāṣyamāṇāyā likhyamāṇāyāḥ śikṣamāṇāyā māraḥ pāpīyān mārakāyikā vā devatā antarāyaṃ na kuryur.[198]

Apparently, some *Prajñāpāramitā* texts already existed at the time when the *Aṣṭasāhasrikā* was created but these texts probably have not survived. It is rather interesting that along with real *Prajñāpāramitā* sūtras there were fakes, i.e. sūtras that were called *Prajñāpāramitā* but did not meet requirements set by the authors of the *Aṣṭasāhasrikā*:

punar-aparaṃ subhūte māraḥ pāpīyān śramaṇa-veṣeṇa-āgatya bhedaṃ prakṣepsyati / evaṃ ca navayāna-saṃprasthitāḥ kulaputrā vivecayiṣyanti na eṣā prajñāpāramitā yām-āyuṣmantaḥ śṛṇvanti / yathā punar-mama sūtra-āgataṃ sūtra-paryāpannam, iyaṃ sā prajñāpāramitā-iti.[199]

Fakes (*prativarṇikā*) of the *Prajñāpāramitā* are also mentioned in Chapter V of the *Aṣṭasāhasrikā*:

utpatsyate hi kauśika anāgate 'dhvani prajñāpāramitā-prativarṇikā.[200]

The authors of the *Aṣṭasāhasrikā Prajñāpāramitā* saw the *Prajñāpāramitā* as the only embodiment of the teaching of all Buddhas, i.e. as *dharmakāya*. Therefore all the respect that should have been paid to the Buddhas was transferred to the *Prajñāpāramitā*. The worship of the *Prajñāpāramitā* text is something that exceeds the worship of all other objects, mainly the worship of relics (*buddhaśarīra*).

In particular, the superiority of the worship of the *Prajñāpāramitā* is manifested in the fact that it can even overshadow the worship of the Buddhas or, rather, that the worship of the *Prajñāpāramitā* includes the worship of the Buddhas:

prajñāpāramitāṃ hi satkurvatā gurukurvatā mānayatā pūjayatā arcayatā apacāyatā kulaputreṇa vā kuladuhitrā vā atīta-anāgata-pratyutpannā buddhā bhagavanto buddhajñāna-parijñāteṣu sarvalokadhatuṣu atyantatayā satkṛtā gurukṛtā mānitāḥ pūjitā arcitā apacāyitāś-ca bhavanti.[201]

Even the Buddhas worship the *Prajñāpāramitā*:

prajñāpāramitā-eva-eṣā subhūte dharmāṇāṃ dharmatā-iti tathāgatā arhantaḥ samyaksaṃbuddhāḥ prajñāpāramitāṃ sat-

kurvanti gurukurvanti mānayanti pūjayanty-arcayanty-apacāyanti.[202]

The *Aṣṭasāhasrikā* extolled the worship of the *Prajñāpāramitā* using different epithets:

evaṃ mahārthikā bhagavatā-uktā prajñāpāramitāyāḥ pūjā kṛtā bhaviṣyati-iti /.../ evam mahānuśaṃsā evaṃ mahāphalā evaṃ mahāvipākā bhagavatā-uktā prajñāpāramitāyāḥ pūjā kṛtā bhaviṣyati-iti.[203]

The advantages of the worship of the *Prajñāpāramitā* seem to be seen in both axiological systems of the *Aṣṭasāhasrikā*. One of these is based on the concept of *dṛṣṭadharmika guṇa* and another on the concept of *puṇya*.

bhagavān-āha – yaḥ subhūte eko bodhisattvo-mahāsattvo yāvaj-jīvaṃ tiṣṭhaṃs-tān sarvasattvān cīvara-piṇḍapāta-śayana-āsana-glāna-pratyaya-bhaiṣajya-pariṣkāraiḥ sarvasukha-upādhānaiś-ca-upatiṣṭhet, tat-kiṃ manyase subhūte api nu sa bodhisattvo mahāsttvas-tato-nidānam bahutaraṃ puṇyaṃ prasavati?

subhūtir-āha - bahu bhagavan, bahu sugata.

bhagavān-āha – ataḥ sa subhūte bodhisattvo-mahāsattvas-tato-nidānaṃ bahutaraṃ puṇyaṃ prasavati, ya imāṃ prajñāpāramitām-antaśo 'cchaṭā-saṃghāta-mātrakam-api bhāvayet.[204]

The urgent need for the worship of the *Prajñāpāramitā* was obviously related to many processes that took place in the Buddhist community in the first centuries BC: the schism and appearance of many schools, the emergence of written texts, etc.

The authors of the *Aṣṭasāhasrikā* apparently thought that the main goal of the worship of the *Prajñāpāramitā* was to prepare the reader or the listener for **the process of the subjectivization of the text**. The set of synonyms of *prajñāpāramitā* played a crucial role in the process along with the worship. The number of synonyms is quite large but most of them are listed in Chapter IX of the *Aṣṭasāhasrikā*:

asatpāramitā	*ma mchis pa'i pha rol tu phyin pa*	non-existent pāramitā
asamasamatā-pāramitā	*mi mnyam pa dang mnyam pa nyid kyi pha rol tu phyin pa*	pāramitā that equals unequalable
viviktapāramitā	*dben pa'i pha rol tu phyin pa*	isolated pāramitā

anavamṛdya-pāramitā	*mi brdzhi ba'i pha rol tu phyin pa*	uncrushable pāramitā
apadapāramitā	*gnas ma mchis pa'i pha rol tu phyin pa*	trackless pāramitā
asvabhāva-pāramitā	*ngo bo nyid ma mchis pa'i pha rol tu phyin pa*	pāramitā without own-being
avacana-pāramitā	*brjod du ma mchis pa'i pha rol tu phyin pa*	inexpressible pāramitā
anāma-pāramitā	*ming ma mchis pa'i pha rol tu phyin pa*	nameless pāramitā
agamana-pāramitā	*'gro ba ma mchis pa'i pha rol tu phyin pa*	non-departing pāramitā
asaṃhārya-pāramitā	*mi 'phrogs pa'i pha rol tu phyin pa*	pāramitā that can not be taken away
akṣaya-pāramitā	*mi zad pa'i pha rol tu phyin pa*	indestructible pāramitā
anutpatti-pāramitā	*mi skye ba'i pha rol tu phyin pa*	pāramitā of non-arising
akāraka-pāramitā	*byed pa po ma mchis pa'i pha rol tu phyin pa*	non-acting pāramitā
ajānaka-pāramitā	*shes pa po ma mchis pa'i pha rol tu phyin pa*	non-recognising pāramitā
asaṃkrānti-pāramitā	*mi 'pho ba'i pha rol tu phyin pa*	pāramitā of non-passing
avinaya-pāramitā	*'dul ba med pa'i pha rol tu phyin pa*	pāramitā without discipline
svapna-pratiśrutkā-pratibhāsa-marīcī-māyā-pāramitā	*rmi lam dang sgra brnyan dang mig yor dang smyig rgyu dang sgyu ma'i pha rol tu phyin pa*	pāramitā of sleep, echo, reflection, mirage and illusion
asaṃkleśa-pāramitā	*kun nas nyon mongs pa mchis pa'i pha rol tu phyin pa*	pāramitā without defilement
avyavadāna-pāramitā	*rnam par byang ba ma mchis pa'i pha rol tu phyin pa*	pāramitā of non-purification

anupalepa-pāramitā	*gos pa ma mchis pa'i pha rol tu phyin pa*	stainless pāramitā
aprapañca-pāramitā	*spros pa ma mchis pa'i pha rol tu phyin pa*	non-spreading pāramitā
amānana-pāramitā	*rlom sems ma mchis pa'i pha rol tu phyin pa*	pāramitā without conceit
acalita-pāramitā	*mi gyo ba'i pha rol tu phyin pa*	unshakable pāramitā
virāga-pāramitā	*'dod chags dang bral ba'i pha rol tu phyin pa*	pāramitā without passion
asamutthāna-pāramitā	*ldang ba ma mchis pa'i pha rol tu phyin pa*	non-arising pāramitā
śāntapāramitā	*zhi ba'i pha rol tu phyin pa*	calm pāramitā
nirdoṣa-pāramitā	*skyon ma mchis pa'i pha rol tu phyin pa*	impeccable pāramitā
niḥkleśa-pāramitā	*nyon mongs pa ma mchis pa'i pha rol tu phyin pa*	unpolluted pāramitā
niḥsattva-pāramitā	*sems can ma mchis pa'i pha rol tu phyin pa*	pāramitā that has no beings
apramāṇa-pāramitā	*tshad ma mchis pa'i pha rol tu phyin pa*	unlimited pāramitā
antadvayān-anugama-pāramitā	*mtha' gnyis mi rtogs pa'i pha rol tu phyin pa*	non-dual pāramitā
asaṃbhinna-pāramitā	*tha mi dad pa'i pha rol tu phyin pa*	undivided pāramitā
aparāmṛṣṭa-pāramitā	*mchog tu mi 'dzin pa'i pha rol tu phyin pa*	untarnished pāramitā
avikalpa-pāramitā	*rnam par mi rtog pa'i pha rol tu phyin pa*	undiscriminated pāramitā
aprameya-pāramitā	*gzhal du ma mchis pa'i pha rol tu phyin pa*	immeasurable pāramitā

asaṅga-pāramitā	*chags pa ma mchis pa'i pha rol tu phyin pa*	unbound pāramitā
anitya-pāramitā	*mi rtag pa'i pha rol tu phyin pa*	impermanent pāramitā
duḥkha-pāramitā	*sdug bsngal ba'i pha rol tu phyin pa*	pāramitā of suffering
śūnya-pāramitā	*stong pa nyid kyi pha rol tu phyin pa*	empty pāramitā
anātma-pāramitā	*bdag ma mchis pa'i pha rol tu phyin pa*	pāramitā without self
alakṣaṇa-pāramitā	*mtshan nyid ma mchis pa'i pha rol tu phyin pa*	pāramitā without marks
sarvaśūnyatā-pāramitā	*stong pa nyid thams cad kyi pha rol tu phyin pa*	pāramitā of all emptinesses
smṛty-upasthāna-ādi-bodhi-pakṣa-dharma-pāramitā	*dran pa nye bar gzhag pa la sogs pa byang chub kyi phyogs kyi chos rnams kyi pha rol tu phyin pa*	pāramitā of the pillars of mindfulness and other *dharma*s of the wings of awakening
śūnyatā-ānimitta-apraṇihita-pāramitā	*stong pa nyid dang mtshan ma med pa dang smon pa med pa'i pha rol tu phyin pa*	pāramitā of emptiness, signlessness and non-attachment
aṣṭa-vimokṣa-pāramitā	*rnam par thar pa brgyad kyi pha rol tu phyin pa*	pāramitā of eight deliverances
nava-anupūrva-vihāra-pāramitā	*mthar gyis gnas pa'i snyoms par 'jug pa dgu'i pha rol tu phyin pa*	pāramitā of nine locations following each other
catuḥ-satya-pāramitā	*bden pa bzhi'i pha rol tu phyin pa*	pāramitā of four truths
daśa-pāramitā	*sa bcu'i pha rol tu phyin pa*	pāramitā of ten (levels)
bala-pāramitā	*stobs kyi pha rol tu phyin pa*	pāramitā of powers

vaiśāradya-pāramitā	*mi 'jigs pa'i pha rol tu phyin pa*	pāramitā of confidence
pratisaṃvit-pāramitā	*so so yang dag par rig pa'i pha rol tu phyin pa*	pāramitā of analytical cognition
sarva-buddha-dharma-āveṇika-pāramitā	*sangs rgyas kyi chos ma 'dres pa thams cad kyi pha rol tu phyin pa*	special pāramitā of all Buddha *dharmas*
tathāgata-tathatā-pāramitā	*de bzhin gshegs pa'i de bzhin nyid kyi pha rol tu phyin pa*	pāramitā of the suchness of Tathāgata
svayaṃbhā-pāramitā	*rang byung gi pha rol tu phyin pa*	pāramitā of self-emergence
sarvajña-jñāna-pāramitā	*thams cad mkhyen pa'i ye shes kyi pha rol tu phyin pa*	pāramitā of the Omniscient's knowledge

The reader (or listener) of the *Prajñāpāramitā* text was only considered to be well prepared for the perception of the text if paradoxical statements caused no negative emotions in him. Along with paradoxical dialogues, the role of the filter that let through only the people who were capable of subjectivizing the *Prajñāpāramitā* text was played by the set of synonyms (the purpose of which was to create the feeling of infinity in the mind).

Numerous epithets of the *Prajñāpāramitā* fulfil the same function. The most frequent epithet in the *Aṣṭasāhasrikā* is *gambhīrā*[205] (*zab mo*) – 'deep'. We would also quote the following epithets:

mahā-guṇa-samanvāgatā[206]	*yon tan chen po dang ldan pa*	having great qualities
aprameya-guṇa-samanvāgatā[207]	*yon tan tshad med dang ldan pa*	having immeasurable qualities
aparyanta-guṇa-samanvāgatā[208]	*yon tan mu med pa dang ldan pa*	having boundless qualities
mahārthikā[209]	*don chen po*	having great benefit
mahānuśaṃsā[210]	*phan yon chen po*	giving great advantage
mahāphalā[211]	*'bras bu chen po*	bearing great fruit
mahāvipākā[212]	*rnam par smin pa chen po*	providing great results

bahu-guṇa-samanvāgatā[213]	*yon tan mang po dang ldan pa*	having many qualities
duranubodhā[214]	*rtogs par dka' ba*	difficult to understand
acintyā[215]	*bsam gyis ma khyab pa*	unthinkable
akṛtā[216]	*ma bgyis pa*	undone
pariśuddhā[217]	*yongs su dag pa*	completely pure
duravagāhā[218]	*gting dpag dka' ba*	difficult to access
durudgrahā[219]	*gzung bar dka' ba*	difficult to grasp
apramāṇā[220]	*tshad med pa*	immeasurable
viviktā[221]	*dben pa*	isolated
atyanta-viviktā[222]	*shin tu dben pa*	completely isolated

According to the authors of the *Aṣṭasāhasrikā*, creating the ultimate state of mind is a process where a Bodhisattva-Mahāsattva should perform certain operations with the *Prajñāpāramitā* text. These operations are denoted by some verbs that form certain chains in the *Aṣṭasāhasrikā*. The most widespread chain consists of the following verbs:[223]

udgṛhṇāti	*'dzin pa*	grasp
dhārayati	*'chang pa*	keep
vācayati	*klog pa*	speak
paryavāpnoti	*kun chub par byed pa*	study
pravartayati	*rab tu 'don pa*	spread
deśayati	*ston pa*	teach
upadiśati	*nye bar ston pa*	direct
svādhyāyati	*kha ton bgyid pa*	repeat
uddiśati	*lung 'bogs pa*	explain

Sometimes the following verbs are added:

likhati[224]	*yi ger 'dri ba*	write
śṛṇoti[225]	*thos pa*	hear
paripṛcchati[226]	*yongs su 'dri ba*	ask

We can quote a passage from Chapter III of the *Aṣṭasāhasrikā* as an example:

> *tasmāt-tarhi kauśika kulaputreṇa vā kuladuhitrā vā kṣipraṃ ca-anuttarāṃ samyaksaṃbodhim-abhisaṃboddhu-kā-*

mena iyam-eva prajñāpāramitā sukhaṃ abhīkṣṇaṃ śrotavyā udgrahītavyā dhārayitavyā vācayitavyā paryavāptavyā pravartayitavyā deśayitavyā upadeṣṭavyā uddeṣṭavyā svādhyātavyā paripraṣṭavyā.[227]

The second level of the subjectivization of the *Prajñāpāramitā* text consists in the performance of the operation that in the *Aṣṭasāhasrikā* is denoted by the verb *śikṣate* (*slob pa*) – 'to learn'. This verb is used everywhere in the *Aṣṭasāhasrikā*[228] but the process of learning is specially considered in the 'Chapter about Learning' (*śikṣāparivarta*).[229]

Since the word *prajñāpāramitā* is used with this verb in the locative case, it apparently does not mean a 'text'.[230] This is also confirmed by the fact that *prajñāpāramitā* in this context is considered to be equivalent to another term denoting the ultimate state of mind – *sarvajñatā*:

> *evam-eva subhūte alpakās-te bodhisattvā-mahāsattvāḥ sattvanikāye samvidyante, ye 'syām sarvajñatā-śikṣāyāṃ śikṣante, yaduta prajñāpāramitā-śikṣāyām.*[231]
>
> *evam śikṣamāṇaḥ subhūte bodhisattvo mahāsattvaḥ śikṣate sarvajñatāyām / evaṃ śikṣamāṇaḥ śikṣate prajñāpāramitāyām.*[232]

The *śikṣā* can be understood as the gradual mastering by a Bodhisattva-Mahāsattva of the *Prajñāpāramitā* that in this context is a text that "came inside".[233] We should bear in mind that 'learning in *Prajñāpāramitā*' does not yet mean that a Bodhisattva-Mahāsattva is at the ultimate state of mind. *Prajñāpāramitā* is still an object for a Bodhisattva-Mahāsattva.

According to the authors of the *Aṣṭasāhasrikā*, the process of *śikṣā* frees a person from the risk of mental and physical faults. This is in fact also *dṛṣṭadharmika guṇa*. Lists of these faults are interesting axiologically and from the point of view of Buddhist studies.

The first list describes the typology of states of mind disappearing with *śikṣā*:[234]

khila-sahagata citta	*tha ba dang ldan pa'i sems*	melancholic mind
viciktitsā-sahagata citta	*the tshom dang ldan pa'i sems*	uncertain mind
īrṣyā-matsariya-sahagata citta	*phrag dog dang ldan pa'i sems, ser snga dang ldan pa'i sems*	envious and greedy mind

dauḥśīlya-sahagata citta	*tshul khrims 'chal ba dang ldan pa'i sems*	immoral mind
vyāpāda-sahagata citta	*gnod sems dang ldan pa'i sems*	evil thought
kauśīdya-sahagata citta	*le lo dang ldan pa'i sems*	lazy mind
vikṣepa-sahagata citta	*gyeng ba dang ldan pa'i sems*	confused mind
dauṣprajñā-sahagata citta	*'chal ba'i shes rab dang ldan pa'i sems*	stupid mind

The second list provides the personology of human types eliminated by learning:[235]

prāṇa-atipātin	*srog gcod pa*	murderer
adatta-ādāyin	*ma byin par len pa*	thief
kāma-mithyā-cārin	*'dod pa la log par spyod pa*	immoral
mṛṣāvādin	*brdzun du smra ba*	liar
piśunavāc	*phra ma smra ba*	slanderer
paruṣavāc	*tshig rtsub po smra ba*	foulmouthed person
saṃbhinna-pralāpin	*tshig kyal pa smra ba*	windbag
abhidhyālu	*brnab sems can*	covetous
vyāpanna-citta	*gnod sems can*	malicious
mithyā-dṛṣṭika	*log par lta ba can*	one who has wrong views

The third list includes human types who have diseases and physical faults that do not occur if a person is engaged in *śikṣā*:[236]

andha	*long ba*	blind
badhira	*'on ba*	deaf
kāṇa	*zhar ba*	one-eyed
kuṇṭha	*rdum po*	dull
kubja	*sgur po*	hunchbacked
kuṇi	*'theng po*	with withered arm
laṅga	*zha bo*	limping
khañja	*grum po*	lame
jaḍa	*lkugs pa*	stunned
lolla	*dig pa*	stutterer
kalla	*rna ba mi gsal ba*	deaf
hīna-aṅga	*yan lag nyams pa*	with tiny limbs

vikala-aṅga	*yan lag ma tshan ba*	deficient in limbs
vikṛta-aṅga	*yan lag mi sdug pa*	with abnormal limbs
durbala	*stobs chung ba*	weak
durvarṇa	*mdog mi sdug pa*	pale
duḥsaṃsthāna	*dbyings mi sdug pa*	bad-looking
hīna-indriya	*dbang po nyams pa*	decrepit
vikala-indriya	*dbang po ma tshang pa*	with defective organs[237]

In the second meaning, i.e. the ultimate state of mind where the full understanding of the *Prajñāpāramitā* will be possible, the term *prajñāpāramitā* is used in the *Aṣṭasāhasrikā* in combination with the verb *carati* (Tib. *spyod*) – 'to act, to move, to practice' – and on the list of the so-called 'six *pāramitās*'.

Prajñāpāramitāyām carati (*shes rab kyi pha rol tu phyin pa la spyod*) can formally be translated into English as 'he acts in *Prajñāpāramitā*'. Apparently, it means 'he has the ultimate state of mind'. It is interesting that a Bodhisattva-Mahāsattva has such a powerful characteristic as *śūnya* only in this context. This probably means that his behaviour is incomprehensible to any external observer. An external observer cannot follow changes in the mind of a Bodhisattva-Mahāsattva ('a Bodhisattva-Mahāsattva does not increase or decrease'). Since a Bodhisattva-Mahāsattva's behaviour is determined by the mind, i.e. by *prajñāpāramitā*, Bodhisattva-Mahāsattva and *prajñāpāramitā* are often used as equivalent terms:

> *na khalu punaḥ subhūte bodhisattvo mahāsattvaḥ prajñāpāramitāyāṃ caran vivardhate vā parihīyate vā / yathā-eva subhūte prajñāpāramitā śūnyā, sā na-eva vivardhate na ca parihīyate evam-eva subhūte bodhisattvo mahāsattvaḥ śūnyaḥ / sa na-eva vivardhate na ca parihīyate, evam-eva subhūte bodhisattvo mahāsattvaḥ śūnyaḥ.*[238]

In this context the term *prajñāpāramitā* has two synonyms: *sāra* (*snying po*) – 'core' and *paramārtha* (*don dam pa*) – the 'ultimate reality' that are opposed to the term *nimitta* (*mtshan ma*) – 'sign':

> *atha kalv-āyuṣmān śāriputra āyuṣmantaṃ subhūtim-etad-avocat – sāre bata-ayam-āyuṣman subhūte bodhisattvo mahāsattvaś-carati, yaḥ prajñāpāramitāyāṃ carati.*[239]
>
> *bhagavān-āha – yaḥ subhūte bodhisattvo mahāsattvaḥ prajñāpāramitāyām carati, sa kva carati? āha – carati bhagavan*

paramārthe / bhagavān-āha – tat-kiṃ manyase subhūte yo bodhisattvo mahāsattvaḥ paramārthe carati, sa nimitte carati? āha – na hi-idaṃ bhagavan.[240]

The term *prajñāpāramitā* also denotes the ultimate state of mind on the list of so-called six *pāramitās* (*ṣaṭpāramitā, pha rol tu phyin pa drug*):[241]

dānapāramitā	*sbyin pa'i pha rol tu phyin pa*
śīlapāramitā	*tshul khrims kyi pha rol tu phyin pa*
kṣāntipāramitā	*bzod pa'i pha rol tu phyin pa*
vīryapāramitā	*brtson 'grus kyi pha rol tu phyin pa*
dhyānapāramitā	*bsam gtan kyi pha rol tu phyin pa*
prajñāpāramitā	*shes rab kyi pha rol tu phyin pa*

The canonical list of six *pāramitās* is part of many Mahāyāna sūtras (e.g. *Vimalakīrtinirdeśasūtra*).[242] But in some Mahāyāna works and Pāli texts we find lists consisting of ten *pāramitās*.[243]

Tantric texts, again, quote six *pāramitās*.[244] The Canadian scholar H. V. Guenther who studies Tantric texts has an opinion that *prajñāpāramitā* ('discriminating awareness born from wisdom') is the last member not only on the formal list of six *pāramitās* but also in Buddhist practice: *pāramitās* are attained in a time sequence starting from *dānapāramitā* and ending with *prajñāpāramitā*.[245] Attaining *prajñāpāramitā* does not mean reaching the ultimate state of mind but only the beginning of the path towards this goal. This means that for Guenther the term *prajñāpāramitā* is equivalent to *bodhicittotpāda* rather than *anuttarā samyaksaṃbodhi*.

Guenther is right if we consider late *Pāramitāyāna* literature only.[246] Gampopa says the same.[247]

In the *Prajñāpāramitā* sūtras, particularly in the *Aṣṭasāhaṣrikā Prajñāpāramitā*, *prajñāpāramitā* is the primary and predominant member among the six *pāramitās*. The other *pāramitās* only exist as the elements of the *ṣaṭpāramitā* list. However, the term *prajñāpāramitā* can also be used outside the context of *ṣaṭpāramitā* (in most cases it is so).

The first five *pāramitās* briefly describe the normative behaviour of a Bodhisattva-Mahāsattva: he should be generous, moral, patient, courageous and capable of meditating, in the special sense of the words. The authors of the *Aṣṭasāhasrikā* argue that not any donation is *dānapāramitā*, not any morality is *śīlapāramitā*, not any patience is *kṣāntipāramitā*, not any courage is *vīryapāramitā* and not any meditation is *dhyānapāramitā*. It means that *dāna* in the word *dānapāramitā* has a meaning that is different from the meaning of *dāna* outside this compound word, etc.

Since these differences have not yet been pointed out in Buddhist studies, I will give some examples from the *Aṣṭasāhasrikā*.

a) *Prajñāpāramitā* is the primary (*pūrvāṃgamā, sngon du 'gro ba*) *pāramitā*:

> *prajñāpāramitā hi ānanda pūrvaṃgamā pañcānāṃ pāramitānām.*[248]
>
> *evam hi subhūte prajñāpāramitāyāṃ śikṣamāṇena bodhisattvena mahāsattvena sarvāḥ pāramitāḥ saṃgṛhītā bhavanti.*[249]

b) *Prajñāpāramitā* is the main and basic *pāramitā*:

> *eṣa hi prajñāpāramitā ṣaṇṇāṃ pāramitānāṃ ... nāyikā pariṇāyikā saṃdarśikā avadarśikā janayitrī dhātrī.*[250]

c) The behaviour of a Bodhisattva-Mahāsattva is described by the terms *dānapāramitā*, etc., only if he has *prajñāpāramitā*:

> *yadā punaḥ kauśika dānaṃ śīlaṃ kṣānti-vīryaṃ dhyānaṃ ca prajñāpāramitā-parigṛhītam bhavati, tadā pāramitā-nāmadheyam pāramitā-śabdam labhate.*[251]

d) The value of *dāna* and other *pāramitās* is considered to be extremely low compared to *prajñāpāramitā*:

> *evaṃ hi subhūte yaś-ca bodhisattvo mahāsattvaḥ prajñāpāramitā-yogam-anuyuktaḥ, anena vihāreṇa viharan yaduta prajñāpāramitā-pratisaṃyuktair-manasikāraiḥ, ekadivasena tāvat-karma karoti / yaś-ca prajñāpāramitā-virahito bodhisattvo gaṅgā-nadī-vāluka-upamān kalpāṃs-tiṣṭhan dānaṃ dadyāt, ayam-eva tato viśiṣyate yo 'yam bodhisattvo mahāsattva evam-ekadivasam-api prajñāpāramitāyāṃ yogam-āpadyate.*[252]

The six *pāramitās* are crucial for a Bodhisattva-Mahāsattva's practice. With their help *prajñāpāramitā* attains perfection:

> *atra hi subhūte prajñāpāramitā pariniṣṭhitā bhavati yaduta ṣaṭpāramitāsu.*[253]

Perhaps, for this reason they have the same epithets as the Buddhas:[254]

śāstṛ	*ston pa*	teacher
mārga	*lam*	path
āloka	*snang ba*	light
ulkā	*sgron ma*	torch
avabhāsa	*snang ba*	shine
trāṇa	*skyob pa*	shelter
śaraṇa	*skyabs*	refuge
layana	*gnas*	place of rest
parāyaṇa	*dpung gnyen*	highest support
dvīpa	*gling*	island
mātṛ	*yum*	mother
pitṛ	*yab*	father

3.3 *Sarvajñatā*

Sarvajñatā (*thams cad mkhyen pa*) is the second term in the *Aṣṭasāhasrikā Prajñāpāramitā* denoting the ultimate state of mind. Its literary and traditional translation into European languages is 'omniscience'.[255] The authors of the *Aṣṭasāhasrikā* did not define this concept unless we can consider the following passage from Chapter XV as a definition:

> *aprameyā hi subhūte sarvajñatā, apramāṇā hi subhūte sarvajñatā.*[256]

However, the *Aṣṭasāhasrikā* provides an interesting list of the concepts that cannot be used to define omniscience:[257]

rūpa	*gzugs*	form
vedanā	*sdug bsngal*	sensation
samjñā	*'du shes*	perception
saṃskārāḥ	*'du byed rnams*	volitional impulses
vijñāna	*rnam par shes pa*	consciousness
prāpti	*thob pa*	achievement
abhisamaya	*mngon par rtogs pa*	reunion
adhigama	*rtogs pa*	realization
mārga	*lam*	path
mārgaphala	*lam kyi 'bras bu*	fruit of the path
jñāna	*ye shes*	knowledge
utpatti	*bskyed pa*	emergence

vināśa	*rnam par bshig pa*	annihilation
utpāda	*skye ba*	birth
vyaya	*'jig pa*	destruction
nirodha	*'gog pa*	cessation
bhāvanā	*sgom pa*	creative imagination
vibhāvanā	*rnam par sgom pa*	detailed creative imagination

The list is followed by a passage directly saying that it is impossible to define *sarvajñatā*:

> *yat-subhūte aprameyam-apramāṇaṃ ... na-api kenacit-kṛtaṃ na-api kutaścid-āgatam na-api kvacid gacchanti na-api kvacid-deśe na-api kvacid-pradeśe sthitam.*[258]

Therefore I cannot agree with Conze who asserts that according to the Mahāyāna, *sarvajñatā* or omniscience includes the knowledge of all individual phenomena: "The Mahāyāna explains that while primarily the Omniscience of the Buddha consists in his acquaintance with the means of attaining heaven and liberation, he also comprehends all things without exception, including such unnecessary pieces of information as the number of insects in the world."[259]

An interesting definition of *sarvajñatā* can be found in the work of the 5th century Chinese Buddhist Seng Chao: "Omniscience is a non-cognitive cognition, in which there is no knowledge."[260] The paradoxical nature of this definition and the closeness of its author to the *Prajñāpāramitā* texts allow us to assume that this definition to some extent reflects how the authors of the *Aṣṭasāhasrikā* understood *sarvajñatā*.

Therefore we can suppose that the authors of the *Aṣṭasāhasrikā* understood *sarvajñatā* first and foremost as a special term, which they used to denote the ability of the ultimate state of mind to grasp the world in its entirety.

Very often *sarvajñatā* occurs in the same context as *prajñāpāramitā*. Sometimes they are considered to be synonymous:

> *sarvajñatā-eva bhagavan prajñāpāramitā.*[261]
>
> *evam-eva subhūte alpakās-te bodhisattvā mahāsattvāḥ sattva-nikāye saṃvidyante, ye 'syām sarvajñatā-śikṣāyāṃ śikṣante, yaduta prajñāpāramitā-śikṣāyām.*[262]

In most cases, however, *sarvajñatā* is a derivative of *prajñāpāramitā*:

> *prajñāpāramitā-nirjātā hi tathāgatānām-arhatāṃ-samyaksaṃbuddhānāṃ sarvajñatā.*[263]

Sarvajñatā is opposed to the concepts of *śrāvakabhūmi* and *pratyekabuddhabhūmi.*[264] Therefore *sarvajñatā* can be considered as a synonym of the terms *bodhisattvabhūmi* and *buddhatva* in these textual situations.

Sarvajñatā is a characteristic feature of the bodhisattvas (*vyākṛta bodhisattva-mahāsattva*[265] and *avinivartanīya bodhisattva-mahāsattva*[266]) and, what is most important, a Buddha. As the Buddhas' omniscience *sarvajñatā* has a parallel term – *sarvajñajñāna* (*thams cad mkhyen pa'i ye shes*) – 'the knowledge of the Omniscient'.

Let us give some examples:

> *tatra hi śrenikaḥ parivrājakaḥ sarvajñajñāne adhimucya śraddhā-anusārī prādeśikena jñānena-avatīrṇah.*[267]

> *eṣa ca kauśika tathāgatasya-ātmabhāva-śarīra-pratilambhaḥ prajñāpāramitā-upāyakauśalya-nirjātaḥ saḥ sarvajñajñāna-āśrayabhūto bhavati.*[268]

> *tathāgataśarīrāṇi hi sarvajñajñāna-āśrayabhūtāni tad api sarvajñajñānam prajñāpāramitā-nirjātam.*[269]

In the *Aṣṭasāhasrikā sarvajñatā* also has some other synonyms such as *sarvajñāna* (*kun tu shes pa*).[270]

The description of how omniscience can be attained is extremely interesting as in the above example of Śrenika who attained omniscience with the help of one-sided (i.e. limited) knowledge based on faith.

But the most significant passage is to be found in Chapter XVII:

> *punar-aparaṃ subhūte avinivartanīyo bodhisattvo mahāsattvaḥ śrāvaka-pratyekabuddha-bhūmi-nirvṛttaḥ sarvajñatāyām pravṛtto bhavati / sa ākāṅkṣan prathamaṃ dhyānaṃ samāpadyate / tathā dvitīyam tathā tṛthīyam tathā caturthaṃ dhyānaṃ samāpadyate / sa ebhiś-caturbhir-dhyānair-viharati, dhyāna-parijayaṃ ca karoti, dhyānāni ca samāpadyate, na ca dhyāna-vaśena-upapadyate.*[271]

Attaining omniscience through meditation (*dhyāna, bsam gtan*) resembles the description of the Buddha's *parinirvāṇa* in the *Mahāparinibbāna-sutta* of the *Dīghanikāya*:

> *Atha kho Bhagavā paṭhama-jjhānaṃ samāpajji. Paṭhama-jjhānā vuṭṭhahitvā dutiya-jjhānam samāpajji. Dutiya-jjhānā*

> *vuṭṭhahitvā tatiya-jjhānaṃ samāpajji. Tatiya-jjhānā vuṭṭhahitvā catuttha-jjhānaṃ samāpajji /.../ Catuttha-jjhānā vuṭṭhahitvā samantara Bhagavā parinibbāyi.*[272]

3.4 *Anuttarā samyaksaṃbodhi*

Anuttarā samyaksaṃbodhi (*bla na med pa yang dag par rdzogs pa'i byang chub*) – 'the highest perfect awakening' – is a very important term denoting the ultimate state of mind. Etymologically and typologically it belongs to the group of terms derived from the root *budh* ('to wake, to be awakened, to understand, to think, to be enlightened') like *bodhi, saṃbodhi, abhisaṃbodhi, avabodha* etc.

In many texts words of this category are the main terms denoting the ultimate state. Thus, we can find *bodhi, saṃbodhi* and *sammā-saṃbodhi* in the Pāli canon and *abhisaṃbodhi* and *samyaksaṃbodhi* in Tantric texts.[273]

The *Aṣṭasāhasrikā*, along with *anuttarā samyaksaṃbodhi*, rarely uses the terms *bodhi* and *saṃbodhi* that have clearly secondary importance in the text. However, very significant is the verb *abhisaṃbudhyate* denoting the moment of attaining *anuttarā samyaksaṃbodhi: anuttarāṃ samyaksaṃbodhim abhisaṃbudhyate* – 'he attains the highest perfect awakening'.

Modern scholars have paid no special attention to the interpretation of the terms of *budh*-family. In the "Encyclopaedia of Buddhism" we cannot find the entry *abhisambodhi.*[274] In Buddhist studies little attention is paid to these terms and very often all of them are reduced to the form *bodhi.*[275] I think that there are some differences between the meanings of these terms that may turn out to be quite significant but this is beyond the scope of this study. Therefore I propose a rather intuitive definition that may be used as a working hypothesis: *anuttarā samyaksaṃbodhi* as it is understood by the authors of the *Prajñāpāramitā* sūtras denotes the state of maximal awareness of mind, whereas the unconscious has practically no control over the person's behaviour.

Anuttarā samyaksaṃbodhi, similarly to *prajñāpāramitā* and *sarvajñatā*, is a state that can be attained through special aspirations. However, the *Aṣṭasāhasrikā* stresses many times how difficult it is to attain it.[276] Chapter III lists the reasons that are human characteristics:[277]

hīnavīrya	*brtson 'grus zhan pa*	uncourageousness
kusīda	*le lo can*	lazyness
hīnasattva	*sems can dman pa*	worthless
hīnacitta	*sems dman pa*	malevolence
hīnasaṃjñā	*'du shes dman pa*	absent-mindedness
hīnādhimuktika	*mos pa dman pa*	viciousness
hīnaprajñā	*shes rab dman pa*	futile awareness

There is a similar list in Chapter XVI:[278]

duṣprajñā	*shes rab 'chal ba*	non-understanding
hīnavīrya	*brtson 'grus dman pa*	uncourageousness
hīnādhimuktika	*mos pa dman pa*	viciousness
anupāyakuśala	*thabs mi mkhas pa*	unskilfulness in means
pāpamitrasaṃsevin	*sdig pa'i grogs po brten pa*	relying on bad friends

Bhagavat's answer to Subhūti's remark also provides four objective reasons:

> *asaṃbhavāt-subhūte durabhisaṃbhavā anuttarā samyaksaṃbodhiḥ / asadbhūtatvāt-subhūte durabhisaṃbhavā anuttarā samyaksaṃbodhiḥ / avikalpatvāt-subhūte durabhisaṃbhavā anuttarā samyaksaṃbodhiḥ / avithapitvāt-subhūte durabhisaṃbhavā anuttarā samyaksaṃbodhiḥ.*[279]

Thus, *anuttarā samyaksaṃbodhi* is a state that does not result from any conscious effort. A bodhisattva who wishes to attain perfect awakening should not consider it as a *dharma*, i.e. a describable object.[280] This is the only way to understand the way of attaining *anuttarā samyaksaṃbodhi* that starts from the series of 'generating the mind of awakening' (*bodhicittotpāda, byang chub sems kyi bskyed pa*) but at the same time *bodhicittotpāda* and *anuttarā samyaksaṃbodhi* are not in a cause and effect relationship:

> *evam-eva subhūte na ca prathama-cittotpādena bodhisattvo mahāsattvo 'nuttarāṃ samyaksaṃbodhim-abhisaṃbudhyate, na ca prathama-cittotpādam-anāgamya anuttarāṃ samyaksaṃbodhim-abhisaṃbudhyate / na ca paścima-cittotpādena anuttarāṃ samyaksaṃbodhim-abhisaṃbudhyate, na ca paścima-cittotpādam-anāgamya anuttarāṃ samyaksaṃbodhim-abhisaṃbudhyate / na ca taiś-cittotpādair-na ca-anyatra tebhyaś-cittotpādebhyo 'bhisaṃbudhyate / abhisaṃbudhyate ca bodhisattvo mahāsattvo 'nuttarāṃ samyaksaṃbodhim.*[281]

Since Bodhisattva-Mahāsattva does not attain the highest perfect awakening as a result of conscious effort, he cannot determine what exactly is the basis for it:

> *evam-eva śāriputra bodhisattvasya mahāsattvasya prajñāpāramitāyāṃ carato na-evaṃ bhavati: ayaṃ dharmo vyākṛto 'nuttarāyāṃ samyaksaṃbodhau, ayaṃ dharmo vyākariṣyate 'nuttarāyāṃ samyaksaṃbodhau, ayaṃ dharmo vyākriyate 'nuttarāyāṃ samyaksaṃbodhau, ayaṃ dharmo 'nuttarāṃ samyaksaṃbodhim-abhisaṃbhotsyate.*[282]

Therefore he cannot even approximately forecast the time of the highest perfect awakening:

> *na ca śāriputra bodhisattvena mahāsattvena evaṃ cittam-utpādayitavyam: cireṇa-anuttarāṃ samyaksaṃbodhim-abhisaṃbhotsyam.*[283]

Nevertheless, a Bodhisattva-Mahāsattva should have the wish to attain this state. But he should realize this wish not in speculations about its nature but in studying the *Prajñāpāramitā* text:

> *tasmāt-tarhi kauśika kulaputreṇa vā kuladuhitrā vā kṣipraṃ ca-anuttarāṃ samyaksaṃbodhim-abhisaṃboddhu-kāmena iyam-eva prajñāpāramitā sukham abhīkṣṇaṃ śrotavyā udgrahītavyā dhārayitavyā vācayitavyā paryavāptavyā pravartayitavyā deśayitavyā upadeṣṭavyā uddeṣṭavyā svādhyātavyā paripraṣṭavyā.*[284]

The *Aṣṭasāhasrikā Prajñāpāramitā* says that Bodhisattvas-Mahāsattvas who want to achieve the highest perfect awakening should follow special norms of behaviour that include respect for all living beings, without exception, complying with the requirements of the six *pāramitās* and incessant care of the spiritual development of other beings.

3.5 *Tathatā*

Now let us take a look at the last term in the structure of the ultimate state of the mind: *tathatā* (*de bzhin nyid*). As we know, this concept has been particularly widely used in Zen Buddhism. Along with *tathatā*, the *Aṣṭasāhasrikā* uses the word *tathatva*, the Tibetan equivalent of which is also *de bzhin nyid*. Apparently, they are absolute synonyms and can replace each other with no limitations.

While modern Buddhist studies have paid little attention to the three previous terms, many pages in articles and books are devoted to the problem of *tathatā*. Let us quote the most characteristic passages from the works that try to define *tathatā*.

Y. Hakeda writes: """Suchness" is a synonym of the Absolute, *chen-ju* in Chinese, *tathatā* or *bhūta-tathatā* in Sanskrit which may be translated literally as "Real Suchness""".[285]

W. S. Karunatilleke writes: "Similarly, consciousness, thought has nothing, but its absolute existence, whereby it becomes incomparable with anything else, and its "such-ness" (*tathatā*) best corresponds to this concept without content. This concept of *tathatā* which is so important for the world-concept of Mahāyāna, cannot be understood properly, unless taken as the simplest expression of the absolute void, which has remained as the single predicate of the thinking process."[286]

D. T. Suzuki writes: "Self-nature in terms of the Prajñāpāramitā is Suchness (*tathatā*) and Emptiness (*śūnyatā*). Suchness means the Absolute, something which is not subject to laws of relativity, and therefore which cannot be grasped by means of form."[287]

H. Nakamura writes:"Buddhists had their unique term *tathatā* also to mean truth."[288]

J. Takakusu writes: """Thusness" or the matrix of "Thus Come" or "Thus Gone" means the true state of all things in the universe, the source of an enlightened one, the basis of enlightenment itself (with no relation to the time or space), but, when dynamic, it is in human form assuming an ordinary way and feature of life. "Thusness" and the "Matrix of Thus Come" are practically one and the same – the ultimate truth. In Mahāyāna, the ultimate truth is called "Thusness""".[289]

The analysis of the *Aṣṭasāhasrikā Prajñāpāramitā* mostly confirms Takakusu's viewpoint.

a) *Tathatā* is a basis for enlightenment:

> *ato bhagavaṃs-tathatāto buddhānāṃ bhagavatāṃ bodhiḥ prabhāvyate.*[290]

b) *Tathatā* can be seen as a term denoting the ultimate state of mind along with the terms *prajñāpāramitā*, *sarvajñatā* and *anuttarā samyaksaṃbodhi*:

atha khalv-āyuṣmān subhūtir-bhagavantam-etad-avocat: kā punar-eṣā bhagavan anuttarā samyaksaṃbodhiḥ?

bhagavān-āha: tathatā-eṣā subhūte anuttarā-samyaksaṃbodhiḥ.[291]

yathā yathā bhagavan bodhisattvo mahāsattva āsannī-bhavaty-anuttarāyāḥ samyaksaṃbodheḥ, tathā tathā prajñāpāramitāyām-avavaditavyo 'nuśāsitavyaḥ, tathā tathā prajñāpāramitāyām avodyamāno 'nuśiṣyamānas-tathatāyā āsannībhavati.[292]

alpakās-te sattvāḥ sattvanikāye saṃvidyante, ye anuttarāyāṃ samyaksaṃbodhau saṃprasthitāḥ / tebhyo 'pi subhūte alpebhyo 'lpatarakās-te sattvāḥ, ye tathatvāya pratipadyante / tebhyo 'pi subhūte alpatarakebhyas-tathatvāya pratipadyamānebhyo 'lpatamās-te ye prajñāpāramitāyāṃ yogam-āpadyante / tebhyo 'pi subhūte alpatamebhyaḥ prajñāpāramitāyāṃ yogam-āpadyamānebhyo 'lpatamās-te bodhisattvā mahāsattvāḥ, ye 'vinivartanīyā anuttarāyāḥ samyaksaṃbodheḥ.[293]

I can also agree with Hakeda and Suzuki. Indeed, as the *Aṣṭasāhasrikā* says, *tathatā* is a kind of transcendental substrate for all phenomena and all *dharmas* and the basis for all ways. It is not subject to change and does not exist in time. *Tathatā* unites all phenomena and all are equal before it. But this is the reason why gradations and hierarchies are significant in the so called phenomenal world:

anujāto 'yaṃ subhūtiḥ sthaviras-tathāgatasya-iti / ajātatvāt-subhūtiḥ sthaviro 'nujātas-tathāgatasya / anujātas-tathatāṃ subhūtiḥ sthaviras-tathāgatasya / yathā tathāgata-tathatā anāgatā agatā, evaṃ hi subhūtiḥ-tathatā anāgatā agatā / evaṃ hi subhūtiḥ sthaviras-tathāgata-tathatām anujātaḥ / ādita eva subhūtiḥ sthaviras-tathāgata-tathatām anujātaḥ / tat-kasya hetoḥ? yā hi tathāgata-tathatā, sā sarvadharma-tathatā / yā sarvadharma-tathatā, sā tathāgata-tathatā / yā ca tathāgata-tathatā, yā ca sarvadharma-tathatā, sā eva subhūteḥ sthavirasya tathatā.[294]

yā ca subhūte pṛthagjanabhūmiḥ, yā ca śrāvakabhūmiḥ, yā ca pratyekabuddhabhūmiḥ, yā ca buddhabhūmiḥ, iyaṃ tathatābhūmir-ity-ucyate / sarvāś-ca-etās tathatāyā advayā advaidhīkārā avikalpā nirvikalpā iti tām tathatāṃ tāṃ dharmatām-avataranti.[295]

yathā tathāgata-tathatā na-atītā na anāgatā na pratyutpannā, evaṃ sarvadharma-tathatā na-atītā na anāgatā na pratyutpannā.[296]

I did not find direct hints of the terms *tathatā* and *śūnyatā* being synonymous in the *Aṣṭasāhasrikā*. Nevertheless, it is obvious that *tathatā* has the same function in the structure of the *prajñāpāramitā* as *śūnyatā* in the structure of *dharma*: it is a term that helps us to get as close as possible to the description of what the authors of the *Aṣṭasāhasrikā* considered to be indescribable.

Apparently, *tathatā* in the *Aṣṭasāhasrikā* denotes the ontological aspect of the ultimate state of mind, after the attainment of which there is no opposition of the subjective and objective, internal and external.

In this connection it is interesting to note that the meaning of the word *tathatā* allowed the authors of the *Aṣṭasāhasrikā* to build up a special (false?) etymology of the term *tathāgata*:

> *iyaṃ sā tathatā, yayā tathatayā bodhisattvo mahāsattvo 'nut-tarāṃ samyaksaṃbodhim-abhisaṃbuddhaḥ san tathāgata iti nāmadheyaṃ labhate.*[297]

Since the etymology *tathā-gata* or *tathā-āgata* is denied in the *Aṣṭasāhasrikā*, the authors of the *Aṣṭasāhasrikā* probably thought that the correct etymology was *tathatāṃ gatah saḥ* ('gone to Suchness').

4. Text as a Teacher

It is known that the logical structure of the text of the *Aṣ-ṭasāhasrikā Prajñāpāramitā* is extremely complicated, even so com-plicated that at first glance the sūtra may seem to be a collection of contradictory and absurd statements. This was probably the purpose of the author (or authors) of the *Aṣṭasāhasrikā* since this text was supposed to play the role of a spiritual teacher for the reader. To put it more precisely, it was the system – the text of the *Aṣṭasāhasrikā* and its reader – that had to play the role of a guru since due to the special structure of the *Aṣṭasāhasrikā* it was possible to particularly actively influence the mind of reader. This special structure is expressed in the instructions that can be encountered in several textual situations. These are all directly aimed at the person who has just read the text preceding the instructions. The instructions refer to the reader's state of mind at a given moment and are not suitable in other textual situa-tions.

4.1 Terms denoting 'shock'

Part of instructions of the *Aṣṭasāhasrikā* can be reduced to one formula:

'If reading this passage does not induce ***state X*** in the Bodhisattva-Mahāsattva, he can continue reading'.

Instructions of this kind are given after textual situations called "conversations about deep *dharmas*" in the *Aṣṭasāhasrikā*. We could give two examples:

> I. *bodhisattvo mahāsattva iti yad-idaṃ bhagavan-ucyate, katamasya-etad-bhagavan dharmasya-adhivacanaṃ yaduta bodhisattva iti? na-ahaṃ bhagavaṃs-taṃ dharmaṃ samanupaśyāmi yaduta bodhisattva iti / tam-apy-ahaṃ bhagavan dharmaṃ na samanupaśyāmi yaduta prajñāpāramitā nāma, so 'ham bhagavan bodhisattvaṃ vā bodhisattvadharmaṃ vā avindan anuphalabhamāno 'samanupaśyan, prajñāpāramitā-apy-avindan anupalabhamāno 'samanupaśyan katamaṃ bodhisattvaṃ katamasyāṃ prajñāpāramitāyām avavadiṣyāmi anuśiṣyāmi?*[298]

> II. *na khalu punaḥ subhūte bodhisattvo mahāsattvaḥ prajñāpāramitāyām caran vivardhate vā parihīyate vā / yathā-eva subhūte prajñāpāramitā śūnyā, sā na-eva vivardhate na ca parihīyate, evam-eva subhūte bodhisattvo mahāsattvaḥ śūnyaḥ / sa na-eva vivardhate, na ca parihīyate / yataḥ subhūte yathā-eva prajñāpāramitā śūnyā, sā na-eva vivardhate na ca parihīyate evam-eva subhūte bodhisattvo mahāsattvaḥ śūnyā / sa na-eva vivardhate, na ca parihīyate / tato bodhisattvo mahāsattvo bodhaye samudāgacchati, evaṃ ca anuttarāṃ samyaksaṃbodhim-abhisaṃbudhyate.*[299]

These examples are typologically very similar to koans in Zen Buddhism: both are based on so-called paradoxical logic.[300] In Zen Buddhism the teacher tries with the help of paradoxes to lead his students to mental shock which should accelerate reaching the *satori* state, and is a kind of threshold for awakening.

In the *Aṣṭasāhasrikā*, however, the absence of ***state X*** is considered to be a necessary precondition for awakening. I think that shock in Zen Buddhism and ***state X*** in the *Aṣṭasāhasrikā* are typologically similar. If it is so, this is the main difference between Zen Buddhism and *Prajñāpāramitā*.

Eight different ways to describe the absence of ***state X*** can be found in the Sanskrit text of the *Aṣṭasāhasrikā*:

1. *cittaṃ na avalīyate na saṃlīyate na viṣīdati na viṣādam-āpadyate, na-asya viprṣṭhī-bhavati mānasam, na bhagna-prṣṭhī-bhavati, na uttrasyati na saṃtrasyati na saṃtrāsam-āpadyate.*[301]

2. *na-avalīyate na saṃlīyate na viṣīdati na viṣādam-āpadyate, na-asya viprṣṭhī-karoti mānasaṃ, na bhagna-prṣṭhī-karoti, na uttrasyati na saṃtrasyati na saṃtrāsam-āpadyate.*[302]

3. *na uttrasyati na saṃtrasyati na saṃtrāsam-āpadyate.*[303]

4. *na uttrasyati na saṃtrasyati na saṃtrāsam-āpadyate na saṃsīdati.*[304]

5. *na saṃsīdati.*[305]

7. *cittaṃ na-avalīyate na saṃlīyate na prṣṭhī-bhavati.*[307]

8. *na bhavati cittasya-avalīnatvam, na bhavati dhandhāyi-tatvam, na bhavati cittasya-anyathātvam.*[308]

As we can see, the discrepancies between different variants are quite large, partly even so large that it does not seem to be a description of the same state.

The existing translations of the *Aṣṭasāhasrikā* into European languages, i.e. translation by Max Walleser into German, and translation by Edward Conze into English, show that the translators did not have a sufficiently clear idea of the essence of the state in question. First, their translations are inconsistent: the same Sanskrit variant has different forms (e.g. version 1. has three different forms both in Walleser's and Conze's translations). Second, both translators (Conze in most cases) prefer to shorten the translation. Is it not indirect proof that they tried to find the same translation for all variants?

Walleser has not translated all chapters and therefore not all variants are reflected.

1. *...(wenn) der Gedanke niedersinkt, nicht zusammensinkt, nicht ängstlish wird, (wenn) nicht seinem Geiste das Rückgrat genommen, das Rückgrat gebrochen wird, er nicht erschrickt, nicht in Schrecken gerät...*[309]

2. *...Gedanke nicht ängstlish wird und erschrickt...*[310]

...nicht erschrickt und nicht sich fürchtet...[311]

3. *...werden sie nicht erschrecken und zittern...*[312]

...nicht erschrickt und nicht fürchtet...[313]

4. *...nicht erschrickt, nicht erzittert, nicht in Schrecken gerät, nicht verzagt...*[314]

5. …*duckt sich nicht, kauert sich nicht zusammen, verliert nicht das Rückgrat, erzittert nicht, erschrickt nicht, gerät nicht in Schrecken, schwankt nicht, zweifelt nicht, ist nicht verwirrt…*[315]

6. …*Gedanke nicht sich duckt, nicht niedersinkt, nicht zusammenbricht…*[316]

7. …*das Denken…nicht niedersinkt, nicht ängstlish wird, nicht in Zweifel gerät, nicht Verwirrung, nicht Veränderung des Gedankes eintritt…*[317]

E. Conze's translation could be a slightly better example, considering our purpose:

1. …*heart does not become cowed, not stolid, does not despair nor despond, does not turn away or become dejected, does not tremble, is not frightened or terrified…*[318]

…*he does not become afraid…*[319]

…*does not make him afraid…*[320]

2. …*will not become cowed nor stolid, will not become cast down nor depressed, will not turn their minds away from it nor have their backs broken, will not tremble, be frightened, be terrified…*[321]

…*will not be demoralized…*[322]

3. …*they will not tremble…*[323]

…*without fear…*[324]

…*he remains unafraid…*[325]

4. …*is not afraid nor loses heart…*[326]

5. …*he does not lose heart…*[327]

6. …*he does not become cowed, or stolid, nor does he turn his back on it; he will not tremble, be frightened, or terrified; he does not hesitate, or doubt, or get stupefied.*[328]

7. …*does not become cowed or stolid in mind, does not turn back…*[329]

8. …*remains unafraid…*[330]

Translation by Kumārajīva into Chinese is much more consistent.[331] There are only two versions represented in it: one consists of four parts and the other of five, whereas the choice of either variant is not based on the Sanskrit text

I 不 驚 不 怖 不 畏 不 没 不 退

***bù jīng** bù **bù** bù **wèi** bù **mò** bù **tuì**;*

II 不驚不怖不没不退

*bù **jīng** bù **bù** bù **mò** bù **tuì***

The main meanings of the characters are as follows (*bu* ('no') is equivalent to *na* in Sanskrit):

a) 驚 *jīng – 'to shock, to surprise, to startle, to alarm'*;
b) 怖 *bù – 'to fear, to be afraid of';*
c) 畏 *wèi – 'to fear, to dread, to be dreaded'*;
d) 没 *mò – 'to sink, to submerge, to disappear'*;
e) 退 *tuì – 'to go back, to retire, to withdraw from, to decline, to reject, to abate, to yield'.*

We can see that although Kumārajīva does not accurately follow the original Sanskrit text, he, unlike Walleser and Conze, uses a certain matrix (the difference between variants 1 and 2 is insignificant). Apparently, this means that for Kumārajīva, Sanskrit variants 1 to 8 described the same state.[332]

Most equivalents, both in Walleser's and Kumārajīva's translations, are related to the notion of fear. Does it mean that the state in question is fear? Apparently, the translators did not think so, although it is obvious that 'fear' is emphasized. However, Conze translated one passage without the word 'fear' ("*...will not be demoralized...*") the passage where several words mean 'fear' in the original Sanskrit text (version 2).[333]

Now let us take a look at the Sanskrit words used in the given versions. They can be divided into three main groups:

a) insecurity (which also embraces incomprehension and doubt) – *avalīyate, viṣīdati, viṣādam-āpadyate, kāṅkṣati, vicikitsati, saṃsīdati;*

b) depression – *viprṣṭhī-bhavati (-karoti), bhagna-prṣṭhī-bhavati (-karoti), prṣṭhī-bhavati, dhandhāyate*;

c) fear - *uttrasyati, saṃtrasyati, saṃtrāsam-āpadyate*.

Haribhadra, the best-known commentator of the *Aṣṭasāhasrikā*, interprets the words that mean 'fear' as follows:

na uttrasyati asthānatrāseṇa;[334]

na saṃtrasyati saṃtatitrāseṇa;[335]

tatra-asthānatrāsa uttrāsaḥ;[336]

saṃtatya trāsaḥ samtrāsaḥ.[337]

As we can see, for Haribhadra *saṃtrāsa* means the same as *saṃtati-trāsa*, i.e. 'strong, lasting fear'. We are more interested in the interpretation of *uttrāsa*, which, according to Haribhadra, means 'fear of insecurity' or 'fear of impermanence' (*asthāna-trāsa*). According to the authors of the *Aṣṭasāhasrikā* 'impermanence' is a normal state for the Bodhisattva-Mahāsattva: he should not abide by permanent norms; on the contrary, his mind should be constantly developing and changing. It is therefore quite understandable that the Bodhisattva-Mahāsattva's mind should remain balanced, even in situations which result in a strong feeling of impermanence for him.

Haribhadra's interpretation enables the group of words, the main meaning of which is 'fear', to be collated with other lexical groups since the notion of 'fear' has the connotation of 'hesitation in the face of impermanence'.

It seems to me that integrating the notions of 'insecurity', 'depression' and 'fear' into the common notion of 'shock' is quite possible since in European languages the word 'shock' may have the same connotations. This notion is also in keeping with the hypothesis given at the beginning of the section as it does embrace all versions describing the state in question. But what is most important, 'shock' also complies with another aspect of ***state X*** – it embraces not only the reader's mind but also his entire psyche and is in fact an uncontrollable state.

The state of shock is a way of protection for a person who does not have the structure of mind which in the *Aṣṭasāhasrikā* is denoted by the term *prajñāpāramitā*. Therefore one cannot say that 'shock' is an undesirable phenomenon. This only determines people who are not capable of going deep into the cycle of the *Prajñāpāramitā* texts.[338]

4.2 *Mārakarma*

The following part of instructions given in the *Aṣṭasāhasrikā* can be reduced to the following form: *A is mārakarma, therefore one has to free oneself from it.*

Chapters XI and XII of the *Aṣṭasāhasrikā* list many *mārakarmas*. Their total number remains open: *subahūni mārakarmāṇi* ('there are very many *mārakarmas*').[339] In terms of content they can be divided into two groups:

a) negative states of mind (e.g. inattention while reading the *Prajñāpāramitā* text,[340] being arrogant with other Bodhisattvas-Mahāsattvas,[341] having doubt in the *Prajñāpāramitā* sūtras[342]);

b) certain external obstacles preventing the spread of the *Prajñāpāramitā* teaching (e.g. quarrels between the teacher and the student[343]).

The whole idea of this kind of instruction is that some phenomena can be denoted by the word *mārakarma*, after which one gets a chance to free oneself from them: 'The Bodhisattva-Mahāsattva should understand them *(mārakarmas*). Once he has understood them, he should get rid of them'.

The term *mārakarma* can be understood in different ways. The first way is to establish a theory based on the idea of a transition stage from mythopoetical thinking to scientific since the *Aṣṭasāhasrikā* is no doubt a kind of scientific text, containing extensive terminology and a well-developed system of proofs. However, it can also be considered as a mythological text since a number of mythical characters appear in it: gods (Śakra, Brahma, etc.), demons, *devaputras* and others. But can we create any satisfactory model of a mythological structure on the basis of the *Aṣṭasāhasrikā*? Can we find in this text all necessary opposite pairs, e.g. 'Māra and Buddha'?[344] At first glance it even seems to be possible. The Buddha (Bhagavat, Tathāgata, Arhat, Samyaksaṃbuddha) tries to help Bodhisattvas-Mahāsattvas[345] and Māra tries to hinder them.[346] Māra can assume the appearance of Buddha, come to bodhisattvas and proclaim the wrong teaching.[347] But is this enough to construct the above-mentioned opposite pair? The bodhisattvas are also helped by śrāvakas and Śakra and hindered primarily by their own emotions.

The *Aṣṭasāhasrikā* characterizes Māra as a mythical figure in a rather restrained way. He is capable of re-embodying and changing his position in space within a moment, and has emotions. If we assume that *mārakarma* is directly related to the mythical Māra, then it can also be translated as 'a deed of Māra', which means the bad effect of the evil mythological being on people.

If we look at Conze's translation, that could be what he thought. In his interpretation, the equivalent of the word *mārakarma* is related to the mythological Māra. The phrase '*idam-api subhūte mārakarma veditavyam*' that is frequent in his translation is: "This also should be known as done by Māra",[348] or "It is also a deed of Māra".[349]

Although this approach has certain charm and is based on tradition, I prefer another, the psychological approach, in which the term *mārakarma* is not a simple compound word, but integral term. The fact that *mārakarma* is a term is also confirmed by its strict use in the situations where the construction in the case of a non-terminological meaning would be different. For example, in the sentence:

> *evaṃ subhūte māraḥ pāpīyān-evam-ādikāni subahūni anyāny-api mārakarmāny-utpādayiṣyati.*[350]

If the word *mārakarma* was used as a non-terminological word, the sentence would look as follows:

> *evaṃ subhūte māraḥ pāpīyān-evam-ādikāni subahūni anyāny-api karmāny-utpādayiṣyati.*[351]

Of course, *mārakarma* is not a term belonging to the level of śāstras, i.e. it did not undergo theoretical development in the period when Buddhist philosophical schools emerged. The reason might be in the term itself – it only has a meaning in the context of the instructions of the *Prajñāpāramitā*.

The word *mārakarma* should primarily be considered as a meditative symbol. Only in this case can we understand why *mārakarma* is a general indivisible term on the level of the terminological analysis of the text. Indeed, the image of the 'evil deity' Māra arises during the meditative imaging of *mārakarma* but this Māra is just an object of meditative imagination that has no connection with mythological theories. Māra as a meditative symbol is created under the full control of the person trying to annihilate him. What happens when a symbol is annihilated is that the phenomenon denoted by the symbol disappears, and this has long been known to researchers of meditation.[352] It allows us to assume that the purpose of using the term *mārakarma* in the *Aṣṭasāhasrikā* was to free people from different mental disorders with the help of meditation.

Heart Sūtra of Transcending Awareness

Edward Conze has said that a Mahāyāna sūtra can be completely understood only after working on it for thirty years.[1] I would say that I do not agree with Conze. I think that even thirty years is not enough: Conze's later works do show that he has deepened his understanding. However, I need to cite Conze when I try to justify myself to my friends who accuse me of translating and publishing anything else except the *Prajñāpāramitā* texts, i.e. the treatises that I have been studying the longest. Still, their reproach is not completely justified since there are some things that I have published, e.g. the Estonian translation of the *Vajracchedikā Prajñāpāramitā* or the "Diamond Sūtra".[2]

It is true, however, that I would now translate it in a slightly different way, and in ten years time, probably in another way. Whatever Conze says, I feel that the Mahāyāna sūtras can never be completely understood. Why? One of the reasons is that they already contain an inherent incomprehensibility; there is something there that directly provokes the reader to repeatedly pose new questions to the text. The *Aṣṭasāhasrikā Prajñāpāramitā* even admonishes the reader just like a real live teacher after a cascade of logical mazes and paradoxes: are you sure you are not puzzled or startled or doubtful or depressed or confused? If you are, do not read further! Contemplate, and only when you think it makes sense, then continue reading.

The Mahāyāna sūtras were first written down (I stress this word since although these sūtras are also based on the pan-Buddhist oral tradition, awareness of the meaning of a written text is important in this case) in the 4th century after Buddha or the 1st century BC. There is sufficient reason to think that the above-mentioned *Aṣṭasāhasrikā Prajñāpāramitā* certainly was one of the first if not the very first of the Mahāyāna sūtras. In any case, the earliest Mahāyāna sūtras are these whose titles contain the word *prajñāpāramitā* ('transcending awareness'). Approximately thirty of these were written over several centuries. Furthermore, the *Prajñāpāramitā* laid a foundation for hundreds of other Mahāyāna sūtras. If there were no *Prajñā-*

pāramitā, there would be no "Lotus Sūtra" (*Sad !harmapuṇḍarīka)*, "Golden Light Sūtra" (*Suvarṇaprabhāsa*), "Flower Garland Sūtra" (*Avataṃsaka*) and many other sūtras.

The *Prajñāpāramitā* texts emerged at the time when Buddhist circles were arguing about whether "Buddha's word" was finally fixed after many canonical volumes (the *Tripiṭakas* in Sanskrit and the*Tipiṭaka* in Pāli) had been written. The majority answered: Yes, it is fixed finally and forever. However, some people found that what the Buddha has said and taught was not meant as the eternal dogmatic truth. The Buddha's purpose was to create in his students the ultimate state of mind that he had attained, rather than to proclaim abstract truths. Therefore the tradition cannot be aimed at maintaining and forwarding the so-called pure original text. You can only communicate what has been verified by the emergence of the similar state of mind in another person. But the teacher can only create a certain state of mind in his student if he takes into account the latter's individual traits. Therefore the Buddha must have given specific (rather than abstractly general) teachings to particular individuals and they in turn to their students who also were specific individuals, and so on. The authors of the *Prajñāpāramitā* saw the development of Buddhism in the first centuries of its history as follows (the scheme is simplified since I only mention one disciple in each generation, although even the first Teacher, Gautama Buddha, Śākyamuni, had many).

The Buddha tried to awaken the ultimate state of mind in disciple *A*. To do this, he gave the teaching ***a***, the text of which was determined by his own state of mind and the disciple's predisposition. The disciple ***A*** became the teacher ***A*** and tried to awaken the ultimate state of mind in disciple ***B***. Of course, he had to bear in mind the latter's special traits. Therefore he could not mechanically cite what he heard from the Buddha even if he remembered it word by word but had to adjust it for the disciple. As a result the teaching ***a*** was modified and became the teaching ***ab***. The disciple ***B*** became the teacher ***B*** who had the disciple ***C***, the teaching was transformed into ***abc***, etc, etc.

The above scheme explains much about the development of Buddhism. It also explains why in the 1st century BC when texts were first written down, there emerged quite a lot of canons belonging to different schools. It also explains why the Buddha who taught in the 6th and 5th century BC (rather than the teacher ***A***, ***B***, ***C***, etc.) is still seen as the main author of the texts placed in all these canons. The whole process that lasted for several centuries can be considered as a general text-generating mechanism started up by the Buddha. Indeed, all the schools agree that the first sūtra in the history of Buddhism was the *Dharmacakrapravartana*, which can be translated as "Starting up the Wheel of Dharma", and considering that *dharma* or the teaching primarily means a text, the title of the sūtra can quite unambiguously be translated as "Starting up the Text-generating Mechanism". This sounds somewhat modern but we should not forget that at a scientific meta-level the attempt to understand the inner essence of cultures through terminology that we can understand, is not only permissible but also necessary.

The majority of Buddhists, however, saw the development of Buddhism in a rather different way. They believed that the Buddha's "original" text was communicated from generation to generation in its "pure" form until it was finally written down. For them it was set in concrete and nothing could be added to it. All very wonderful but for the fact that this majority was divided into different schools with their own written canons which did not quite match the others. According to the *Prajñāpāramitā* scheme, this was supposed to happen, but the purist majority started arguing amongst themselves by using the touchingly primitive scheme also known in other religions: ""We" are right and all others, i.e. "they" are wrong." This must be the reason why the proponents of the *Prajñāpāramitā* started calling the majority "Hīnayāna", i.e. the 'Small Vehicle' that can only carry a small group. They named their own universal, pluralist and tolerant tradition "Mahāyāna" or the 'Great Vehicle'. It could be supposed that the schools of majority would still be arguing about them being right and the others being wrong if most of them had not simply ceased to exist. Only one of them – Theravāda – has survived due to the happy coincidence of many circumstances. Mahāyāna has become a truly worldwide religion, probably the only one in which numerous schools and traditions do not want to perish the others but accept others next to them, or inside them or even themselves inside others.

As I already said, Mahāyāna started from the *Prajñāpāramitā*. The first sūtras of this tradition were written in the 1st century BC when the canons of Hīnayāna schools were also fixed in writing. However, the *Prajñāpāramitā*, unlike Hīnayāna, did not finish the production of texts at the level of sūtras. On the contrary, the *Prajñāpāramitā* sūtras declare that more sūtras will appear in the future. History has shown that the predictions of the authors of the *Prajñāpāramitā* have come true: the emergence of canonical Mahāyāna literature is largely dated as the period from the 1st century BC to the 5th century AD.

It seems paradoxical that we do not know the authors of the Mahāyāna sūtras, although the process of their creation lasted for more than five centuries. They all start with the standard introduction: "Thus have I heard. Once Bhagavat stayed ..." Moreover, many sentences in the sūtras are ascribed to Bhagavat (i.e. the Buddha) himself and even if he does not speak he sits next to the speakers either in a state of concentration (*samādhi*) or otherwise, encouraging the discussions of disciples by his presence. Could the sūtras be falsified, as proponents of Hīnayāna often accused Mahāyāna? Most probably not even from the point of view of modern textual critics, if we consider the idea of the "text-generating mechanism". The Wheel of Dharma was started up by the Buddha (Bhagavat) and later the mechanism simply continued working. Moreover, the initial sentence of the sūtras – "Thus have I heard" – can be interpreted as some kind of reservation: the Buddha's words are conveyed by another person.

Still, as I already said, this other or, rather, others (since there apparently were quite many of them) should not be seen as the authors of the Mahāyāna sūtras. The author is still the Buddha and the text-generating mechanism he started up. Interestingly enough, the Mahāyāna sūtras are in a way quite similar and this similarity justifies the above-mentioned. They are similar in terms of vocabulary and style and, most importantly, regarding their intellectual power and persuasiveness. In this respect they certainly differ from the works of Buddhists who lived in the same period and wrote under their own names. The writings of Nāgārjuna, Asaṅga, Vasubandhu, Aśvaghoṣa and others might have been more persuasive in terms of their logical structure, and their language might have been better but they lacked the special fluidity that the Mahāyāna sūtras possess.

The "Heart Sūtra" is one of the shortest *Prajñāpāramitā* texts. If you are not familiar with other sūtras, it might seem rather incomprehensible. However, it should still be read as one of the first, since the questions that it raises, or the semi-clarity that it induces, may urge a thinking reader to seek answers. Some of the answers can definitely be found in the *Bodhicaryāvatāra* by Śāntideva and even more answers in the *Aṣṭasāhasrikā Prajñāpāramitā.*

The scene of the activities of the sūtra is Rājagṛha, one of the most important cities at the time of the Buddha. The Buddha must have stopped there quite often. This time the Buddha is surrounded by disciples: *bhikṣus* (mendicant monks) and bodhisattvas (both monks and laymen who think not only about their own liberation but also about the liberation of all sentient beings). All bodhisattvas are characterized by compassion. The bodhisattva Avalokiteśvara is the embodiment of compassion *par excellence*. It is not likely that he had a definite prototype in "real" life. Most probably, he was a generalized figure that emerged in the process of text-generation.

Avalokiteśvara is asked questions by Śāriputra, a *bhikṣu* who is well known from Hīnayāna texts and is apparently a historical person. However, it is important that the most intelligent Hīnayāna *bhikṣu* here only asks questions. The bodhisattva Avalokiteśvara (he also has another epithet, *mahāsattva*, meaning 'great being') is the one who teaches. What is he saying? He is saying that all *dharmas* are empty. But what are *dharmas*? In the most general sense, *dharma* is the text-generating mechanism that has already been discussed, the one that creates the ultimate state of mind. *Dharma* also is the ultimate state of mind itself and the text that is created by the ultimate state of mind. But in this sūtra, *dharma* does not mean so much a text as a whole, but rather a element of text or a minimum text or, in other words, the most significant terms used in Buddhist texts. The number of *dharmas* is different in different schools (70 to 140) but some of them coincide in all schools. I am not quoting the list of *dharmas* here. More important is that "all *dharmas* are marked by emptiness" (*sarvadharmāḥ śūnyatālakṣaṇāḥ*).

What does it mean? It does not mean, as it is often believed, that *dharmas* do not exist and that they are illusory deceptive images. In fact, 'emptiness' (*śūnyatā*) means that *dharmas* or text-generating mechanisms, in this case basic Buddhist terms contain an infinite number of opportunities to fill them with different content. It means that, for example, the word *rūpa* ('form') is not a defined and forever fixed concept but, in the process of inner text-generating (mental activity), it can be filled with one or another or third or hundredth or thousandth meaning. In other words, in the whole process of thinking we should make sure that defined concepts are not too limited: although Buddhists have defined all basic terms and treat the definitions with great respect, all definitions are temporary, and relevant for one or another specific state of mind. This by no means implies that Buddhism avoids mental activity. On the contrary, taking *śūnyatā* into account enabled it to use extremely sophisticated logic. In this case, words, concepts, ideas or sentences are not prisons but provide a chance to implement what is really human (animals who, as Buddhists believe, lack abstract thinking, are obviously incapable of attaining ultimate states of mind).

Thus, "all *dharmas* are empty". Only a person whose mind is not defiled (*acittāvaraṇa*) and whose consciousness is clear can fully understand it. This state of mind can be attained by reading the *Prajñāpāramitā* texts since one should rely on the "Transcending Awareness of bodhisattvas". 'Transcending Awareness' is the equivalent of *prajñāpāramitā* in English. It means the awareness that helps to overcome the ocean of *saṃsāra*. There is no reason to translate *prajñāpāramitā* as 'intuition', which, unfortunately, was done too often in earlier times. This would imply a connotation disparaging mental activity.

Dialogue in the *Bodhicaryāvatāra*

One can have no doubt that there is dialogue in the *Bodhicaryāvatāra*.[1] It is particularly clear in Chapter IX, although it is not difficult to find signs of dialogue in other chapters as well. However, it is not so easy to find out who the dialogue involves.

It might be assumed that one participant in the dialogue is the author himself, the 7th–8th century Buddhist thinker and poet Śāntideva who represents the "right" viewpoint and "criticizes" *somebody's* wrong ideas and views. There is some truth in this assumption. Indeed, what we perceive as Śāntideva's own ideas are really *his* ideas but we should also find out who this *somebody* is in order to provide a full answer to this question. It also seems obvious that there are very many opponents and that Śāntideva criticizes all of them: the Hinduist and the Hīnayāna Buddhist, the layman and the hermit, the active person and the inactive person. In order to make this clear, let us take Chapter IX which is entitled *Prajñāpāramitā*. It primarily considers the problems that we could (conventionally) call philosophical: the arrangement of the world, the existence of the Creator, perception, etc. The commentator of the *Bodhicaryāvatāra* Prajñākaramati and also commentators in Tibet[2] understood this chapter primarily as a criticism of different Hinduist and Buddhist schools from the position of the *mādhyamika-prāsaṅgika* school using the *prasaṅga* method, i.e. reducing the opponent's statements to the absurd (*reductio ad absurdum*).

If this is the case, there should be many opponents: these are the proponents of the Hinduist *sāṃkhya, nyāya, vaiśeṣika* and *vedānta* schools, *vaibhāṣika, sautrāntika* and *yogācāra* Buddhists and even *cārvāka* materialists. Still, their views are criticized correctly: their standpoints are presented in a form similar to what is called quoting in the European tradition.

However, Śāntideva nowhere defines his opponents[3] or says that these are *nyāya* standpoints and those are Hīnayāna views. Moreover, the whole chapter looks like a continuous stream of thought moving fluently from "criticising" one system to another. For instance, in verse IX, 59 commentators think that the first sentence and the first half of the second sentence criticize the *cārvāka* school and the end of the second sentence is aimed against the *sāṃkhya* school: "I am neither the flesh nor the sinews. I am neither heat nor wind. I am neither the orifices nor, in any way, the six consciousnesses."

This makes us think that Śāntideva "criticizes" certain views rather than certain schools and that he is not interested in whether the idea ***a*** really belongs to a proponent of the school ***A***. Moreover, the "criticized" seems to be the same person changing his views depending on the general stream of thought in the chapter.

Who is then the person "criticized" by Śāntideva? This is Śāntideva himself. Śāntideva is arguing with Śāntideva. It means that the dialogue in Chapter IX of the *Bodhicaryāvatāra* is an internal dialogue. Śāntideva, a proponent of the *mādhyamika* school, is arguing with doubting Śāntideva, uncertain Śāntideva. Śāntideva who understands the meaning of emptiness – *śūnyatā* – is arguing with Śāntideva who assumes that all phenomena are real in the sense that they have their own nature. If we use Buddhist terminology, we can say that Śāntideva's *prajñā* is arguing with Śāntideva's *avidyā*, i.e. the aware Śāntideva is arguing with the ignorant Śāntideva. This is the dialogue between *prajñā* and *avidyā*, awareness and ignorance. *Avidyā* incessantly creates all kinds of ideas and logical constructions, ending with the creation of a closed world model. *Prajñā*, on the contrary, reduces these ideas and constructions to the absurd and creates an open world model.

Does it mean that the dialogue in the *Bodhicaryāvatāra* is between the developed mind and undeveloped mind? It does, partly, but in a much more specific sense. The fact is that *avidyā* is deformed rather than undeveloped intelligence. It is first on the list of so-called *kleśas* or defilements of the mind (*cittakleśa*). Since other *kleśas* are what in European psychology could be called emotions (mostly negative) such as passion, hate, pride, envy, etc., and one can become free from *avidyā* only after having rid oneself of the other *kleśas*, it can primarily be defined as intelligence with a negative emotional background.

Prajñā, on the other hand, is the leading link on the list of the so-called six *pāramitās*, the other members of which can be considered as what European psychology calls positive emotions: generosity, morality, patience, vigour and concentration. In the Buddhist context these can be treated as intellectually directed emotions.

Thus, one can say that in a more general sense the dialogue in the *Bodhicaryāvatāra* is between emotionality and intellectuality.[4] We could also see it in the previous chapters where an entirely intellectual analysis was aimed at preparing the ground to strengthen positive emotions and overcome negative emotions. Thus, forbearance overcomes hate (VI, 1–2: "This worship of the Sugatas, generosity, and good conduct performed throughout thousands of aeons – hatred destroys it all. There is no evil equal to hatred, and no spiritual practice equal to forbearance. Therefore one should develop forbearance by various means, with great effort."), vigour overcomes sloth (VII, 2: "What is vigour? The endeavour to do what is skilful. What is its antithesis called? Sloth, clinging to what is vile, despondency, and self-contempt."), concentration overcomes distraction: (VIII, 1–2: "Increasing one's endeavour in this way, one should stabilize the mind in meditative concentration, since a person whose mind is distracted stands between the fangs of the defilements. Distraction does not occur if body and mind are kept sequestered. Therefore, one should renounce the world and disregard distracting thoughts.")

Now we would ask the last question: "Is the *Bodhicaryāvatāra* only a reflection of the dialogue between Śāntideva's emotionality and intellectuality?" Śāntideva himself writes: "Nothing new will be said here, nor have I any skill in composition. Therefore I do not imagine that I can benefit others. I have done this to perfume my own mind." (I, 2.)

However, immediately after that he continues: "While doing this, the surge of my inspiration to cultivate what is skilful increases. Moreover, should another, of the very same humours as me, also look at this, then he too may benefit from it." (I, 3.) It means that, according to Śāntideva, the *Bodhicaryāvatāra* has a more universal meaning and reflects the general principles of the human mind.

The Light Path and the Dark Path

Chapter VIII of the *Bhagavadgītā* contains the following verses:

23.
But at what times to non-return,
And (when) to return, disciplined men
Dying depart, those times
I shall declare, bull of Bharatas.

24.
Fire, light, day, the bright (lunar fortnight),
The six months that are northward course of the sun,
Dying in these, go
To Brahman Brahman-knowing folk.

25.
Smoke, night, also the dark (lunar fortnight),
The six months that are southward course of the sun,
In these (when he dies) to the moon's light
Attaining, the disciplined man returns.

26.
For these two paths, light and dark,
Are held to be eternal for the world;
By one, man goes to non-return,
By the other he returns again.

27.
Knowing these two paths, son of Pṛthā, not
Is any disciplined man confused.
Therefore at all times
Be disciplined in discipline, Arjuna.[1]

It seems to me that these verses have not received as much attention as they deserve. Indeed, commentators have emphasized the fact that there is something similar in the *Chāndogya Upaniṣad* and the *Bṛhadāraṇyaka Upaniṣad*. F. Edgerton has even concluded that these verses interpret the conception of the *Upaniṣads* in the wrong way.[2] Edgerton would be right if the ideas of the *Bhagavadgītā* were considered as genetically related to the *Upaniṣads* and only the *Upaniṣads*. In this case the verses would not, indeed, deserve special attention. However, since this is just an assumption and not a proven fact, at least now these verses should be accorded generous attention, and only the information that we obtain from them should be considered.

Nevertheless, this significantly differs from the ideas offered to us by the *Upaniṣads*. The *Upaniṣads* talk about the gradual transition of a dead person from one state to another but the *Gītā*, it seems to me, names the terms that are considered meaningful in both the light and dark paths:

LIGHT PATH: sun, light, leaving (and not coming back);

DARK PATH: moon, darkness, returning.

As we can see, these words might also be considered as opposite pairs (since the light path and dark path already make an opposite pair): *sun – moon; light – darkness; leaving (without returning) – returning*.

The quoted verses already show that the path of the *Gītā* is a light path. It means that the consideration of the 'dark path' should in a way be contrasted to the teaching of the *Gītā*, at least in the sense that the other main terms of both systems should also form opposite pairs.

I have not managed to find such a text among ancient Indian texts. But this does not mean that it does not exist. Interesting results, however, can be obtained from the comparison with other cultural traditions.

The cluster of concepts of the 'dark path' reminds us Taoism: Taoists' attachment to the moon and moonlight is widely known. *Darkness* and *returning* are also undoubtedly basic Taoist concepts. Therefore I think that when we look for the 'dark path' we should analyse and compare the *Bhagavadgītā* and Taoist texts. In this article an attempt is made to demonstrate the opposite pairs that I managed to find in the course of the comparative analysis of the *Bhagavadgītā* written in Sanskrit and the Ancient Chinese text *Daodejing*. The opposite pair *sun – moon* has not been found on the basis of the two texts since the sun has a very important position in the *Gītā* but the *Daodejing* does not even mention the moon.[3] Let us first take a look at the opposite pairs that were named above.

LIGHT – DARKNESS

'Light', 'radiance', 'flame' (*tejas, bhāsa)* are the properties of the most important concept of the *Gītā* – God, or to be precise, a divine person:

XI, 12.
Of a thousand suns in the sky
If suddenly should burst forth
The light, it would be like
Unto the light of that exalted one.

17.
With diadem, club, and disc,
A mass of radiance, glowing on all sides,
I see Thee, hard to look at, on every side
With the glory of flaming fire and sun, immeasurable.

30.
Devouring them you Thou lickest up voraciously on all sides
All the worlds with Thy flaming jaws;
Filling with radiance the whole universe,
Thy terrible splendors burn, O Viṣṇu!

XIII, 17.
Of lights also it is the light
Beyond darkness, so 'tis declared;
Knowledge, the object of knowledge, and the goal of knowledge;
(It is) settled in the heart of all.

In the *Gītā*, as in many other Indian texts, there are many expressions such as the 'illumination of knowledge', 'fire of knowledge', etc.:

IV, 37.
As firewood a kindled fire
Reduces to ashes, Arjuna,
The fire of knowledge all actions
Reduces to ashes even so.

XIV, 11.
In all gates (orifices) in this body
An illumination appears,
Which is knowledge; when that happens, then one shall know
Also that goodness is dominant.

In the *Daodejing*, on the contrary, the epithet of the main term 道 *dao* is *xuan* 玄 which can be translated as 'duskiness', 'darkness', 'profound', 'primordiality':

1. ...*nemad ilmuvad ühe ja samana*
ometi lahknevad nimetamisel
ühe ja samana

öeldud tumedana
tumedast veel tumedam
kõigi saladuste värav.

(*...these two together emerge;*
but have different names
being together
is called dark
darker than dark
it is the door of all mysteries.)[4]

Light and brightness are not acceptable in the *Daodejing*. They should be reduced and limited:

4. ...*tuhmista ta sära*... (...*dull its brightness*...),

56. ...*tuhmista sära*... (...*dull the brightness*...).

The light of knowledge is also undesirable. The people should stay in the dark:

65.
ennemuiste head teinud kulgejad
ei nad valgustanud rahvast
hoopis jätsid tumedaks...

(*ancient good-hearted followers of course*
did not enlighten people
rather left them in darkness...).

LEAVING (UNRETURNABILITY) – RETURNING

The purpose of the teaching of the *Bhagavadgītā* is to leave *saṃsāra* for the Highest Personal God:

XII, 6.
But those who, all actions
Casting on Me, intent on Me,
With utterly unswerving discipline
Meditating on Me, revere Me,

7.
For them I the Savior
From the sea of the round of deaths
Become right soon, son of Pṛthā,
When they have made their thoughts enter into Me.

8.
Fix thy thought-organ on Me alone;
Make thy consciousness enter into Me;
And thou shalt come to dwell even in Me
Hereafter; there is no doubt of this.

Those who do not aspire to the goal, return:

> IX, 3.
> *Men who put no faith*
> *In this religious truth, scorcher of the foe,*
> *Do not attain Me, and return*
> *On the path of endless round and deaths.*

On the contrary, the ideal of the *Daodejing* is to return, i.e. an eternal circle:

> 40.
> *kulgedes liigub naasja vaid ...*
> (*it is only the one who returns who moves in the course ...*),

> 25. ...
> *ütlen suur*
> *suure ütlen möödduvaks*
> *mööduva ütlen kaugenevaks*
> *kaugeneva ütlen naasvaks...*

> (...
> *I say great*
> *I say that great is transient*
> *I say that transient is moving away*
> *I say that moving away is returning...*).

People also return – to the state of a child, to a natural state, to the state of infinity (see Chapter 28).

Further, we would consider those opposite pairs identified during the comparative analysis of the the *Bhagavadgītā* and the *Daodejing*. Most concepts included in these texts are more or less about the words denoting what I conventionally call Higher Reality.[5] Higher Reality in the *Bhagavadgītā* is the Divine Person (*puruṣottama*), in the *Daodejing* – *dao* (course, the way things normally go). In the narrower sense either concept reflects only one aspect of higher reality.

Both the *Bhagavadgītā* and the *Daodejing* agree that Higher Reality has two aspects: describable and indescribable. In the *Gītā* the describable aspect is personal God – Kṛṣṇa[6] – and the indescribable aspect is Brahman, whereas the indescribable (i.e. Brahman) is inside the describable:

> XIV, 27.
> *For I am the foundation of Brahman,*
> *The immortal and imperishable,*
> *And of the eternal right,*
> *And of absolute bliss.*

XI, 37.
And why should they not pay homage to Thee,
Exalted One?
Thou art greater even than Brahman; Thou art the
First Creator;
O infinite Lord of Gods, in whom the world dwells,
Thou the imperishable, existent, non-existent,
and beyond both!

The subordination of the indescribable to the describable is explained by the fact that a person's religious attitude to a divined person is considered to be more acceptable than aspiring to the impersonal absolute (Chapter XII):

Arjuna said:

1.
Those who are thus constantly disciplined,
And revere Thee with devotion,
And those also who (revere) the imperishable unmanifest –
Of these which are the best knowers of discipline?

The Blessed One said:

2.
Fixing the thought-organ on Me, those who Me
Revere with constant discipline,
Pervaded with supreme faith,
Them I hold to the most disciplined.

3.
But those who the imperishable, undefinable,
Unmanifest, revere,
The omnipresent and unthinkable,
The immovable, unchanging, fixed,

4.
Restraining the throng of the senses,
With mental attitude alike to all,
They (also) reach none but Me,
Delighting in the welfare of all beings.

5.
Greater is the toil of them
That have their hearts fixed on the unmanifest;
For with difficulty is the unmanifest goal,
Attained by embodied (souls).

The *Daodejing* already mentions two aspects of Higher Reality in Chapter 1.:

...nimetu on taevasmaa algus
nimetatu on musttuhandete ema...

(...nameless is the beginning of heaven and earth
named is the mother of the myriad...).

The *Daodejing* prefers to be silent about the indescribable aspect. The describable aspect is what is called *dao* or *course*. It is not just a term but first and foremost a metaphor describing the flow of a river:

32.
...kulgemise võrdluspilt taeva all
jõed ja ojad merre voolavad...

(...the course under heaven can be compared to
rivers and streams flowing towards the sea).

Therefore the word 'course' can be used as an equivalent of *dao* in translation, particularly considering that *dao* is not so much a way, along which one moves to and fro, but an internal direction, the course of things, a natural process.

The *Daodejing* talks only about the describable aspect of Higher Reality but the reader should always bear in mind that there is also an indescribable (unnamed) aspect and that the describable aspect is subordinated to it.

Thus, the higher aspects of Higher Reality also form opposite pairs in both texts:

DESCRIBABLE – INDESCRIBABLE.

As noted previously, *dao* means a course, process or the natural motion of things. In any case *dao* is movement and Lao-zi's book confirms this:

25. *...kõikjal liigub väsimata...*
(...everywhere moving but tirelessly).

The *Bhagavadgītā* characterizes God as something stable and immovable:

II, 17.
But know that that is indestructible,
By which this all is pervaded;
Destruction of this imperishable one
No one can cause.

18.
These bodies come to an end,
It is declared, of the eternal embodied (soul)
Which is undestructible and unfathomable. ...

20.
He is not born, nor does he ever die;
Nor, having come to be, will he ever more come not to be.
Unborn, eternal, everlasting, this ancient one
Is not slain when the body is slain.

Therefore the following opposite pair is also quite justified:

MOVEMENT – STABILITY.

The movement of *dao* is the returning. Moreover: it is movement downwards. Chapter 32. of the *Daodejing* says that the picture with which *dao* can be compared is the flow of rivers and streams and they apparently flow from a higher place to a lower place. Therefore everything that is good in the world is like water going down to where the flow takes it:

8.
ülim headus on kui vesi
vesi on hea musttuhandetele
ta ei võistle
ta läheb sinnagi
mida peetakse halvaks
nõnda ta ongi kui kulg...

(*the highest good is like water*
water is good for the myriad
it does not compete
it even goes where
people do not like
therefore it is like a course...)

People must also go along with this movement downwards:

28.
...ole jõgi taeva all...

(*...be a river under heaven...*).

Therefore all people who want to be influential in the world should place themselves on a lower level:

66.
suured jõed ja mered
saavad ojakeste kuningaiks
nemad asuvad allpool
sellest saavad ojakeste kuningaiks
sellepärast
tahad olla rahva peal
südames end madalda

tahad olla rahva ees
südames end taganda...

(great rivers and seas.
may become the kings of streams
they are sited lower
then they become the kings of streams
for this reason
if you wish to be above the people
you must lower yourself in your heart
if you wish to lead the people
you must stay retreat behind them
in your heart).

The path of the *Bhagavadgītā*, on the contrary, leads up from below. One of the most widespread epithets in the *Gītā* is 'supreme'. The purpose is to reach heights. Chapter VI describes it as follows:

VI, 5.
One should lift up the self by the self,
And should not let the self down;
For the self is the self's only friend,
And the self is the self's only enemy.

6.
The self is a friend to that self
By which self the very self is subdued;
But to him that does not possess the self, in enmity
Will abide his very self, like an enemy.

7.
Of the self-subdued, pacified man,
The supreme self remains concentrated (in absorption),
In cold and heat, pleasure and pain,
Likewise in honor and disgrace.

8.
His self satiated with theoretical and practical knowledge,
Immovable, with subdued senses,
The possessor of discipline is called (truly) disciplined,
To whom clods, stones and gold are all one.

Therefore the following opposite pair can also be presented:

MOVING UP – MOVING DOWN.

Another opposite pair can be noted:

HILLTOP – VALLEY.

It was already mentioned that the *Gītā* considers 'reaching the top' as a goal of human being. However, this word also denotes 'the Highest':

XV, 18.
Since I transcend the perishable,
And am higher than the imperishable too,
Therefore in the world and the Veda I am
Proclaimed as the highest spirit.

The *Daodejing*, on the contrary, speaks about a valley:

28.
...ole oruks taeva all...
(*...be the valley under the heaven...*);

6.

surematut oruvaimu
kutsutakse ürgemaks...

(*the valley spirit never dies*
it is called the primordial mother...).

This primordial mother is *dao*. In the whole text of *Daodejing* *dao* represents the female and from there we go to the next opposite pair –

FATHER – MOTHER.

Dao is naturally the mother:

1.
...musttuhandete ema...

(*...mother of the myriad...*);

20.
...kuid ma hindan toitvat ema...

(*...but I value the sustenance providing mother*);

25.
...küllap taevasmaa ema...

(*...it can be regarded as the mother of heaven and earth...*);

52.
...emaks taevaalusele...

(*...that is the mother of all under heaven...*).

As the mother, *dao* gives birth to all and everything:

42.
kulg sünnitab ühe
ühest sünnib kaks
kahest sünnib kolm
kolmest sünnivad musttuhanded...

(*the course begets one*
one begets two

two begets three
three begets a myriad...).

In the *Bhagavadgītā* Kṛṣṇa names himself the father of everything:

XIV, 4.
In all wombs, son of Kuntī,
Whatsoever forms originate,
Of them great Brahman is the womb,
I am the father that furnishes the seed.

Arjuna also addresses him as a father:

XI, 43.
Thou art the father of the world of things that move and move not,
And Thou art its revered, most venerable Guru;
There is no other like Thee – how then a greater? –
Even in the three worlds, O Thou of matchless greatness!

LORD – NON-LORD

Arjuna addresses Kṛṣṇa using the word *īśvara*. Kṛṣṇa also calls himself *īśvara*. The word *īśvara* could be translated as 'Lord'.

XI, 37.
And why should they not pay homage to Thee, Exalted One?
Thou art greater even than Brahman; Thou art the First Creator;
O infinite Lord of Gods, in whom the world dwells,
Thou the imperishable, existent, non-existent, and beyond both!

The *Daodejing* stresses that *dao* is not Lord[7]:

34.
...katab ja toidab musttuhandeid
ometi ei pea end isandaks...

(*...clothes and feeds the myriad*
but still does not see himself as Lord...).

To conclude this part of the article, we would present one more opposite pair:

HUMAN-LIKE GOD – *DAO*-LIKE HUMAN.

Kṛṣṇa as an *avatāra* appears in the form of a human being. However, the cosmic body of Kṛṣṇa is also anthropomorphic as he is described in Chapter XI. He has a "great many mouths and eyes" (10), "innumerable arms, bellies, faces and eyes" (16). Arjuna addresses him:

XI, 23.

Thy great form, of many mouths and eyes,
O great-armed one, of many arms, thighs, and feet,
Of many bellies, terrible with many tusks, –
Seeing it the worlds tremble, and I too.

The human ideal of Lao-zi is the one following *dao*:

23.
sellepärast ole kulgeja
kulgeja on sama mis kulg

(... *therefore, one who devotes himself to the course*
is one with the course...).

Probably, another opposition may be seen behind it:

HUMAN – NATURE.

Descriptions of *dao* use natural objects such as a river, water or a valley, while in the *Gītā* even for the Highest God, the standard is human and not just human but a personality *(puruṣa)*.

Further opposite pairs are related to social life. The problems of society and the state play an important role in the *Daodejing*. As far as the *Bhagavadgītā* is concerned, it seems that they are less significant compared to philosophical and theological problems. Still, a number of opposite pairs can also be found at this level, for example

EMPIRE – SMALL COUNTRY.

The ideal of Lao-zi is a very small country where even the dogs barking and the roosters crowing in the neighbouring countries can be heard (80). As far as a big country is concerned, it should be ruled as a small country (60). An empire should consider itself to be lower than a small country, to show humility to a small country (61).

The *Bhagavadgītā*, as well as the whole of *Mahābhārata*, pronounces the idea of establishing an empire. Kṛṣṇa also announces this to Arjuna:

XI, 33.

Therefore arise thou, win glory,
Conquer thine enemies and enjoy prospered kingship; ...

KEEPING THE PRESENT – ASPIRING TO THE PAST

According to Lao-zi all he is aspiring to has already existed in the past. Then the world was dominated by ideal small countries (80). There were also wise men who lived in accordance with the *course* (15, 65) and now we should naturally follow suit.

The *Gītā*, on the contrary, assumes that the existing social situation should be preserved. Indian society was based on a caste system. Kṛṣṇa says in the *Gītā*:

> IV, 13.
> *The four-caste-system was created by Me*
> *With distinction of Strands and actions*
> *(appropriate to each);*
> *Altho I am the doer of this,*
> *Know Me as one that eternally does no act.*

The purpose of each person is to fulfil their duty to society (see XVIII, 41–44). The fulfilment of this duty is a precondition to moving towards even higher goals.

(RIGHTEOUS) WAR – PEACE

The duty of a *kṣatriya* is to take part in a righteous war.

> II, 31.
> *Likewise having regard for thine own (caste) duty*
> *Thou shouldst not tremble;*
> *For another, better thing than a fight required of duty*
> *Exists not for a warrior.*
> 32.
> *Presented by mere luck,*
> *An open door of heaven –*
> *Happy the warriors, son of Pṛthā,*
> *That get such a fight!*
> 33.
> *Now, if thou this duty-required*
> *Conflict wilt not perform,*
> *Then thine own duty and glory*
> *Abandoning, thou shalt get thee evil.*

War is not only a social phenomenon but also a cosmic one. Kṛṣṇa says:

> XI, 32.
> *I am Time (Death), cause of destruction of the worlds,*
> *matured*
> *And set out to gather in the worlds here.*

Even without thee (thy action), all shall cease to exist,
The warriors that are drawn up in the opposing ranks.

For Lao-zi, any war is unacceptable:

31.
relvad pole õnne riistad
olendid neid vihkavad
sellepärast
kulgejad ei tarvita
(weapons are not the tools of good fortune
beings hate them
therefore
followers of the course do not use them).

In the same chapter Lao-zi refutes the arguments of Confucians who advocate righteous war:

räägitakse
ülemvõimu valdaja pidagu peiesid
laibavirnade kohal nuta kurvastades
võidad sõja
pea peiesid

(it is said
the bearer of supreme power is to hold
the mourning rites
in sorrow and grief beside the piled up dead
if you win the war
hold the mourning rites).

Chapters 30 and 46 also mention negative attitudes to war.

The Course of Translation

Although Europeans were aware of the existence of China long before the great geographic discoveries, and the first direct influences of Chinese culture on Western Europe date back to the 17th century, one of the masterpieces of Chinese literature, the *Daodejing* by Lao-zi, only reached the West in 1788, translated into Latin by an unknown Jesuit missionary. Another half century passed before, in 1842, Stanislas Julien published a translation of Lao-zi into French. Since then Europeans have shown considerable interest in this work. The *Daodejing* has become one of the most frequently translated works in world literature. In the countries with a rich tradition of Chinese studies, the number of translations is also impressive: there are, for example, about fifty translations into English.

If non-experts compared all these translations, they could get the impression that these had been translated from different sources. Indeed, already the differences in form are noteworthy: some texts are in prose, some are in verse, in some translations prose and verse are mixed; some translations seem surprisingly compressed compared to others that are bulky volumes where most of the text is in brackets, which seems to indicate the opinion that Lao-zi can only be understood if we add copious words to the original.

If we now take the time to review the translations more thoroughly, we will find some that use abundant Chinese vocabulary and some that are full of terminology borrowed from Latin. Some translators remain faithful to their mother tongue. Reading the translations provides an even more multiform picture. We find with amazement that Lao-zi was a philosopher who could be associated with very different philosophical schools: according to some translations, he was a materialist and others seem to treat him as a subjective idealist. We have no difficulty finding passages that make Lao-zi almost a Christian, a Buddhist, a shaman or even a Muslim.

Browsing the translations at random, one can easily come to the conclusion that the original text of the *Daodejing* allows very different and even directly opposite interpretations. Furthermore, Lao-zi was a very intelligent man who understood that all ways led to One and therefore he described all ways in his work. Taking this a step further, we realize that everyone has to find their own translation, which is in keeping with their own beliefs, expectations and aspirations.

However, such conclusions are by no means correct. On the contrary, the truth is that the differences in the translations do not come from the original Chinese text of the *Daodejing* but depend on how much the original was ignored. Indeed, many aspects have not been taken into account: the structural features of the original, the definitions and comparisons given in the text, the place and function of the work in the cultural space of ancient China, etc.

Is there any translation at all that has taken heed of all the original features? The only answer we can give is "no", and such a translation is unlikely to appear. One of the reasons is that our knowledge of the past always remains incomplete. Another reason is that even the best translations are made in their own time and place and inevitably reflect other aspects too, alongside the nature of the original.

Still, we should and could select from this enormous bulk of translations the ones that attempt to convey original features in the best possible way. Of course, these translations are also different since the parameters of space and time were different when the text was translated but the *attempt* to only convey the original and not to *intentionally* add anything else is quite obvious. Some translations seem to intentionally try to make Lao-zi a herald of Christianity (for noble reasons, of course – to prove that great virtues flourished in China) or Islam (of course, to improve the image of this religion in the eyes of Europeans: you can see that even such a great man as Lao-zi said something like that ...) or something else. Some even argue that Lao-zi, following the example of Greek natural philosophers, spoke about the four elements of nature, although it is a well-known fact that Chinese systems are based on five elements.

Of course, such intentions remain foreign to translations aimed at *understanding* Lao-zi's own ideas. Such translations, which could be denoted as scientific ones, form something similar to a line or, rather, ascending pillar, in which later translations, based on previous discoveries are trying to find something new that would bring the general trend closer to Lao-zi's original. These translations are actually part of a collective international process and I would class them under the concept *the course of translation*. I think that this concept also includes a great number of research works considering the text of Lao-zi in one way or another and helping us to understand it better.

Translation in this *course of translation* is a process of creating a kind of *metatext*. Of course, this process is neither integral nor uniform or free from contradictions. Here one can also notice deviations in one direction or another but the main trends can be clearly outlined.

The trend that has become ever more pronounced in the past decades is the attempt to convey the structure of the form and structure of the original Chinese text as accurately as possible. In fact, this task is not as simple as it might seem at first sight. The problem is that the *Daodejing*, as well as other classical Chinese texts, is for certain considerations generally presented in the form of an unstructured text in which the lines run from the beginning of a page to the end and a new line does not necessarily mark a new meaningful unit. This is the case even with poems and texts where verse and prose intermingle. Due to the rhythm, tones and rhymes, an expert can unmistakably tell verse from prose. An experienced reader has no difficulty finding verses, stanzas or poems in the uniform text.

The Europeans have long been aware of the fact that the *Daodejing* is not a prose text in the conventional meaning of the word. However, it was also obvious that it was not normal verse: some passages could easily be structured in accordance with the rules of ancient Chinese poetry, and in some cases verses seemed to interchange with prose. Therefore, several translations that at the time significantly advanced understanding the *Daodejing* were done using a mixed method: part of the text was translated in verse and part in prose. The viewpoint that the originally pure poetic text had suffered throughout the centuries due to amendments and other contortions and that the translator should correct such "mistakes" started to gain ground in the first decades of the twentieth century. Entire lines were left out from some translations that appeared at the time. Still, these translations can be considered as part of the course of the translation since they also worked towards the trend of discovering the internal structure of the *Daodejing*.

The Russian sinologist Vladimir Spirin provided a probable solution for the problem in his book published in 1976 where he proved that ancient Chinese canonical texts (*jing*), including the *Daodejing*, were schematic texts divided into chapters with a complicated configuration.[1] The scheme plays an important role in understanding the text, and therefore the translations should reflect schematising possibilities hidden in the text as accurately as possible. Although I cannot agree with all Spirin's conclusions – for example, his opinion that all chapters of the *Daodejing* can be divided into nine sub-units is not particularly convincing – his method is convincing enough to make the structural approach to the *Daodejing* and other canonical texts (*jing*) a norm.

To illustrate the importance of the internal structure of the *Daodejing*, let me quote the three-line block at the beginning of Chapter 63 with some translation examples.

爲無爲
事無事
味無味

wéi wú wéi
shì wú shì
wèi wú wèi

Yang Hing-shung (1950):

Нужно осуществлять недеяние, соблюдать спокойствие и вкушать безвкусное.[2]

A. Waley (1934):

It acts without action, does without doing, finds flavour in what is flavourless.[3]

R. Wilhelm (1921):

Wer das Nichtsein übt,
Sich mit Beschäftigungslosigkeit beschäftigt,
Geschmack findet an dem, was nicht schmeckt...[4]

D. C. Lau (1963):

Do that which consists in taking no action; pursue that which is not meddlesome; savour that which has no flavour.[5]

E. Schwarz (1970):

Handle – doch nie der natur zuwieder
tu – doch nicht der taten wegen
schmeck – doch nicht um geschmack zu finden[6]

W. Chan (1963):

Act without action.
Do without ado.
Taste without tasting.[7]

G. Feng & J. English (1972):

Practice non-action.
Work without doing.
Taste the tasteless.[8]

Let us now give an example from an earlier translation which, nevertheless belongs to the course of translation:

J. Legge (1891):

(It is the way of the Tâo) to act without (thinking of) acting; to conduct affairs without (feeling the) trouble of them; to taste without discerning any flavour.[9]

What can we say about these examples? Legge is only interesting from the historical point of view since he shows how "meaning" was added to Lao-zi in brackets because this attitude was predominant at the time – also in translations from other languages. As we can see, there are no brackets in later translations but the translations still differ to a certain extent.

Looking at the original, we can see that the first and third character in each line is the same and the one in the middle means negation. The meaning of the first line – *wéi wú wéi* – is well known to sinologists from many other Taoist and Zen Buddhist works and its idea was correctly conveyed by Waley and Chan. The second line is correct in the translations made by Waley, Chan and to some extent Feng and English. The third line is only correct in Chan's translation but Waley deviates from what should be directly imposed by the structure of the block: the first line of the block is generally decisive in understanding the meaning of the other lines. It is amazing that Chan managed to convey the entire block in translation without knowing theoretical justification by Spirin (unfortunately, he was not so consistent with some other blocks). In Estonian I conveyed the meaning of this block as follows (with the English rendering in brackets):

toimi toimimata
tegutse tegutsemata
maitse maitsmata[10]

(*act without action*
do without doing
taste without tasting),

although other possible versions would be:

toimi ilma toimimata
tegutse ilma tegutsemata
maitse ilma maitsmata

(which in English is equivalent to the first version)

or

toimi mitte toimides
tegutse mitte tegutsedes
maitse mitte maitstes

(*act not acting,*
do not doing,
taste not tasting).

Now let us take a quick look at the schematising principles in the *Daodejing*. The basic unit of the scheme is a line, followed by a block, chapter and then the text as a whole.

Defining a **line** might seem easy at first glance: a line is a sequence of characters that has a closed grammatical form and expresses a completed meaning. If we consistently followed this wording, a line and a sentence would turn out to be identical concepts. Indeed, a whole number of translations seem to follow this principle.

In fact, such a definition does not follow the structural features of the *Daodejing* and primarily with what Spirin called 'universal parallelism'. Therefore it seems to be more correct to define a line as (1) the most minimal element of structural parallelism and (2) words or phrases belonging to the external framework (where, in addition to the possibilities mentioned by Spirin, I would place a word or a phrase that equally belongs to each line of the following block). For example, at the beginning of Chapter 2 the formula of two characters *tiān xià* – 'under heaven' should be considered as a separate line as it belongs to both parts of the block:

天下
皆知美之爲美
斯惡已
皆知善之爲善
斯不善已

tián xià
jiē zhī měi zhī wéi měi
sī è yǐ
jiē zhī shàn zhī wéi shàn
sī bù shàn yǐ.

In my translation into Estonian:

taeva all
kõik mõistavad ilusa ilusaks
siit ka inetus
kõik mõistavad hea heaks
siit ka halb,

(*under heaven*
all understand beautiful as beautiful
hence the ugliness
all understand good as good
hence the evil).

(The phrase 'under heaven' should conceptually be repeated before the second part of the block: *under heaven all understand good as good ...*).

The middle part of Chapter 51 should be schematized as follows:

故
道
生之
德
畜之
長之
育之
亭之
毒之
養之
覆之

gù
dào
shēng zhī
dé
xù zhī
zhǎng zhī
yù zhī
tíng zhī
dú zhī
yǎng zhī
fù zhī

and translated as:

sest
kulg
sünnitab neid
vägi
kasvatab neid
juhib neid
toidab neid
hooldab neid
korrastab neid
kostitab neid
katab neid

(*because*
the course
begets them
the power
raises them
leads them
feeds them
maintains them
arranges them
entertains them
covers them).

Parallel lines or line complexes that follow each other form a **block**. A block is not a mechanical unity of lines but fulfils a function of forming the meaning as we could see when we analysed the first block of Chapter 63 quoted previously. Each block is characterized by unity of content. Blocks also determine the meaning of the lines that form them – a line can only be fully understood in the context of a block (which, of course does not mean that a line could not function independently). Blocks can follow each other directly or have lines between them belonging to the external framework. In the latter case such lines also determine the meaning of the block.

A **chapter** may consist either of one (for example, Chapter 18) or of several blocks and the lines that form the external framework. The schemes of the three chapters can be presented as an example (frames designate blocks, numbers inside the frames denote the number of lines in the block, and number 1 represents a single line):

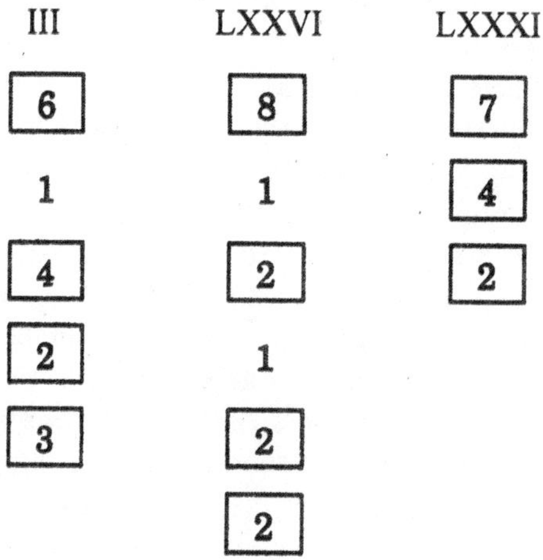

Now we may ask what is the **text** of *Daodejing* **as a whole**? Is it a philosophical treatise presented as a schematic text or can we consider it as a long poem as, for example, Nikolai Konrad does?[11]

In order to answer this question, we should first find out whether the words in the *Daodejing* are philosophical terms or concepts that also involve images. Let us take, for example, the phrase from Chapter 42:

萬物
負陰而抱陽

wàn wù
fù yīn ér bào yáng

If we translate it literally, it would be absurd: "Ten thousand things are bearing *yin* and have *yang* in their hands". It does not make sense even if we translate *yin* and *yang*: "Ten thousand things are bearing a shadow and have light in their hands".

What is wrong? *Wànwù* does mean 'ten thousand things' if translated literally. However, as well as the Greek *μυρίος*, the Chinese *wànwù* also means an enormous amount or innumerable quantity, i.e. what has been brought into European languages as the loan word 'myriad'. In Chinese philosophical and semi-philosophical texts *wànwù* is associated with the meaning of 'myriad'. The character *fù* originally meant 'to bear' and *bào* 'to hold in one's hands' but in the middle of the first millennium BC they acquired a more universal meaning. The line in question should express at least three ideas: (1) all phenomena are affected by two opposite powers – *yin* and *yang*; (2) all that lives grows from the earth to the heaven; (3) human beings are the synthesis of heaven and earth. The figurative approach should be able to convey all this laconically: "Myriads embracing shadow are stretching into light". Or if we try to see something that looks like a passive construction in the Chinese sentence, we could keep the initial meanings of the characters: "Myriads borne by the shadow are taken into the light". This, however, is also figurative.

The idea that the concepts of the *Daodejing* are used figuratively is confirmed by the fact that even *dao* is explained through a metaphor in the figurative way in Chapter 32: "The course under heaven can be compared to rivers and streams flowing towards the sea."

If we consider that the *Daodejing* has other features typical of verse (rhymes, emphases, etc.), it seems that there should be no doubt regarding the poetic nature of the text. Still, the *Daodejing* has the character of a philosophical treatise and, in particular, it was considered as such in medieval China. The answer is seemingly that the *Daodejing* belongs to the period when the transition from mythopoetical thinking to a theoretical one was ongoing. Therefore the *Daodejing* cannot only be seen as a myth or a poem but neither can it be seen as a purely philosophical treatise. How can it be rendered in translation?

The form should follow the scheme of the original as accurately as possible. Since it is impossible to keep the number of syllables in a line due to the laconism of the ancient Chinese language, one should not even try to do it. Considering that the number of syllables is different in lines belonging to different blocks, which brings about intermittent rhythms within a chapter, the most adequate form for the translation of the *Daodejing* should be a free verse structure.

The course of the translation in the past decades has brought about many new approaches to the understanding the meaning of characters in the *Daodejing*. In the works of J. Needham, A. Waley, H. Welch, G. Creel and many others we can find numerous pages explaining the meaning of one or another key word. In spite of the fact that researchers' opinions do not always coincide, here we can also see the common trend of finding fewer similarities between Lao-zi's teaching and European religions or philosophies.

Therefore Western philosophical and religious terminology has been removed from translations. It does not mean, however, that it is absolutely impossible to find equivalents to the words of Lao-zi (and other thinkers from the East). It is possible to find them but one should understand the simple fact that the terminology of any system of thought is based on everyday colloquial language. Eastern philosophies raised other words to the level of terms than Greek or German philosophies (the terminology of which we usually consider as the only ones possible). Since colloquial languages, due to their stronger connection to real life, are less different from each other than philosophical languages, the key for translating Eastern philosophical texts is as follows. First, one has to find out the meaning of the word in everyday language of the original and then try to find as close an equivalent as possible in the language of translation, not worrying about whether or not this word is used in contemporary philosophical and religious literature. In a translation such a word will inevitably attain the position of a term. This trend in particularly has been promoted by the researcher of Tibetan Buddhist texts H. V. Guenther over recent decades and is now the main trend in the translation of Lao-zi and other ancient Chinese philosophers as well. For example, after the publication of A. Waley's translation it was almost generally recognized that the most proper equivalent in English for the Chinese term *de* is not 'virtue' in its moral or ethical meaning, but 'power'.

This trend can be clearly seen in the interpretation and translation of *dao*, the main term of Taoism and ancient Chinese philosophy in general. In the first Latin translation *dao* was rendered as *Ratio* in the sense of 'divine mind'. In the 1820s this trend was continued by Abel Rémusat using the following words: "Ce mot me semble ne pas pouvoir être bien traduit, si ce n'est par le mot λόγος dans le triple sens de souverain Être, de raison, et le parole."[12] His successor in the chair, the publisher of the first French translation of the *Daodejing*, Stanislas Julien, apparently used the word *la Voie* – 'Way' – to translate *dao* for the first time. Since then the 'way' has become one of the most widely used equivalents of *dao*, although in the last quarter of the nineteenth century it was already understood as a natural process rather than a structure created on earth, having certain borders and leading to a particular place or a sum of certain orders and instructions, as Mr. Balfour said: "When the word is translated Way, it means the Way of Nature, – her processes, her methods, and her laws."[13]

In the first decades of the twentieth century, we again notice that *dao* is translated as 'Logos' or 'intellectual principle'. For example, Carus – 'Reason', R. Wilhelm – 'der Sinn'. Richard Wilhelm even gave a rather strange theoretical excuse for translating *dao* as anything at all: "Im Grunde genommen kommt auf den Ausdruck wenig an, da er ja auch für Laotse selbst nur sozusagen ein algebraisches Zeichen für etwas Unaussprechliches ist. Es sind im wesentlichen ästhetische Gründe, die es wünschenswert erscheinen lassen, in einer deutschen Übersetzung ein deutsche Wort zu haben."[14]

However, the return to *Ratio* was not permanent. First *dao* was translated as a 'way' again. Based on it, French intellectuals supporting Islam (R. Guénon and others) started looking for analogies between Taoism and Islam but this was refuted by the prominent sinologist H. Maspero: "Although the word 'dao' means 'way', it has nothing to do with the 'Path' of Christian or Moslem mystics."[15]

The way in the meaning of *dao* is not something along which you go ahead or come back but the internal course of things, a process. Chinese scholars started reminding Europeans about it as early as the 1930s. Hu Shih wrote: "So, the new principle was postulated as the Way (Tao), that is a process, an all-pervading and everlasting process."[16] The most prominent Chinese philosopher of 20th century Fung Yu-lan has said: "... when we talk about Tao, we speak from the aspect of activity of all things."[17] By the way, Fung Yu-lan also wrote the article about Taoism for the Russian "Encyclopaedia of Philosophy I", where he notes: "His (Lao-zi's – L. M.) main concept is *dao* – the natural course of things that does not depend on God or humans and is the general law of the movement and transformation of the world."[18] One of the greatest researchers of the Chinese history of science J. Needham notes: "The Tao or Way was not the right way of life within human society, but the way in which universe worked, in other words, the Order of Nature."[19]

Almost all prominent sinologists have emphasized in the past decades that *dao* is not a 'way' in the usual sense but rather a process, the 'order of things'. This trend is well summarized by Alan Watts: "Thus the Tao is the course, the flow, the drift, or the process of nature ..."[20] And further: "Tao is the flowing course of nature and the universe..."[21]

But let us come back to Richard Wilhelm: *dao* is just an algebraic sign to denote the inexpressible. This argument seems to be an excuse for not translating or interpreting *dao*. Those who tried it, however, encountered great difficulties with the *Daodejing*, for example, in Chapter 77 opposing 天之道 *tián zhī dào* ('the *dao* of heaven') and 人之道 *rén zhī dào* ('human *dao*'). What are these if *dao* is just an inexpressible and immovable basis for all that exists? Indeed, even Feng and English, who otherwise did not translate *dao* preferred to translate the expression *rén zhī dào* as 'way of men'! Does the *Daodejing* speak about one *dao*, two *daos* or even several *daos*? A European might overcome this difficulty by using capital letters and opposing *dao* to *Dao* or even *DAO*. Lao-zi and other ancient Chinese philosophers could not even think in such a way since, as we know, there are no capital letters in Chinese.

What does Lao-zi himself say about the inexpressible and unnamed? In the very beginning of Chapter 1 it is said that (as I have translated it into Estonian, with the English rendering in brackets):

> *nimetu on taevasmaa algus*
> *nimetatav on musttuhandete ema*
>
> (*the unnamed is the beginning of heaven and earth*
> *the named is the mother of the myriad*).

Therefore the inexpressible or the unnameable also has an expressed or named aspect. The word *dao* is the named aspect of the inexpressible since it is not a sign with no meaning such as *x*, *y* or *z*. Of course, Lao-zi is aware that a name does not completely express the inexpressible and that alongside something that can be discussed there is something that cannot be discussed, but the word *dao* has not been chosen by chance, although Chapter 25 could make us think so:

ma ei tea ta nime
sellepärast ütlen kulg
suvaliselt annan nimetusi

(*I do not know its name*
therefore I say course
I give names arbitrarily).

However, Chapter 32 refers to the fact that the word *dao* has been chosen primarily as a metaphor – it also denotes the flow of rivers and streams. Comparing *dao* with the flow of water is also characteristic of other Taoist texts, for example *Zhuang-zi*, and what Chapter 25 says after the above passage also shows that the word *dao* is intended to denote movement:

ütlen suur
suure ütlen mööduvaks
mööduva ütlen kaugenevaks
kaugeneva ütlen naasvaks

(*I say great*
I say that great is transient
I say that transient is moving away
I say that what is moving away is returning).

Therefore it does make a difference if we replace *dao* in translation with something or leave it untranslated. Respect for the author implies that we use the word which would allow us to exploit the same metaphors and images in the language of translation as in the original text. Still, we should bear in mind that it all has an unnamed, i.e. inexpressible aspect. It might be difficult for Europeans to understand it, since they have always tried to discuss what cannot be discussed (for example, proofs of God) but Taoists as well as Buddhists prefer to be silent about the inexpressible. They discuss what can be discussed. Lao-zi was not silent: thus, he did not talk about the inexpressible.

However, *dao* is not just Lao-zi's word. This is also the central concept in other Chinese philosophical schools, even in Legalism. We have no reason to think that Lao-zi was the first one to use it. Later *dao* became more and more terminological, so that it has even been defined. The *Zhongyong*, a text ascribed to Confucius but apparently created after him (which is, by the way, also highly valued by Taoists) says (Chapter 1):

järgida loomust
sellest on öeldud
kulg

(*to follow nature*
it is said to be
the course).

More attention has been paid in recent decades to the place of the *Daodejing* in ancient Chinese philosophy as an integral system. A. Waley makes valuable observations concerning the relationship between Taoism and Legalism in his commentaries. Yang Yong-guo refers to the passages that could be critical of Mo-zi.[22] Most sinologists seem to think that Lao-zi's book criticizes Confucianism.

Indeed, a closer look at the teachings of other ancient Chinese schools seems to offer new possibilities for the clarification of "confusing" and "vague" passages in the *Daodejing* – unfortunately, there are still too many.

Chapter 31 has caused much confusion and incomprehension among researchers. D. C. Lau wrote: "The text of this chapter is obviously in disorder and needs rearrangement..."[23] Indeed, if we look at the translations that have so far been published, we can see that the beginning of the chapter calls upon people to abandon weapons completely, but later, the use of weapons is allowed for righteous purposes. Yang Hing-shung's translation fairly accurately reflects the level of the comprehension regarding this chapter:

> "A good army is a means that causes misery and all creatures hate it. Therefore a person who follows *dao* does not use it.
>
> A nobleman prefers to be respectful in peacetime and uses violence in wartime. An army is a means of misery and is not a means for a nobleman. He only uses it when he is forced to do so. The main principle is to maintain peace but not to exalt oneself if one wins. To exalt oneself after a victory means to be happy to kill people. The one who is happy to kill people cannot win support in the country. Well-being is created by respect and misery comes from violence.
>
> Leaders of the units line up to the left and the commander stands on the right. People say that they should be met by a funeral ceremony. If many people are killed, one should cry bitterly over it. The victory should be commemorated by a funeral ceremony."[24]

The chapter becomes quite understandable if we assume that Lao-zi is quoting a Confucian in the middle of it. And, indeed, opposed are *youdaozhe* ('the one who follows the course') as a Taoist and *junzi* ('the nobleman') as a Confucian. The first is completely against using weapons and the other one resorts to this opportunity in a hopeless situation. Lao-zi is categorical when he answers the Confucian: even a victory won in a righteous war should be commemorated with a funeral ceremony:

relvad pole õnne riistad
olendid neid vihkavad
sellepärast
kulgeja ei tarvita

õilis arvab
rahuaegu hindan vasemat
sõdides hindan paremat
relvad pole õnne riistad
pole õilishinge riistad
tarvitan kui teisiti ei saa
ülimaks pean rahu
võidan küll kuid ilusaks ei pea
ilusaks kui peaksin
rõõmustaksin inimtapust
rõõmustaksin inimtapust
püüdlused ei täituks taeva all
pidupäevil hindan vasemat
murepäevil hindan paremat

abipealik lahingus on vasemal
ülempealik lahingus on paremal

räägitakse
ülemvõimu valdaja pidagu peiesid
laibavirnade kohal nuta kurvastades
võidad sõja
pea peiesid

(weapons are not instruments of happiness
beings hate them
therefore
those who follow the course do not use them

but a nobleman thinks
in peacetime I value left
but while warring I value right
weapons are not instruments of happiness
or instruments of a nobleman
I use them if I cannot avoid it
but I place peace above all
I win but I do not think it would be good
if I should

rejoice over human slaughter
if I rejoice over human slaughter
my aspirations would not be fulfilled
under heaven
on festive days I value left
on days of woe I value right
assistant commander is on the left in the battle
supreme commander is on the right in the battle

people say that
he who commands the highest power
should hold a funeral ceremony
cry over the piles of the dead
you win the war
you must hold the funeral ceremony).

The beginning of Chapter 41 can also be interpreted differently from how it has been done previously. I think that the hierarchy presented there (*shàngshì, zhōngshì, xìashì*) does not express the gradation of people's abilities but accurately represents the Confucian hierarchy of officials as it is recorded in Meng-zi's book.[25] Let us quote Lau's translation:

When the best student hears about the way
He practices it assiduously;
When the average student hears about the way
It seems to him one moment there and gone the next;
When the worst student hears about the way
He laughs out loud.
If he did not laugh
It would be unworthy of being the way.[26]

First, it is not possible to practice *dao* in Taoism. It is only possible to return to *dao*. However, it can be done in Confucianism (in my own translation):

inimene
ülendab kulgu
kulg
ei ülenda inimest

(man
elevates the course
the course
does not elevate the man).[27]

Second, the laughter of the bad student seems to be derisive in the Lau's translation. In fact, Taoists considered laughter to be a very good and necessary activity since it shows that everything is going as it should (i.e. flows or courses). Third, Taoists took no heed of Confucian hierarchy but thought that people climbing up a hierarchical ladder lose their naturalness. Therefore it seems that the person mentioned in the first line, a high official, does not understand *dao* but confidently thinks that it can be practiced (moved). The third line is about a medium-level official, but in China, as anywhere else, he has no opinion of his own. The lower official has preserved his humanness. He is saying nothing but laughing. It is natural behaviour. So, my translation of the chapter is as follows:

kõrgõpetlane kulgemisest kuuldes arvab
liigun ja liigutan teda
keskõpetlane kulgemisest kuuldes arvab
nagu oleks nagu poleks
allõpetlane kulgemisest kuuldes
naerab selle üle valjult

pole naeru
pole kulgu

(*the high scholar hearing about the course thinks*
I will move myself and move it
the medium scholar hearing about the course thinks
maybe it is maybe it is not
the lower scholar hearing about the course
laughs out loud

if there is no laughter
there is no course).

I am not aware of any other Oriental text which is so difficult to understand. Naturally enough, the interpretation of this text, the central word of which is 'course' can be best described as the 'course of translation'.

Undoubtedly, this course is not going to end now or later. Many unclear passages in the *Daodejing* still need explanation. The clarity of the "clear" passages can also take a different turn. For example, if we manage to prove that the word *xiang* that is present in each line of the second block of Chapter 2 meant 'it' in Lao-zi's time, the block might look as follows:

olev
olematu seda sünnitab
raske
kerge seda valmistab
pikk
lühike seda mõõdab...

(existing
non-existing gives birth to it
heavy
light prepares it
long
short measures it...)

and so forth and so on.

Buddhist Mythology

(Article written for the Encyclopaedia of Mythology)

Buddhist mythology is a collection of mythological images, figures, characters and symbols related to the religious and philosophical system of Buddhism that emerged in the 6th and 5th centuries BC in India and was widespread in South, South-East and Central Asia and the Far East.

Buddhism is conventionally divided into three traditions: Hīnayāna (the 'Small Vehicle'), Mahāyāna (the 'Great Vehicle') and Vajrayāna (the 'Diamond Vehicle') that are in fact not three stages in the development of Buddhism. These three traditions probably had direct common or close sources in early Buddhism but later developed relatively independently. Written Hīnayāna canons and the first Mahāyāna sūtras appeared approximately at the same time (1st century BC). The first known Vajrayāna texts date back to the 3rd century AD. These traditions that accentuated different aspects of early Buddhism do not differ in terms of the main principles. Common plots and figures in their mythologies enable us to speak about the existence of Buddhist mythology in general.

There has been little study of the beginnings and development of Buddhist mythology, particularly of its early stage, since there are practically no texts that clearly date back to the time of so-called early Buddhism.

Sources used to study Buddhist mythology include numerous texts created and shaped throughout the centuries in India and other countries that were influenced by Buddhism. The main source of Buddhist mythology in general and Hīnayāna mythology in particular is the *Tipiṭaka*, a body of canonical texts from the Hīnayānist Theravāda lineage recorded in the Pāli language in the 1st century BC in Sri Lanka (Ceylon) (according to this tradition, the oral version was summarized in its final form immediately after Śākyamuni's death but in reality it underwent some remaking and rethinking before it was written down). The *Vinayapiṭaka* ('Basket of Discipline') and the *Suttapiṭaka* ('Basket of Sūtras') are the most interesting, in terms of mythology, of the three so-called baskets (*piṭakas*) of the *Tipiṭaka*.

The canonical literature of Mahāyāna is vast. The development of the Mahāyāna canon in Sanskrit lasted a long time, probably from the 1st century BC to the 9th or 10th century AD. "The Lotus Sūtra" (*Saddharmapuṇḍarīka*), "Sūtra of the Happy Land" (*Sukhavatī-vyūha*), "Sūtra of the Entering Lanka" (*Laṅkāvatāra*), "Sūtra of the Transcending Awareness in Eight Thousand Lines" (*Aṣṭasāhasrikā Prajñāpāramitā*), "Sūtra of the Transcending Awareness in Hundred Thousands Lines" (*Śatasāhasrikā Prajñāpāramitā*), "The Diamond Sūtra" (*Vajracchedikā*), "Teaching of Vimalakīrti" (*Vimalakīrtinirdeśa*) and some others are essential to the Mahāyāna mythology.

The sources of Vajrayāna mythology largely include the canonical texts of this tradition, the so-called tantras. The most important of these are *Guhyasamājatantra* (probably 3rd century), *Hevajratantra* (6th–8th century), *Vajrabhairavatantra* (7th–8th century). Considerable information on Buddhist mythology can also be found in non-canonical Buddhist texts (commentaries to sūtras and tantras, treatises, biographies of outstanding Buddhists, etc.).

The basic features of Buddhist mythology formed in India within 1500 years (from 6th century BC to the beginning of the second millennium AD). Śākyamuni, whose teachings constitute the basis of Buddhism, apparently had much lesser influence on the development of mythology than on some other aspects of Buddhism (philosophy, psychology and ethics) but much of what is included in Buddhist mythology undoubtedly dates back to his time. The degree of mythologisation of Buddhism has been constantly growing throughout its history: for example, the texts of the first millennium AD are much richer in mythological plots and images than those of the late first millennium BC. However, we cannot say that Buddhism was originally relatively free from mythology (such ideas were suggested by European scholars in the late 19th and early 20th centuries).

In terms of its attitude towards mythology, Buddhism is quite different to other religions. This is related to the main concept of Buddhism, according to which humans (and only humans) have a special place in the hierarchy of all (including mythological) beings, since only they have a chance to liberate themselves from the burden of beginningless *saṃsāra* (i.e. become an Arhat or a Buddha). All the others (including gods and other mythological figures) cannot directly attain *nirvāṇa* (for this purpose they should be born as humans), and in this sense their status is lower than that of humans, although they may possess some qualities that humans do not have (the Buddhas and bodhisattvas surpass all other beings in this respect as well).

Buddhism also has a special attitude to the reality of mythological figures. While in popular Buddhism, they were considered to be quite real, philosophical Buddhism saw them as creations of the human mind and thus in fact eliminated the question of their reality or unreality. This attitude provided opportunities for the unlimited expansion of the Buddhist pantheon and the enrichment of its mythological content. The Buddhist pantheon included a great number of gods, demigods and other mythological beings from the mythologies of all peoples and tribes practising Buddhism; they preserved their functions, although they adhered to the principles of Buddhism. Thus, Buddhism borrowed some gods like Brahma, Indra (Buddhist Śakra), Viṣṇu, Gaṇeśa and others, *lokapālas* and *gandharvas* from the mythology of Brahmanism and Hinduism, Gesar and Talha from Tibetan mythology, etc. The Buddhist pantheon was also enlarged due to the mythologization of real persons. Apparently, Śākyamuni and his disciples (Ānanda, Kāśyapa, Maudgalyāyana, Subhūti, Śāriputra and others) turned into mythological figures at a very early stage of the development of Buddhism. In the following centuries this process also involved all the more or less famous teachers, abbots and hermits.

The most unique way of increasing the Buddhist pantheon was the artificial (and quite conscious) creation of mythological images and figures. This process, that might have started as early as at the end of the first millennium BC, culminated in the second half of the first millennium AD with the appearance of the main Vajrayāna *yidams*. Created as anthropomorphic symbols for meditation, these characters soon acquired mythological features, and were included in the Buddhist mythological pantheon. Dynamism and the tendency to be enlarged and enriched are typical of Buddhist mythology as a whole, as well as of individual images and figures. Thus, the bodhisattva Avalokiteśvara was transformed into the female deity Guanyin in China, and some legends emerged in Tibet around *yidam* Yamāntaka trying to explain his origin.[1]

The relationship between the theoretical, philosophical and mythological levels is also quite special in Buddhism. Buddhist philosophers who were aware of the difference between abstract, theoretical and mythopoetical thinking did not deny the importance of the latter since they saw it as a means of attaining *nirvāṇa*. Therefore, ideas and concepts of Buddhist philosophy and psychology were often filled with mythological content (which, in particular, was supposed to simplify their comprehension). On the other hand, some mythological features (for example, the form and details of the images of *yidams*) were explained as the symbolic representation of one or another theoretical conception. Thus, the nine heads of Vajrabhairava (one of the forms of Yamāntaka) symbolize the nine parts of the Buddhist canon, his two horns represent the absolute and relative truths, his sixteen legs denote the sixteen aspects of the concept of emptiness, etc.

GENERAL BUDDHIST MYTHOLOGY, which in many aspects is close to Brahmanist and Hinduist mythologies, has probably experienced some influence of non-Aryan Indian mythologies. Buddhist mythology might also reflect some of the mythological ideas of the Indus civilization. Some elements of Brahmanist mythology were remodelled in Buddhist mythology: primarily, cosmology and attitudes towards gods. Therefore, the characteristic features of the cosmological ideas of Buddhist mythology are on a grand scale and attempt to increase all elements of the universe to infinity. Innumerable worlds are grouped into huge world systems (*sahāloka*) which, according to the vivid simile from Buddhist texts, are more numerous than the grains of sand in the Ganges River. Each individual world is a flat disk of land; it lies on water, water floats in air and air is in space (*ākāśa*). A huge mountain called Meru or Sumeru is in the centre of the world, and the sun, moon and stars revolve around it. Meru is concentrically surrounded by seven mountain ridges that are separated by circular lakes. Behind them there are four continents: Pūrvavideha in the East, Jambudvīpa in the South, Aparagodānīya in the West and Uttarakuru in the North. Each is surrounded by 500 islands washed by the huge world ocean. The world ocean is surrounded by the rocky wall Cakravāla.

The life of people living on the four continents is different: the shortest in Jambudvīpa, the happiest in Uttarakuru where there is no private property, grain ripens on its own and people do not work. Nevertheless, the most successful birth is in Jambudvīpa (which mainly coincides with India) where people are brave, witty and pious. The Buddhas appear exclusively in Jambudvīpa. The continents are also inhabited by animals. Deep under the ground there are *pretas* and, deeper still, the different levels of hell (*naraka*). *Asuras,* the demigods, live mostly at the foot of Meru. Gods, who in Buddhist mythology are divided into hierarchical groups, live partly on Meru but mostly above it. Lowest are the "Four Great Kings" *(caturmahārāja)* – Dhṛtarāṣṭra, Virūḍhaka, Virūpākṣa and Vaiśravaṇa who respectively rule *gandharvas*, *kumbhāṇḍas*, *nāgas* and *yakṣas*. The "Heaven of Thirty Three Gods" (*trāyastriṃśa*) headed by the god Śakra (Indra) is above them, on the top of Meru. Higher still there are heavens – Yāma, Tuṣita, Nirmāṇarati and Paranirmitavaśavartin. Gods living in these heavens, as well as people, animals, *pretas*, *asuras* and the inhabitants of hells, constitute the so-called sphere of desires (*kāmāvacara* or *kāmadhātu*) since the main motive of their actions is the aspiration to satisfy their own desires. Other gods reside in the two other spheres. There are sixteen (sometimes seventeen are mentioned) lower heavens of Brahma (*brahmaloka*) in the "sphere of the forms" (*rūpāvacara* or *rūpadhātu*). The "sphere of non-forms" (*arūpāvacara* or *arūpadhātu*) above them is divided into four higher heavens of Brahma.

According to Buddhist mythology, gods as well as all other beings live by the laws of karma. They can exert certain influence on what happens in the world, but the world changes mainly due to the universal law of karma. Existence as a god is just one of the transient forms of existence in *saṃsāra*.

In spite of the fact that *saṃsāra* on the whole has no beginning, each individual world emerges, develops and perishes over time. A world exists during one *mahākalpa* which is divided into four incalculable kalpas (*asaṃkhyeya kalpa*), each lasting billions of years. There are two kinds of *mahākalpas*: *buddhakalpas* when the Buddhas appear in the world and 'empty *kalpas*' (*śūnyakalpas*) when no Buddhas appear. The present *kalpa* is a *buddhakalpa* and is considered to be extremely lucky since a thousand Buddhas should appear during the whole *kalpa*. In Buddhist mythology six Buddhas are named who have appeared before Śākyamuni – Viśvabhū, Vipaśyin, Śikhin, Krakucchanda, Kanakamuni and Kāśyapa – and one who is going to appear in the future – Maitreya.

The image of a Buddha is the main subject of Buddhist mythology. The Buddhas appear in all worlds (although not in all *kalpas*) and therefore their number is also incalculable. The Buddhas start their path towards awakening as bodhisattvas. During many *kalpas* (the word 'incalculable' is often used here) they reincarnate in the shape of different beings and do good deeds. Finally, after attaining perfection they stay in the heavens for a long time (in different versions either in Tuṣita or Akaniṣṭha). Their birth in the world as humans is accompanied by many miraculous events (earthquakes happen, flowers fall from the sky, etc.). The Buddhas have such powers and capabilities that they surpass all other beings, including gods. Only the Buddhas can affect the course of events in other worlds and not just in their own world. After reaching *nirvāṇa* they teach their *dharma* (i.e. the teaching that helps people to attain *nirvāṇa*).

Dharma is not eternal. It is particularly powerful during the first 500 years and then gradually fades away. Finally, when the world sinks into the obscurity of ignorance, the time is ripe for a new Buddha. The way of a bodhisattva and the state of a Buddha are generally described in Buddhist literature using the example of Śākyamuni, the Buddha of the present time.

Along with the Buddhas and bodhisattvas, Buddhist mythology mentions some other categories of human beings who have attained perfection (in the sense of the highest stage of their personal development). In Buddhist mythology there are two such categories: *arhats* and *pratyekabuddhas*.

It is very important for Buddhist mythology to describe and explain the miraculous powers of the Buddhas and other persons who have achieved perfection or are striving to achieve it. These powers are either mental (understanding intentions or thoughts of other people, or knowing past and future reincarnations – one's own and other's) or physical (flying, walking on water, becoming invisible, etc.).

Elements of flora and fauna also have a certain place in Buddhist mythology. The most often mentioned flower is the lotus symbolising purity, wonderful birth, spiritual enlightenment and compassion. Gods (as well as the inhabitants of Sukhavatī and other "pure lands" in Mahāyāna mythology) and even some outstanding people in this world (e.g. Padmasabhava) are born from lotus flowers.

The main tree in Buddhist mythology is the bodhi tree ('the tree of awakening'), belonging to an actual species called *Ficus religiosa*, under which Śākyamuni attained awakening (*bodhi*). The bodhi tree has become an inseparable attribute of all Buddhas of all times and in all worlds. Attaining awakening is only considered possible under it. But Buddhist mythology also knows purely mythological trees: these are primarily the so-called *kalpavṛkṣas* that are found on all four continents and exist during the whole kalpa. The tree Cittapāṭalī grows in the land of *asuras*. It is the apple of discord between *as*uras and gods. Only gods can reach the fruit because the tree is incredibly tall.

Looking at fauna, it is *nāgas* (mythological snakes or dragons), often partly or fully anthropomorphic, that have an important place in Buddhist mythology. *Nāgas* are interested in the Buddha's teaching. They guard holy texts and give them to the people who are ready to understand them. Buddhist mythology has also included mythological birds *garuḍas*, the marine animal *makara*, etc., from Hinduist mythology. The zoomorphic symbols of different Buddhas and bodhisattvas are the peacock, the turtle, the horse, the bull, the elephant and the lion. The favourite animals are deer: it is believed that two of them were the first who listened to Śākyamuni's teachings (therefore there is often a picture of two deer, with the Wheel of Dharma between them, placed above the doors of Buddhist temples). Bodhisattvas can also assume the aspect of an animal in order to teach *dharma* to animals. There are many legends about Śākyamuni's previous births as an animal (ape, bird, deer, etc.) in the Buddhist world.

Buddhist mythology in general could be seen as a summary of the mythologies of different Buddhist traditions, but it apparently does not represent the so-called early Buddhism which had quite a low degree of mythologization.

HĪNAYĀNA MYTHOLOGY. As a separate tradition in Buddhism, Hīnayāna had acquired its completed form by the 1st century

BC. Hīnayāna is not the name used by the supporters of this trend of Buddhism. The proponents of Mahāyāna used this word to denote the Buddhist schools whose teachings they considered to be limited (e.g., in Hīnayāna the way of a bodhisattva is not seen as universal and attainable to all). Nevertheless, this term, along with Mahāyāna and Vajrayāna has become part of the terminology in Buddhist studies. According to some sources, the number of Hīnayāna schools at some point reached eighteen but only one of them, Theravāda, has survived. We have a most general idea of the specific features of Hīnayāna mythology since the canons of Hīnayāna schools have only survived in fragments (only the Theravāda canon *Tipiṭaka* has been preserved in its entirety). Differences between Hīnayāna mythology and general Buddhist mythology are relatively small and are mainly regarding details in the description of different figures, images and plots. In all probability, Buddhist mythology was from the outset open, dynamic and capable of changing and enriching its content. Hīnayāna mythology, on the contrary, demonstrated some conservative tendencies striving to preserve the existing system of mythological ideas (but, as the history of Theravāda in Sri Lanka and the countries of South-East Asia shows, this was not quite possible).

MAHĀYĀNA MYTHOLOGY. Mahāyāna formed as an independent Buddhist tradition in approximately the first centuries BC on the basis of the Buddhist school of Mahāsaṅghika. Unlike Hīnayāna, Mahāyāna is characterized by the universal nature of the idea of liberation: the possibility of attaining the state of a Buddha is given to all beings since they already have a Buddha nature. The central image in Mahāyāna is a bodhisattva who cares not just about his own liberation but also about the liberation of all beings.

Mahāyāna mythology is one of the richest mythologies in the cultural history of mankind. The aspiration to create mythological images and plots that is so typical of Buddhism is particularly strongly manifested in Mahāyāna. Almost any Mahāyāna sūtra (the Mahāyāna canon contains hundreds of these) in a way offers its own mythology to some extent different from other sūtras. Mahāyāna mythology is united not by a system or similar mythological images and plots but by a common approach (strivings to increasingly mythologize Buddhism) and a host of common principles, on the basis of which mythological elements are developed.

The number of the Buddhas in Mahāyāna is infinite. They have always appeared in *saṃsāra* that has no beginning and will appear until its end but they all have the same nature that is expressed in the concept of *dharmakāya* – the 'body of dharma'. Infinite is also the number of bodhisattvas who in Mahāyāna texts are either purely mythological characters or mythologized historical figures.

One of the main elements of Mahāyāna is the mythologization of the process where sūtras were created. According to Mahāyāna, Buddha Śākyamuni teaches *dharma* not only to his disciples. He is surrounded by bodhisattvas, gods, *nāgas* and other mythological characters, the number of which is often said to be incalculable. At the same time an incalculable number of Buddhas teach the same *dharma* in other worlds to a similar circle. The places where Śākyamuni taught were also mythologized. They are represented in Mahāyāna not so much as particular cities, rivers, mountains and forests where Śākyamuni stayed for some time but as eternal symbols of attaining awakening. For example, according to Mahāyāna, Śākyamuni taught on Mount Gṛdhrakūṭa near the city of Rājagṛha not only during his lifetime but teaches there throughout the ages, and Mount Gṛdhrakūṭa is not just in a particular place in India but in all the worlds.

Along with the mythologization of real places, Mahāyāna often describes mythological countries and cities. In some sūtras they are largely located in Jambudvīpa in our world (according to a description from the *Aṣṭasāhasrikā Prajñāpāramitā*, the mythical city of Gandhavatī, the residence of the bodhisattva Dharmodhgata, is somewhere to the East of Jambudvīpa, and the mythical city of Vairocanavyūhālaṃkāragarbha of the *Gaṇḍavyūhasūtra* is in the South). These mythical cities and countries with their ideal order and jewels, of which even houses are built, can be seen as a kind of Buddhist utopia.

Buddhist utopias also include so-called fields of the Buddha (*buddhakṣetra*) – entire worlds created by the Buddhas' mental effort and therefore different from other worlds in terms of ideal order and the possibility of reaching *nirvāṇa* with no special effort (but with the help of the Buddha who created this particular field of the Buddha). The best known Buddha fields, Abhirati and Sukhavatī, have been created respectively by the Buddhas Akṣobhya and Amitābha, and they are incredibly distant from our world: there are myriads of worlds between these worlds and our world.

The word *bodhisattvayāna* (the 'Vehicle of Bodhisattvas') is often used as a synonym to Mahāyāna since the image of a bodhisattva as the ideal of human aspirations has a central place not only in the doctrine of liberation but also in the mythology of Mahāyāna, the canonical literature of which is full of descriptions of the deeds of mythological (Avalokiteśvara, Mañjuśrī, Kṣitigarbha, Maitreya, etc.) and semi-mythological bodhisattvas. Some bodhisattvas (e.g. Avalokiteśvara) are honoured equally to the Buddhas and in some cases even more. The image of a Buddha in Mahāyāna mythology has also undergone some changes. In the theory of the 'three bodies of Buddha' the 'body of dharma' (*dharmakāya*) is endowed with absolute nature and is, in fact, common for all Buddhas. The concept of Ādibuddha emerged on the basis of this assumption in late Mahāyāna and was particularly popular in Vajrayāna mythology.

VAJRAYĀNA MYTHOLOGY. Vajrayāna (other names: Mantrayāna, Tantrayāna, Sahajayāna, Buddhist Tantrism) is seen either as part of Mahāyāna or as an independent third tradition (different from Hīnayāna and Mahāyāna) in the development of Buddhism. Apparently, Vajrayāna formed as an independent Buddhist tradition in the middle of the first millennium AD. In the late 19th and early 20th centuries, European scholars repeatedly attempted to prove the origin of Vajrayāna from Hinduist Tantrism but the latest theories (Govinda, Guenther, Bharati) proving the independent development of Vajrayāna from earlier sources seem to be more convincing.

Vajrayāna is based on the same common Buddhist principles that are also based on Hīnayāna and Mahāyāna. But unlike the other two traditions, Vajrayāna emphasizes that it is possible to attain the state of a Buddha in a person's present life. To do this, a Buddhist should, along with methods constituting the way of a bodhisattva, do certain yogic exercises (contemplation on an *yidam*, meditation, reading mantras, etc.). Respect towards the guru (spiritual teacher) is particularly important in Vajrayāna.

Characteristic to Vajrayāna is the tendency to systematize the pantheon and other mythological ideas. But it is not a closed system.

It is open to new mythological characters (especially bodhisattvas, *yidams* and *lokapālas*) from the mythology of peoples that live in Vajrayāna's sphere of influence. Some *yidams* are created by prominent gurus (who allegedly acquired them from a Buddha, particularly from Vajradhara). The presence of a great number of *yidams* is most typical of the Vajrayāna pantheon. There are a host of semi-mythological characters in Vajrayāna mythology – famous yogis and teachers, the creators of different Vajrayāna schools and traditions, like 84 Mahāsiddhas, Padmasambhava, the founders of Buddhist monasteries etc. They are often worshiped along with the highest figures of the Buddhist pantheon and their biographies that are full of mythological details are in fact quite similar to legends about purely mythological characters. Female figures such as female bodhisattvas (e.g. Tārā), female equivalents of *yidams* (*prajñās*) and others have a special place in Vajrayāna mythology. Vajrayāna mythology also knows its own utopia. This is the country of Śambhala, the mythical homeland of the mystical teaching of the 'Wheel of Time' (*kālacakra*). An era of justice and bliss will arrive in the world after the so-called Śambhala war between good and evil forces.

An interesting tendency of mythologising real life became apparent in late Vajrayāna, particularly in Tibet. Certain persons, mainly high-ranking spiritual hierarchs, were proclaimed the earthly reincarnations of mythical characters, mostly bodhisattvas (Avalokiteśvara, Mañjuśrī and others).

With the spread of Buddhism in China, Tibet, Korea, Japan, Mongolia, Buryatia, Sri Lanka, Burma, Thailand, Laos, Cambodia and Vietnam, the religious and mythological systems of many local peoples experienced significant changes in concepts and dogmas, but the general basis of Buddhism and Buddhist mythology remained the same as in India. Innovations in Buddhist mythology were primarily about the rethinking of some insignificant aspects and including in the pantheon local deities who were often identified with the Buddhas and bodhisattvas. Of the three main traditions, the mythologies of Mahāyāna and Vajrayāna underwent major changes, mainly in the countries north and north-east of India. Taoism and related popular beliefs had the greatest effect on Buddhist mythology in China.

Assimilation of Chinese mythological concepts and images was particularly rapid under the Song dynasty (960–1279). The Buddhas and bodhisattvas were endowed with the attributes of local deities. Sometimes their appearance (cf. Kṣitigarbha) and even sex (Avalokiteśvara transformed to the goddess Guanyin) changed. Mythological characters partly lost their religious significance as symbols of attaining *nirvāṇa*. Instead, people consider worshiping them as a means of achieving mundane purposes. The Chinese tended to associate mythological characters with Chinese history and geography. Thus, the god Yama was identified with a civil servant who died in 592, and Mount Wutaishan, a major Buddhist cult centre, was said to be the residence of Mañjuśrī.

In Tibet the pantheon of Buddhist mythology was enlarged particularly intensively by including local deities from Bön mythology and from many local cults (they all were proclaimed protectors of Buddhism). Thus, the pantheon included the legendary Tibetan king Gesar, the god of war Talha, the deity Pehar and others. All founders and leaders of the main Buddhist schools (e.g. Marpa and Milarepa, Tsong Khapa), abbots of monasteries (e.g. Trungpa) and all other more or less significant figures were included in the pantheon in a semi-mythologized form. Most of them were associated with mythological bodhisattvas and Buddhas. Thus, Dalai Lamas were said to be reincarnations of Avalokiteśvara, and Panchen Lamas were seen as reincarnations of Amitābha. Tibetan Buddhist mythology spread in Mongolia, Buryatia, Tyva and Kalmykia where the development of the pantheon experienced similar trends.

The same trends are typical to Buddhist mythology in Korea and Japan (Buddhism spread into these countries from China). In Japan, throughout its history, Buddhism coexisted with the national Japanese religion Shinto, which left its considerable mark on the mythology of Japanese Buddhism. Shinto gods (*kamis*) were included in the Buddhist pantheon as bodhisattvas and Amaterasu was even seen as a reincarnation of the Buddha Vairocana.

In Sri Lanka and the countries of South-East Asia, Buddhism spread mostly in the form of Hīnayāna. Since Hīnayāna mythology was less capable of assimilation of local traditions, the mythologies of these countries did not have any particular effect on Buddhist mythology. Still, the coexistence of local mythological ideas with Buddhism can be noticed there: for example, the spirit of Adam's Peak is worshiped in Sri Lanka and so-called *nats* (local spirits) are honoured in Burma.

Buddhist mythology is one of the richest and most versatile in the world's cultural history. It is an interesting example of the emergence and development of mythological images and plots in interaction with deep philosophy. The ability of Buddhist mythology to systematically expand and enrich itself made it one of the most widespread mythologies in the world.

The images and plots of Buddhist mythology had an effect on the development of literature and art both in India and many other Asian countries. Mythological Buddhist themes were used by the great poets of India (Aśvaghoṣa, Śāntideva), Tibet (Milarepa, Longchenpa), China (Yü Xin, Zuoran, Hanshan Zi, Wang Wei, Bo Juyi, Du Fu, Li Bo). Many statues, bas-reliefs and icons using Buddhist mythological plots decorate ancient and medieval temples in India, Nepal, Tibet, China, Japan, Sri Lanka, Burma, Thailand, Cambodia, Laos, Vietnam, Bhutan, Mongolia and Korea.

Buddhist mythology has had a great effect on the mythologies of many religious systems (Jainism, Hinduism, Bön, Taoism, Shinto, etc.) and on popular beliefs.

The Cultural Model of Tibet

The headwaters of the major Eastern rivers are located in Tibet.[1] Tibetan waters flow to the fields of South, East and South-East Asia. There are also some other truisms, for example, that Tibet is sparsely populated and that the standard of living has always been low.[2]

The truisms do not suffice when we focus our attention on Tibetan culture. Even scholars do not agree on what is typical for Tibetan culture or how high the cultural level of Tibetans actually is. People who are not experts might think that most Tibetans are illiterate and undeveloped in terms of culture. There is also quite the opposite opinion: Tibet is the centre of the highest spiritual civilization.

We hardly need to discuss the irrelevance of these two viewpoints. Of course, Tibet is not a country where literacy and culture are non-existent but neither is it the "cradle of future humankind"[3] as argued by the prominent Russian painter N. K. Roerich.

Until recently, Tibet was a feudal country, with a culture generally comparable to the cultural level of medieval Europe. Still, this culture was rather original. In some areas it was ahead of the European culture of the time (which, however, does not mean that it did not lag behind in other areas).

Tibetan studies have been developing quite rapidly over recent decades. This primarily concerns the studies of Tibetan texts: more and more Tibetan literary and cultural works are being published and translated into European languages every year. Therefore the contours of Tibetan cultural history have already been outlined quite clearly. The point is that this culture no longer seems static, stagnant or fearful of new trends.[4] Latest research has shown that Tibetan culture has in fact been dynamic and open to enrichment through borrowing from other cultures throughout its history. However, some people think that there has been a certain stagnation in the development of Tibetan culture in the past two or three centuries but there is substantial proof refuting this viewpoint.[5] We can only speak about the relative stagnation of Tibetan culture, as compared to European culture which has developed much faster over recent centuries.

Exploring Tibetan culture and history, one should bear in mind that written documents can be seen as a more or less reliable source of information only when we are studying the second millennium.[6] As far as the first millennium is concerned, much critical work needs to be done with the few sources that were definitely written during its final centuries.[7] The earliest period of Tibetan history still needs deciphering: thorough archaeological research would provide more information on what is vaguely mentioned in epics, legends and myths.

Still, we can already say that some small incessantly fighting feudal kingdoms emerged in the basin of the river Tsangpo (Brahmaputra) at the beginning of the first millennium. The Yarlung kingdom came to the forefront in the 3rd century. However, the formation of the centralized Tibetan state was not completed until the early 7th century when it was carried out by Namri Lontsen (? – 627), a representative of the Yarlung dynasty.

His son Songtsen Gampo (627-650) expanded the borders of the kingdom. His conquests and educational activities laid the foundation of the Tibetan civilization in the broadest sense of the word.[8] As a military and political empire, Tibet was no weaker than such mighty powers of the time as Tang China or the Empire of Harsha in India. The imperial spirit that dominated in Tibet in the 7th to 9th centuries, freed Tibetan thought from tribal narrow-mindedness and promoted the spread of new cultural values and ideals. Tibet had contacts with many countries[9] but its neighbours India and China had the strongest cultural and economic influence on it. Therefore it seems quite logical that Songtsen Gampo's first wife was the daughter of the king of Nepal and his second wife was one of the daughters of the Chinese emperor. Each arrived in Tibet accompanied by a big retinue including many artisans who gave impetus to the development of a number of crafts. Official Tibetan historiography also tells us that Songtsen Gampo sent a group of young people to India to develop the Tibetan literary language.[10] Most of them died because of the unbearable climate. Thönmi Sambhota was the only one who returned and, as Tibetan sources say, he created Tibetan writing modelled on ancient Indian alphabets, wrote the first Tibetan grammar and translated the Mahāyāna sūtra "A Detailed Description of the Basket of Virtues of Avalokiteśvara."[11] Literary Tibetan was formed on the basis of Thönmi Sambhota's grammar in the 7th and 8th century.

This introduced the first stage of written Tibetan culture which can conditionally be called the period of textual imitation, since the bulk of literature consisted of translations of Buddhist texts, mainly from Sanskrit and Chinese.[12]

Tibetan historiography associates the introduction of a written language in Tibet with the need to propagate Buddhism which was advocated by Songtsen Gampo, although in this case imperial interests apparently prevailed. The borders of the vast empire created by the great king stretched well beyond Tibet including some regions in the North of India, West of China and a number of Central Asian areas where Buddhism was not yet replaced by Islam.

Buddhist ideas started penetrating Tibet well before the reign of Songtsen Gampo. They came both from Central Asia where there was a community of Tibetan monks in Khotan and from adjacent Indian kingdoms and later also from neighbouring China, where the Tang emperor, a contemporary of Songtsen Gampo, patronized Buddhism in his empire.

Under Songtsen Gampo, Buddhism began strengthening its position in Tibet. Whatever later Buddhist historiography says, Songtsen Gampo himself apparently never became a Buddhist.[13] However, he was sympathetic to the new religion. Songtsen Gampo might have seen Buddhism as a means to enhance centralized power[14] or to limit the influence of priests who possessed great real power both at the court and among the people. Songtsen Gampo's Nepalese and Chinese wives who practised Buddhism undoubtedly had a certain influence on him.

Buddhist monks from India, Khotan and Nepal began to arrive in Tibet. Initially the spread of Buddhism was limited to the royal family and people close to it and was strongly opposed by priests. However, as early as in 779 the Tibetan king Trisong Detsen (755-797) proclaimed Buddhism the state religion of Tibet.

Two Buddhist traditions competing with each other appeared in Tibet in the second half of the 8th century: Indian and Chinese. Indian Buddhism was represented by Kamalaśīla and Chinese by Hoshang.

Kamalaśīla propagated the teaching of what was fixed in the works of his predecessors Śāntarakṣita and Śāntideva.[15] The main point was that a bodhisattva's way had to be gradual. In order to reach the level of a Buddha, he had to diligently study the theory of *dharma* and the practice of *pāramitās* thereby accumulating the virtues that in the end would lead to transition from *saṃsāra* to *nirvāṇa*.

According to Hoshang, liberation is a spontaneous act that can take place in any person regardless of personal effort. It is not difficult to understand that Hoshang represented the chan (zen) tradition.

In 792 in the Samye Monastery[16] there was a debate between Kamalaśīla and Hoshang arbitrated by the king of Tibet.[17] Later Buddhist historiography argues that Kamalaśīla brilliantly won the debate. However, this is not confirmed by the official documents of the time. The edict of the arbitrating king only says that it is necessary to follow the middle way taught by the Buddha Gautama, with which both opponents agreed.[18]

Soon after the dispute, Chinese monks were deported from Tibet, which reflected political rather than religious controversy between Tibet and China. The Tibetan court wanted to stop the increasing Chinese influence in the country since China was an enemy of the Tibetan empire, and only the peace treaty signed in 822 put an end to numerous military conflicts.

A new local religion was developing in Tibet at the same time. It developed into its final form in the early second millennium AD and was named Bön (a certain category of priests was denoted by this word in the popular religion).[19] Popular beliefs were one of the sources of Bön but even a cursory glance at its holy scriptures and iconography shows such similarity to Buddhism that there can be no doubt: Bön is modelled on Buddhism. But officially, representatives of Bön have always stressed their opposition to Buddhism and said that their religion was founded by somebody called Shenrab who allegedly arrived from the West.

In the late 8th and early 9th centuries the number of Buddhist texts translated from Sanskrit grew significantly. A Commission on Translation of Buddhist Texts was set up in 826 under the king Relbachen (815-838). It unified translation of Buddhist terms and instructed translators to strictly observe this unification, threatening even severe punishment to those who failed to follow the instructions. Basic Buddhist scriptures were translated from Sanskrit during the following centuries and the translations were later united in two enormous collections: *Kangyur* (*bka' 'gyur*) including texts ascribed to the Buddha himself (sūtras and tantras) and *Tengyur* (*bstan 'gyur*) containing commentaries to *Kangyur*, treatises by Indian Buddhist scholars (Nāgārjuna, Asaṅga, Vasubandhu, Bhāvaviveka and others) as well as treatises by Indian scientists on medicine, grammar, poetry, astrology and icon painting.

An Indian, an expert in Sanskrit and one or two Tibetans normally participated in the translation of a text.[20] An obligatory translation style was developed. This style was extremely accurate in rendering Sanskrit words, expressions and grammatical constructions. Although Tibetan is very different from Sanskrit, these translations enable the Sanskrit texts to be restored fairly easily if these have not survived.[21] Of course, this kind of translation is to some extent artificial for the Tibetan language and is not perceived as a living text by the ordinary reader. Nevertheless, the style took root among the Buddhist elite and was even used later in original writings.[22]

Tibetan lotsawas[23] who translated sacred Sanskrit texts avoided phonetic loans and even rendered the meaning of the terms that were difficult to translate through use of their mother tongue. Thus, the term *pāramitā* is rendered by the phrase *pha-rol-tu-phyin-pa* or 'leaving for the other [bank]', or, to be precise, 'going outside', i.e. leaving the cycle of rebirths. Even proper names were often translated rather than transcribed: thus, Ānanda (the disciple of Buddha) – 'Joyful', Akṣobhya (the name of a Dhyānibuddha) – 'Imperturbable', Aśoka (the name of the Indian king who advocated Buddhism) – 'Untroubled', which are equivalent to the meaning of the Sanskrit words but sounds quite differently in Tibetan. Even place names were mostly translated. For example, Rājagṛha (a city in India) is translated as 'King's House', which is semantically correct but phonetically the Indian and the Tibetan name have nothing in common.

It is interesting to note that Chinese translations of Sanskrit texts extensively used phonetic borrowing even in rendering easily translatable Buddhist terms such as *mahāsattva* ('great being').

Tibetan lotsawas definitely knew all this because Chinese translations of Sanskrit texts were done much earlier. However, Tibetan lotsawas rejected phonetic borrowing.

Along with Indian Buddhist texts, many Indian treatises in all spheres of medieval science were translated into Tibetan and later included in the Buddhist canon. The best samples of Indian literary works were also translated into Tibetan.

Thus, along with Buddhism, Tibetans gradually adopted the science and culture of Buddhist India and the Buddhist way of life. This process could not even be stopped by the persecution of Buddhists under King Lang Darma in 842 and the subsequent stagnation that lasted for approximately a hundred and fifty years. A resurgence began in the early 11th century. Outstanding Indian teachers arrived in Tibet and many Tibetans travelled to Indian Buddhist centres and joined such famous monastic universities as Nālanda and Vikramaśilā.[24]

Buddhism in India was not uniform. Sometimes three main traditions – Hīnayāna or the 'Small Vehicle', Mahāyāna or the 'Great Vehicle' and Vajrayāna or the 'Diamond Vehicle'[25] – co-existed within one monastery. Each tradition was divided into different schools and each school had its own authorities in the past and present, its own scriptures and its own ideas of *nirvāṇa* and the way leading to it.

The theory of Hīnayāna accentuating personal liberation was not attractive for Tibetans. However, they accepted the monastic code of the Hīnayāna that still regulates the life of Tibetan monks.

Mahāyāna was much more to their liking since it combined sophisticated logical thinking[26] with positive emotionality expressed in the concept of compassion: a bodhisattva can sacrifice his own life and even his *nirvāṇa* in order to save other living beings. This compassion and aspiration to help other people and all other beings is declared in Mahāyāna texts by many Buddhas and bodhisattvas.[27] For example, the *Bhaiṣajyaguru-vaidūryaprabha-rāja-sūtra* that has become the basis of the Buddhist medical canon says that the Supreme Healer, the patron of doctors when he was still a bodhisattva promised that after attaining the state of a Buddha he would help living beings with many things, including the treatment of diseases.

Vajrayāna, or Buddhist Tantrism, also attracted Tibetans. In a strictly Buddhist sense it is not so much an independent branch but rather a part of Mahāyāna.[28] Tireless meditation that may liberate a person from the burden of *saṃsāra* within one lifetime rather than the practical implementation of compassion to all living beings in everyday life is extremely important in Vajrayāna. For intensive *yoga* practice one needs a competent teacher, guru,[29] and occasional seclusion from worldly life.

All these traditions did not exist in their pure form in Tibet. Most often Mahāyāna was combined with a Hīnayāna monastic code. There were also people who did not take monastic vows but were very well-versed in both Mahāyāna and Vajrayāna.

The period of textual imitation ended by the 10th century. The 11th century marked the beginning of a new period in the development of Tibetan culture which can be called a "period of text-generation". Literary activities took place in new religious organizations – monastic orders or schools that in the situation of feudal fragmentation in Tibet became a real political force.

The founder of the first school in Tibetan tradition was Atīśa (982–1054), an Indian Buddhist scholar and the abbot of the Vikramaśilā monastery, who arrived in Tibet in 1042 invited by the king of the small but influential state of Gugé.[30] Historians of the Geluk school argue that he was invited because it was necessary to cleanse Buddhism of distortions. Atīśa was then sixty. He was considered to be an outstanding teacher in the whole Buddhist world of the time. He stayed in Tibet until his death in 1054. Due to Atīśa, Tibetans learned about some new trends in Indian Buddhist thought such as the teaching the 'Wheel of Time' (*kālacakra*) which later played a major role in the spiritual life of Tibetans. Together with *kālacakra*, Tibetans adopted a new chronology based on sixty-year cycles (the first year of the first cycle is the year 1027 according to our chronology). Atīśa introduced in Tibet the cult of Avalokiteśvara, the bodhisattva of compassion,[31] and propagated the idea of special relations between a teacher and a pupil, i.e. the concept of a 'guru'. In spite of Atīśa's great influence on Tibetan spiritual life, the Kadam school founded by his student Dromdön played no significant role in the cultural and political life of the country until the reforms of Tsong Khapa.[32]

Sakya was the most influential school of the time. The founder of this school is considered to be Drokmi (992–1072) who travelled a lot around India collecting texts. Sakya had many great scholars and writers. Particularly outstanding among them were Sakya Pandita (1182–1251) who wrote philosophical, grammatical and poetical treatises, Phakpa (1235–1280), the creator of ancient Mongolian writing and Putön (1290–1364), the historian and codifier of the Tibetan Buddhist canon.[33]

The Kagyu school provided many creative persons. The predecessors of this school founded in Tibet by Marpa are the Indian yogi Tilopa and his disciple Nāropa.[34] The Tibetan Marpa (1012–1096) was Nāropa's (1016–1100) disciple for sixteen years. Having returned to Tibet with an excellent collection of manuscripts, Marpa did not take monastic vows but promoted the development of the school by translating, from Sanskrit, tantras and treatises as yet unknown in Tibet. He had many disciples, the most famous of whom was no doubt the greatest poet of Tibet, Milarepa (1040–1123).[35]

The poems of Milarepa could have been collected and written down and maybe even edited by his disciples.[36] They are similar to folk songs but their content proves that Milarepa had an excellent knowledge of Buddhist philosophy, although he asserts that he was not interested in it at all.

As a teacher Milarepa was the polar opposite of Marpa: gentle, patient and meek. His best disciple was Gampopa (1079–1153) who, unlike Marpa and Milarepa, became a monk.[37] The monastery founded by him became one of the most important Tibetan cultural centres. Since only monasticism could guarantee the existence of a school, it is by no means an exaggeration to consider Gampopa as the actual founder of the school.

The unity of Kagyu lasted for a very short time. Already Gampopa's students organized the first sub-schools. The most influential in Tibet became the Karma Kagyu branch that received its name from the nickname of its founder Tüsum Khyenpa (1110–1193) – Karmapa ('one who understands karma'). Karmapa became the title of all future heads of this sub-school. They were considered to be reincarnations of Tüsum Khyenpa and the bodhisattva Avalokiteśvara at the same time. Thus, it was the idea of Karma Kagyu monks that an outstanding spiritual figure could choose the place of his new rebirth and that certain signs could be used to find him.[38]

Another Kagyu sub-school, Pakmo - founded by Gampopa's disciple Pakmodrupa (1110–1170) – had a notable role in Tibet's political life in the 14th–15th centuries. The leaders of this school even managed, with the help of the Mongols, to push the Sakya school into the background.

The traditions of the three main schools – Kadam, Sakya and Kagyu – date back to the early 11th century in India. Followers of these schools never denied their Indian origin - on the contrary, they were proud of it. Close relations with India existed until the destruction of Indian Buddhist monasteries during the Muslim conquests in the early 13th century.[39]

One more school developed at the same time. Its followers declared that it was founded by the semi-legendary Padmasambhava, the first teacher of Vajrayāna Buddhism in Tibet.[40] The school is called Nyingma and some of its traditions undoubtedly date back to the 8th century, to the time of Padmasambhava. The main bulk of Nyingma literature that is ascribed to Padmasambhava is said to have been hidden by him in different places in Tibet and found centuries later. The process of looking for hidden texts (*terma*) lasted until recently and was used as a means of according a new text the highest authority. Therefore, it is no wonder that not only European scholarly critics but other Tibetan schools also doubt the authenticity of these texts.

Nevertheless, Nyingma literature is very diverse and interesting.[41] The book that is best known in Europe is the so-called "Tibetan Book of the Dead".[42] Longchenpa (14th century), a versatile scholar who systematized the scriptures of this school, had a great influence on the development of philosophical thought.

As early as the beginning of the 13th century, Tibet was covered with monasteries belonging to different monastic orders, and their number grew from year to year: monks from major monasteries founded new monasteries that were subordinate to the former. Later some new monasteries became relatively independent: this meant a new sub-school with its reincarnations, traditions, relics and customs.[43] The interests of feudal aristocracy often played a decisive role in the emergence of a new sub-school.

Thus, during the 13th and 14th centuries Tibetan society formed an incredibly complicated structure where temporal power was interwound with the spiritual. Monasteries acquired ever greater political power and secular aristocrats ensured their influence by sending their sons to prestigious monasteries where they later took leading positions. Reincarnations of abbots were often found in noble families.

Relations between different schools and sub-schools were complicated and their nature depended on many particular circumstances (organizational, doctrinal, local, personal, family, etc.) that were constantly changing. Therefore it is impossible to talk about eternal friendship or eternal enmity between particular schools or monasteries: there were both. But the most important aspect was that a person (apart from reincarnations and major hierarchs) was not attached to one or another school during his lifetime. There were many cases when a young monk studied with outstanding teachers from different schools and made his final choice in favour of one or another school at a very mature if not old age.

Theoretical debates between schools were largely about insignificant issues. As far as the essence of the teaching is concerned, it was interpreted in the same way in all schools. Tibetan Buddhism as a whole is the closest analogue of the Buddhism that was spread in North India in the late first and early second millennia.[44] Therefore most researchers at the present time no longer use the term 'Lamaism' that emerged in European science at the end of the 19th century.

There must have been thousands of monasteries in Tibet even in the Middle Ages. Most of them were small (with ten to a hundred monks) but there were also huge monastic cities with populations of several thousand.[45]

While small and medium-sized monasteries were primarily religious institutions where monks were involved in religious practices, the function of the large monasteries was much more complicated. Of course, they also functioned as religious centres but it would be a simplification to see them just as religious establishments. They were great educational centres and they are rightly compared to medieval European universities. Tibetan university-monasteries were also divided into colleges.

In the first college sūtras and philosophical works of great Indian teachers, primarily Asaṅga and Nāgārjuna, were studied. There were no strict deadlines for graduating from the college. There were students who graduated in one or two years. Others spent twelve or even more years there. After exams, students had to participate in open debates and then, depending on their success, they received their academic degree: geshe (*dge bshes*), geshe lharampa (*dge bshes lha ram pa*) etc.

After graduating from the "general college" the student could choose a course in other colleges. The most prestigious were the colleges of tantra (*rgyud*) and medicine (*sman*). In the college of tantra students acquired complicated Vajrayāna methods (which, incidentally, have a certain resemblance to techniques used by some branches of modern psychotherapy – psychoanalysis and gestalt therapy). In the medical college the student had to study all the courses related to healing. The reader can obtain an idea of the level of difficulty from the collection of illustrations in the treatise "The Blue Beryl" which were also used as teaching materials in medical studies. After successful graduation from the faculty the student received the menrampa (*sman ram pa*) degree, which gave him the right to engage in medical practice.

The heights of knowledge were, of course, available to few. Most monks, having mastered a trade, practised it for the rest of their lives. Many trades were needed for the normal functioning of a monastery: tailors, shoemakers, jewellers, smiths, printers, etc. These crafts were also taught in monasteries.

Architecture and art were also seen as crafts in Tibet. Painters, sculptors and other artists were at a rather low level in the monastic hierarchy and so there was no particular concern regarding preservation of their names. Nevertheless, Tibetan artists were professionals in the best sense of the word. They created the magnificent buildings of Tibetan monasteries and fine pieces of art – *thangkas*, bronze statuettes, illuminated manuscripts and xylographs.[46]

Other arts also developed in monasteries. Special ritual dances were performed, often as part of theatrical performances about the lives of great sages and ascetics.

Medieval Tibetan monasteries were not only cultural but also big economic centres. They controlled a great extent of land, most of which was rented out to thousands of farmers who were obliged to perform certain duties. Even trade became increasingly concentrated in monasteries over the years. All in all, the monastery was a centre of Tibetan social life where the most important problems were solved.

Such was the situation in Tibet in the early 15th century when a new school emerged that completed all the trends that could be seen centuries earlier, and turned the country into a centralized theocratic state. A man born in Amdo and called Losang Drakpa, known more by his another name Tsong Khapa, is considered to be the founder of this school, which was later named Geluk.

Tibetan Buddhists believe that he was a reincarnation of the bodhisattva of wisdom Mañjuśrī. He was born in 1357 and already in his early youth was ordained by the Fourth Karmapa. Later he also learned from teachers belonging to other schools. Most of all he liked Kadam and the teaching of Atīśa. He founded the Ganden Monastery which became the cradle of the Geluk school. European scholars judge Tsong Khapa's work differently. Some see him as a reformer who, similarly to Martin Luther, renewed the church. For others, he is a restorer who cleansed Tibetan Buddhism of some improper influences and brought it closer to its Indian origins.[47] He might have done both but his main purpose was to establish monasteries with a strict internal order. Since he was very much supported by the Lhasan aristocracy, he concentrated his activities in Lhasa and later made it the centre of his school. The major monasteries of future Tibet were founded near Lhasa during his lifetime: Drepung in 1416 and Sera in 1419.

Tsong Khapa died in 1419. His disciple Gedündrup (1391–1475), the prior of the Drepung monastery, played a decisive role in the establishment of the new school. As well as the hierarchs of other schools, he declared before his death that he would be reincarnating (as far as Tsong Khapa is concerned, Tibetans see him as another Buddha who went to *nirvāṇa* and would therefore not be reincarnated ever again).

The next reincarnation of Gedündrup was, of course, found. He was called Gedün Gyatso (1476–1542). During his life the school of "Yellow hats"[48] expanded its influence. His reincarnation Sönam Gyatso (1543–1588) turned the Geluk school into a political power. He had very good relations with Altan Khan of Mongolia who granted him the honourable title of Dalai Lama[49] during their meeting in 1578. His two predecessors were also posthumously denoted by this title.

The great grandson of Altan Khan, Yönten Gyatso, became the fourth Dalai Lama and this choice determined fate of the Geluk school. The "Yellow hats" spread their influence using the support of Mongolian troops and the fifth Dalai Lama Ngawang Losang Gyatso (1617–1682) saw himself as the ruler of all Tibet. His reign is usually labelled as the era of Tibet's new grandeur. Indeed, his country was strong and he managed to free it from the influence of other countries: the Mongolian state was already weak and the new rulers of China – Manchus – could not yet dictate their will.

While enhancing the power of his sect, the fifth Dalai Lama gradually limited the influence of other schools, sometimes using forceful methods. However, almost all schools continued to exist and some of them even flourished.[50] In any case, Geluk had a favourable effect on them through some reforms: introducing academic titles, setting the rules of debates, requiring the postulates of logic to be observed, etc. Only the Kagyu Jonang school, the last great representative of which was the historian Tāranātha, disappeared completely.

During the fifth Dalai Lama Tibetan culture was at its prime. Dalai Lama was a gifted person. He wrote a commentary to the *Abhidharmakośa*, a well-known work by the Indian scholar Vasubandhu and a number of treatises on poetry and astrology.[51] He surrounded himself with talented people. A remarkable person among them was regent Sangye Gyatso. who wrote some historical, astrological and medical works.

The building of the Potala Palace that was to become the symbol of Tibet's grandeur was started in 1644 on the site of the former palace of king Songtsen Gampo. The name Potala was borrowed from Indian mythology. Legend has it that the bodhisattva Avalokiteśvara lives on a mountain called Potala in South India. In Tibet Avalokiteśvara was honoured more than any other figure of the pantheon and was seen as the patron and protector of the country. Proclaiming Dalai Lama a reincarnation of Avalokiteśvara was meant to enhance the supreme power of the main Geluk hierarch. Since then there have been two reincarnations of the bodhisattva of compassion in Tibet – Karmapa and Dalai Lama. For Buddhists, there is no contradiction in this since a bodhisattva may have many reincarnations.

Potala was meant to become the largest building in the world at the time. Its size, indeed, was enormous. The building works dragged on. The fifth Dalai Lama died in 1682 with the palace unfinished. What to do next? Regent Sangye Gyatso was afraid of unrest and unexpected changes and he therefore concealed the death of the Dalai Lama - declaring that the hierarch was in deep meditation.

This step may have had a crucial effect on the future of Tibet. What happened in the early 18th century undermined the greatness of Tibet. Could the main reason be that the new Dalai Lama was a young boy who under the circumstances could not be raised properly (the former Dalai Lama being officially alive)? The young man who was expected to be a man of action turned out to be a dreamy poet, although an excellent one.[52] He could have initiated a new stage in Tibetan poetry or in Tibetan culture as a whole. He could have had followers. But he remained one his own and lonely. Was this the fault of Sangye Gyatso? Or could the recession in Tibet have been caused by objective historical reasons? What are the boundaries of the role of an individual in history?[53]

Tibetan waters are still flowing to other countries. And so does Tibetan wisdom. Tibetan cultural values are now shared by the whole world.

Once More about Yamāntaka

This study attempts to find an answer to the question that is, both in form and content, one of the major issues in European science: "What came first?"[1] In this case the question is: "What came first, the anthropomorphic symbol[2] of Yamāntaka or the Tibetan legend retelling the myth about the origin of the deity Yamāntaka?"[3]

The legend is as follows.

There was once a hermit who had lived in a cave for a long time. He needed to contemplate there for a full fifty years to attain *nirvāṇa*. There was just one day to go when two robbers entered the cave.

They were dragging a stolen bull which they then killed by cutting off his head. But when they saw the hermit they decided to kill him as well because he had witnessed their crime. They cut off his head, although he begged them not to. But the hermit had already acquired supernatural powers. He placed the bull's head on his shoulders and turned into the terrible deity Yama. Yama killed both robbers and drank their blood. Thus he lost any hope of reaching *nirvāṇa*. Infuriated, he threatened to kill all Tibetans. The Tibetans asked the bodhisattva Mañjuśrī to help them. Mañjuśrī assumed the terrifying figure of Yamāntaka (which also had a bull's head) and drove Yama into subterranean domains.[4]

The anthropomorphic symbol of Yamāntaka (*Yamāntaka* – 'The One Who Ended Yama') comes in several modifications that have different names (Yamāntaka, Kṛṣṇayamāri, Raktayamāri, Yamāri, Vajrabhairava), a different number of heads (1, 3 or 9), arms (2, 6, 14 or 34) and legs (2 or 16), different symbols in their hands and some other attributes. All Yamāntakas belong to the same family (*kula*) of Buddhas and have identical basic mantras: OṂ YAMĀNTAKA HŪṂ and OṂ YAMĀNTAKA HRĪḤ STRĪḤ VIKṚTĀNANA HŪṂ HŪṂ PHAṬ PHAṬ SVĀHA. The most sophisticated Yamāntaka associated with the above legend is probably Vajrabhairava who has 9 heads, 34 arms and 16 legs.

I tried to formulate the question that needs to be answered as precisely as possible, having clearly defined two levels (related to the two different types of thinking – meditative and mythological) in the structures of which Yamāntaka has quite different functions. If we do not distinguish between the two levels, the question can be asked in a simplified form: "What came first, the image of Yamāntaka on *thangkas* (icons) or the Tibetan legend about the origin of the deity Yamāntaka?"

The question seems to have been recently raised in this form by the Leningrad scholars L. N. Gumilev and B. I. Kuznetsov[5] who also suggested an unambiguous answer – the legend came first.[6] They think that the legend emerged as some kind of reflection of actual political events that took place during the reign of Trisong Detsen, i.e. in the 9th century. Later the mythical image and maybe even the whole myth was represented as a pictogram in order to propagate Buddhism among illiterate Tibetans.[7] Since the myth emerged in Tibet, according to the view of Gumilev and Kuznetsov the Indian origin of Yamāntaka is out of the question.[8]

Unfortunately, while constructing this rather interesting and clever scheme, L. N. Gumilev and B. I. Kuznetsov failed to pay attention to a number of facts which enable the opposite answer to the question. Let us start with the fact that all the names of anthropomorphic symbols belonging to the Yamāntaka group (i.e. Yamāntaka, Vajrabhairava, etc.) are Sanskrit names. Indeed, they all have Tibetan equivalents[9] but so do almost all Indian names that can be encountered in Tibetan Buddhist texts. On the other hand, anthropomorphic symbols or mythological images that have been created or have emerged in Tibet have only Tibetan names.[10]

Yamāntaka can be found in many Sanskrit texts, where there is no doubt about the Indian origin:

1. The *Sādhanamāla*[11] was created not later than the 12th century. It is a collection including 312 *sādhanas*, i.e. instructions for meditation on anthropomorphic symbols. *Sādhanas* 279 and 280[12] in the *Sādhanamāla* are devoted to Yamāntaka, *sādhanas* 274-278[13] to Kṛṣṇayamāri and *sādhanas* 268-272[14] to Raktayamāri. Furthermore, Yamāntaka is mentioned in some other *sādhanas*.[15] Vajrabhairava is also mentioned once.[16]

2. The *Mañjuśrīmūlakalpa* which is probably the most voluminous work of the Vajrayāna literature belongs to an earlier period.[17] Out of 55 chapters of the *Mañjuśrīmūlakalpa*, three are devoted to

Yamāntaka[18] and Yamāntaka's connection with the bodhisattva Mañjuśrī can also be noted elsewhere in this work.[19]

3. The *Guhyasamājatantra*[20] might be considered one of the oldest Vajrayāna works and it also mentions Yamāntaka on several occasions.[21]

In all these Indian scriptures Yamāntaka is represented as an anthropomorphic symbol for meditative thinking rather than a mythological image.[22]

I think that this clearly enough proves Indian origin of Yamāntaka and enables us to give the following answer to the question that was asked at the beginning of the article: "The anthropomorphic symbol of Yamāntaka was before the Tibetan legend telling the myth about the origin of the deity Yamāntaka".

Thus, we have two opposite answers to the same question. I would say that the reason is not only due to the use of different materials. L. N. Gumilev and B. I. Kuznetsov argued that the image of Yamāntaka was based on *myth.* Is this approach not due to the idea widespread among many scholars, according to which mythological thinking precedes other types of thinking? I believe that the opposite process took place in the case of Yamāntaka: the myth emerged on the basis of the anthropomorphic symbol, i.e. meditative thinking existed before mythological thinking.[23] However, since anthropomorphic symbols were created consciously within quite scientific (Buddhist) psychology, we can say that, in this case, scientific thinking came before mythological thinking.

1, ∞ and 0 as Text Generators and States of Mind

This article considers the text types that can be reduced to certain formulae. These formulae focus on the words that mean the same as the symbols **1**, ∞ and **0**.

Such texts constitute a noteworthy part of the Indian cultural heritage. The use of mathematical symbols in this study can be justified by the fact that they have been formed under the influence of such texts and maybe even while these texts were being created.

The most ancient formula is most likely the following:

(1) $\Sigma = \mathbf{1}$,

where the symbol Σ ('all') designates any quantity, but the word 'all' is not necessarily used in a particular text. The formula is valid in all possible tenses and these tenses may also be present in one particular text, whereas their sequence and the nature of this sequence may vary, e.g. "was, is and will be", "will be because it was", "was and will be because it is", etc.

Texts of this type have appeared at all stages of the known Indian cultural history. This tendency is most obvious in the Veda-Brahmanist tradition (the *Vedas*, *Upaniṣads* and *Vedānta*).

The second text type can be described using the following formula:

(2) $\mathbf{1} \leftrightarrow \infty$.

This formula can be interpreted in two ways: **1** and ∞ are interrelated, both on the essential and descriptive level: the nature of their interrelation is determined by their mutually attractive force. What is designated by Σ ('all') in formula (1) is also subordinated to this force. It is either reduced to 'one' or grows to 'infinity' (both operations are often performed synchronically and univocally).

This text type is particularly common in the Hinduist tradition (e.g. in the *Bhagavadgītā*) but is not totally uncommon in Buddhism either.

A text based on the following formula should be considered as a classical Buddhist text type:

(3) $A = \mathbf{0}$,

where A means the defined units of the text-generating mechanism (but also the mechanism as a whole). The frequently used formula:

(4) $\Sigma A = \mathbf{0}$

also enables an ontological interpretation where ΣA should be understood as "all describable manifestations of existence". **0** or 'emptiness' (in Sanskrit both are denoted by the word *śūnya(tā)*) means not so much the absence of something (although it does mean the absence of a fixed unchangeable existence) but the possibility of emergence. 'Possibility' is defined by the properties 'unlimited' or 'endless'. Therefore the formula

(5) $\mathbf{0} < \infty$

is also quite possible.

Formulae quoted here constitute a basis for different kinds of texts: poetic, religious, philosophical, scientific, etc. Only very few of them (which appear to be relatively recent) attempt to prove their validity using logical deductive methods. Therefore it seems to be credible that they initially were not summaries of any verifying or descriptive text. They were, rather, axiomatic statements, behind which there were apparently some creative states of mind.

Texts based on these formulae also exist in other traditions. However, while formulae (1) and (2) have been known in the Western tradition for a long time, formulae (3), (4) and (5) have only recently emerged in modern science (for example, the idea of vacuum – emptiness as the endless possibility for the emergence of the universe). Here we can make the conclusion that the formulae are not related to certain types of thinking, i.e. they do not come from a cultural context but express what can be called universal human states of mind.

Semiotics as a Possibility for the Study of Religious Texts Under Communist Dictatorship

For many nations, the decades-long dictatorship by communists in Eastern Europe was one of the most difficult periods in history. The monopolistic position of the communist empire was expressed not only in the total centralization of the economy but also in the imposition of Marxist ideology on every sphere of intellectual activity. This does not imply that all regions of the empire were leveled down to a common standard, although there were tendencies towards such leveling. The relatively more favored nations were the so-called People's Democracies in Eastern Europe; one step lower, with regard to the level of freedom, stood the Baltic republics, Georgia and Armenia and, as paradoxical as it may seem, Moscow, the heart of the empire. Therefore, it is very difficult to determine with all certainty the possibilities of carrying out academic research in these places, for in addition to spatial boundaries there were temporal coordinates to take into account.

So, for example, the renowned Saint Petersburg school of Buddhist studies was able to continue its work for well over ten years after the October Revolution, although the ruling party had had a new Marxist school of studies established which viewed Buddhism as a more "reactionary" ideology, intended to defend the interests of the "exploiters". This school was so successful that, in the 1930s, a thorough purge was carried out, destroying not only all serious Buddhist studies but also all Buddhist institutions on the territory of the Soviet Union, Mongolia and Tyva (Tuva). As the number of monasteries and shrines prior to the destruction had been almost a thousand, it is no overstatement to say that of all religions, it was Buddhism that the communists hated the most. True enough, after the war two monasteries were restored in Buryatia and one in Mongolia for reasons of foreign policy, but a true renaissance of Buddhism did not begin until the late 1980s.

However, the renaissance of Buddhist studies began much earlier mostly due to two extraordinary persons, both of whom emerged in 1956. The first of these, George Roerich, came from India. He was the son of Nikolai Roerich, a Russian artist who had gone into exile after the revolution. The other was Bidya Dandaron, an incarnation of Kumbum Tulku who had received many teachings from the Buryat Lamas and Leningrad scholars before being sent to the Gulag in 1937.

Roerich and Dandaron revived Buddhist studies in the Soviet Union; their activities resulted in the emergence of three schools, which may be called the Roerich school, the Dandaron school and the Roerich-Dandaron school. The latter included Alexander Piatigorsky, Oktyabrina Volkova and Yuri Parfionovich. Roerich died in 1960; Dandaron settled in Buryatia and began a restoration of Buddhism for which he was once again sent to Gulag where he died in 1974. In the years that followed, anyone who had had the slightest connections with Dandaron was persecuted, so that in the 1970s and the early 1980s, the development of Buddhist studies in the Soviet Union was once again paralyzed.

However, Alexander Piatigorsky had participated in the seminars of semiotics that had taken place in Moscow in the early 1960s which laid the foundation for what came to be called the Tartu-Moscow school of semiotics. This school is geographically defined by the two cities, because several scholars from Tartu also belonged to it, including the chief ideologist of the school, Yuri Lotman. The tradition of summer schools on semiotics in Tartu, where new ideas and methods were developed, began in 1964 and became famous all over the world. The presence of Marxism was completely ignored, discussions focused on such basic concepts as sign, text, culture, noosphere, semiosphere, etc. Of course, the communist authorities realized that the whole business was not ideologically sound, but due to the relatively liberal situation in Estonia, on the one hand, and to the complexity of semiotic terminology, on the other, they did not interfere until the mid-1970s. One more session was held in 1986, which was connected with an amusing incident. The final festive dinner, which took place in a restaurant in Tartu, was interrupted by the director of the restaurant after one of the participants (Dr. Leskis) had proposed his traditional toast: to drink to the health of the Queen of England. The director intimated that KGB officers had overheard the whole event and had phoned him. Such absurdities even happened in the first years of *perestroika*.

I am speaking about semiotics, because scholars of many religions participated in the work of the summer schools. Considering the number of presentations, Buddhism prevailed over Christianity, Islam, Hinduism or shamanism. I should like to draw your attention to some of the concepts for a description of Buddhism that were developed in the summer schools.

As noted above, the terminology of the Tartu-Moscow school is fairly complicated. One of the reasons for this may of course have been an attempt to prevent the authorities from seeing the point, but a more important reason was to develop an exact description, a precise metaterminology, which would serve to convey Buddhist concepts with the greatest possible degree of adequacy, avoiding any transfer of the ideas and terms of Christian and Western philosophy.

Let us begin by evaluating Buddhist texts from the position of the transmission of the so-called true message of the Buddha. Contrary to very common attempts among Buddhist scholars at the time to find the "original Buddhism", to restore the "original Buddhist text", we proceeded from the premise that it is essentially an impossible task, and moreover, an unnecessary one, as it is not in conformity with the well-known truth in Buddhism that a teaching is not a petrified dogma but is subdivided into concrete texts (or messages) that are then offered to specific persons. Since the recording of texts did not begin until centuries after the passing of the first text generator (Gautama Buddha), and because of a very long oral tradition, it is altogether impossible to find out whether the Buddha transmitted only one "original Buddhism", or whether there were several of them. Today, moreover, all Buddhist texts that have been fixed in writing can be viewed on an equal basis as mechanisms generating similar states of mind that have functioned in different cultural contexts.

At this point we come to one of the most crucial concepts of Buddhism, *dharma,* which several generations of Buddhist scholars have taken great pains to unravel. They agree that *dharma* is an ambiguous term, its meaning ranging from the Buddha's teachings to a state of mind and an element of existence or a phenomenon.

From the point of view of semiotics, however, this is not a solution. If a term that has obviously had a certain meaning in a certain cultural context cannot be interpreted unambiguously, that is, if we cannot find an adequate equivalent to translate it, one of the explanations may be that in our culture there has never been a word which could correspond to it. But there is another possible explanation: there is a word but no such cultural context that would enable it to be transformed into a term. We believe that, as a result of the work of the Tartu-Moscow school of semiotics, this context has been established, and that there is a term which functions within this context in a manner similar to the term *dharma* in Buddhist texts. This term is *text*. A Buddhist teaching is a text, which may appear either in written form or as a speech or inner monologue or even in the form of gestures or facial expressions or in objects of nature. But a phenomenon in itself is not a text; for example, a book becomes a text only when someone is reading it.

For example, a very important Buddhist text, the *Aṣṭasāhasrikā Prajñāpāramitā*, deliberates on the difference between a sūtra that is constantly being read, promulgated, chanted and copied, and a sūtra that is buried in a *stūpa*. It concludes that in the first case it is a "living body of the text" (Sanskrit: *dharmakāya*), while the other represents a "dead body of the text" (Sanskrit: *dharmaśarīra*).

And yet, a text cannot be understood as a certain delimited phenomenon. *Dharma* (text) is both the whole body of Buddhist scriptures and an individual part of it, such as a sūtra. But a text, or *dharma*, is also a word belonging to the so-called list of *dharmas* (for example, *rūpa* or form) and, in a broader perspective, every single word that represents an important concept in a "large text".

I have said above that a book, for example, will become a text only when it is being sensibly rendered, i.e. when there is a mind working on it. A text is always connected with a mind. Understanding a text always implies reaching a certain state of mind. The process of understanding is in essence a process of creating a text, and consequently, a state of mind can also be viewed as a text. So we have come to the conclusion that the Buddhist concept *dharma* corresponds in all its aspects to the word *text* – or, to be consistent with what was said above, the text *text*.

The above interpretation can also be applied to interpret a very important concept in Buddhism, namely, *śūnyatā*. This word, denoting in common language "emptiness", has been interpreted by Buddhist scholars in various ways, and depending on the interpretation, Buddhism has been seen as relativism, nihilism and many other things. In semiotic interpretation, *śūnyatā* indeed means 'emptiness', as well as 'zero', but not in the sense of absence of anything but in the sense of an infinite number of possibilities. Thus, the important Buddhist formula *sarva-dharma-śūnyatā* (the emptiness of all *dharmas*) does not mean 'absence of any phenomena', but 'infinite possibilities (to interpret) all texts', or 'openness of all texts'.

I shall content myself with the examples given here and conclude that using semiotics in Buddhist studies has given us an opportunity not only to avoid Soviet pseudo-science, but also to open aspects of Buddhism that have previously been overlooked.

The Concept of Humanistic Base Texts

The shifts in society that occur with the passing of time, or history, can be described and interpreted from various aspects. First and foremost, the choice of aspect depends on which phenomena and tendencies the describer or interpreter considers as being decisive or even as having motive powers. Thus, for example, changes in production and commerce, i.e. in the economy, have been regarded as such, or else the events within or between countries (for instance, in diplomacy or on the battlefield), i.e. in politics.

Likewise, the alterations, renewals and decay of mythological, religious, philosophical, artistic and ideological ideas, or changes in the spiritual world, have also been held responsible, as have, indeed, many other things. I regard *humanistic base texts* as the greatest influencing factor in the history of recent millennia.

Despite their major impact, the number of humanistic base texts is not really large. They were created, or they appeared or took shape (the use of several words above refers to the complex nature of the formation process of the texts) in various parts of the Old World within a definite period of time. This is characterized by the distinct formation of the new social dimension which had started to evolve much earlier, but was left unrecognized for a long time, denoted by different words in different places at that time, but which can at present be termed, in the most general sense, as culture.

It must have become obvious at that period that mankind was more than just a part of the surrounding nature, and that the human being was more than merely a member of the tribe or people or *polis* or state, but a transmitter of traditions, and mythological and religious beliefs. The burden of personal existence must have become apparent to people for the first time at approximately the same time, and this found expression in the questions addressed to oneself and to others: "How to be?", "Why to be?", "What to do?", "How to improve or change myself or, how to become different or new?". All these questions presuppose an awareness of the sense of duty and responsibility, and I would like to add at this point that the so-called existential questions in the manner of "To be or not to be?" were probably not popular at that time.

Although in the absolute time scale this period and, as a result, the formation of humanistic texts do not exactly coincide by regions, one could still maintain as a generalization that this took place between the 6th century BC and the 2nd century AD, while some of the texts have attained their final shape even later.

Among such texts, I am now including: from the Chinese tradition, the *Lunyu*, from the Indian tradition, the *Bhagavadgītā* and many Buddhist texts, belonging to the *Suttapiṭaka*, from the Near East traditions the Gospels of Matthew, Mark and Luke. My interpretation of the texts is based on the originals, the majority of which, except for the gospels, I have also translated into Estonian. In this English-language article , however, let me use the generally accepted English translations: the *Lunyu* by Chan and Legge, the *Bhagavadgītā* by Edgerton. Quotations of the Gospels are taken from "The New English Bible".

Understandably, the above-mentioned list is not final. And naturally, I could not range the above-mentioned texts by their value, or even claim that the texts written later have been influenced by those written earlier. On the contrary, I think that the writing of each text is connected with a particular cultural context, prevalent in a particular region.

By a particular cultural context I also mean a definite religious background, the traces of which can be detected in the humanistic base texts to a greater or lesser degree. Moreover, it is mainly due to this very context that these texts have engendered different religious and ethical-philosophical doctrines, and in the course of the development of these over various periods, the humanistic ideas remained entirely unnoticed. I shall now take a closer look at the problems that emerged while studying these texts.

Texts can be studied in various ways and using different methods. This also applies to texts that are commonly called scriptures in some religious traditions and base texts in modern semiotics. When investigating these texts, the tradition itself, and particularly the commentary and explanatory literature developed within it, are normally taken into account. Undoubtedly, such an approach has yielded brilliant results, and is largely to be credited for the excellent translations through which the scriptures and base texts have been made available to us and which continue to have considerable influence on the development of mankind.

However, it is always possible to use other ways and different methods. At this stage I would only like to point out the following: if we eliminate from the texts everything that has to do with the definite cultural environment, the common element that remains is what I have denoted by the term 'humanistic base texts'.

We shall now attempt to sum up the meaning of this notion. The word 'base text' refers, logically enough, to the text that has been a basis for other texts; thus we have a text here that over the ages has functioned as a text generator. A genuine base text has the ability to give rise to an indefinite number of new texts over an indefinite period of time which do not have to be put down in writing but, as indeed they mostly do, may exist either in the form of oral speech or discussion or even as a speculative act (deliberation, reflection, contemplation, meditation).

A humanistic base text has a specific tendency, expressed by the word 'humanistic'. In English, the semantic range of this word has been conveyed by mainly two equivalents: 'humane' and 'human', in the sense of being 'characteristic of man'. The semantic range of these both, as is generally known, is rather vague. Thus, to be more specific, a 'humanistic base text' is a base text that on the one hand is characterized by elevating man as such (in other words, as a species and an individual) to the central and determining phenomenon of existence, and on the other hand, by an emphasis on such 'humane' qualities as dignity, philanthropy, compassion, non-violence, responsibility, sense of duty, respect, etc. in human relations.

I repeat: although each humanistic base text has evolved within the context of a definite culture, reflecting the latter's influence both in its form and content to such an extent that at first glance it may seem difficult, if not entirely impossible, to find a common denominator for them, there are still enough similarities and common features that allow us to do so, relating to both the formation process and structure of the texts (**A**) and the doctrines they contain (**B**), as well as the direct and indirect impact they make (**C**). I shall now present the most essential ones:

A1. Humanistic base texts evolved in a relatively developed cultural environment, characterized by the existence of the art of writing and the generally accepted and, in some cases, the sole religious and mythological thought system, as well as by an aspiration to establish, in one form or the other, a social hierarchy. At the same time, we can detect a tendency to reinterpret the existing and to present new ideas and doctrines.

By the middle of the first millennium B.C., the urban culture that the invading Aryans had destroyed about a thousand years earlier had been restored in India. There is enough evidence to presume that the new script had likewise emerged by that time. The dominant religion of India during that period was polytheism that had a rich mythological background and was based on the Aryan holy scriptures, the *Vedas*. Yet the monotheistic Brahmanism, initiated by the *Upaniṣads*, was rapidly spreading, accepting the social hierarchy and the supremacy of brahmans. It seems there was much discontent with such an order of things and it was from among the class of the military-rulers, or the *kṣatriyas* that several teachers emerged who laid the ground for new traditions. The *Suttapiṭaka* contains many references to the different contemporary teachers, many of whom have been commonly classified as *ājīvaka*.

The development of culture had been more consistent in China and no such strictly structured caste-system evolved there as in India. Yet the constant wars were undermining the very basis of culture, and the traditional religion, in which the ancestor-cult played a major part, was disintegrating. There, too, a great number of different teachers emerged in the middle of the millennium, offering a way out of the predicament. The *Lunyu* touches upon several of those.

Palestine was occupied by Rome at the time of Jesus, but since the Judaic tradition was very strong, there was a constant movement for freedom. This served to consolidate the Judaic social order, where the leading role belonged to the Pharisees. But there, too, the time was ripe for the emergence of new ideas, as the later prophets and sects like the Essenes prove.

A2. These texts have nominal authors, referred to by the same texts and the tradition based on them.

These nominal authors are not Masters themselves but their disciples, or the disciples of their disciples, or just other persons. It is obvious that the evangelists Mark, Matthew and Luke belonged to the teaching tradition, as did Ānanda who recited suttas in the *Suttapiṭaka*. The authorship of the *Bhagavadgītā* has been ascribed to the legendary Vyāsa, the author of the entire *Mahābhārata*, but the narrator of the text itself is legendary Sanjaya. It is likewise quite evident that Confucius himself did not record the *Lunyu*, and that this text was formed on the basis of the notebooks of his disciples.

A3. These texts present a definite Teaching. This Teaching has been expressed directly by a definite Master, who has a definite mission to preach it.

The texts describe, to a greater or lesser extent, the life story of the Master, but none of these present the full biography of the Master, least of all the *Bhagavadgītā*, with Kṛṣṇa as Master who is mainly called *Śrī Bhagavan.*

The *Lunyu* touches upon the life of the Master more often, but mainly in the form of references to the regions he taught at different times. His dicta are mostly preceded by the phrase *Zi yue* that has been translated in a number of ways, for example, as "the Master said". Quite frequently, the name of *Kong Zi* is used, less often *Qiu* and *Kong Qiu.*

We do not find a thorough description of the Master's life in the *Tipiṭaka*, despite its length, although there are numerous references to separate incidents and the people he met. *Siddhārtha, Gautama, Śākyamuni* – all these names occur there, although *Bhagavan* is the most frequent one. The last days of his life have been described in the *Mahāparinibbāṇa-sutta.*

The Gospels are considerably more biographical in this respect, ranging from the times before the birth of Jesus to the Crucifixion, and even Resurrection. Yet we learn nothing of the boyhood and youth of Jesus there. He is called Jesus *(Iēsous),* Christ *(Christos),* also Lord *(Kyrios)* and Teacher or Master *(didaskalos).* According to the Gospels, he preferred to call himself simply the Son of Man (*ho hyios tou anthrōpou).*

A4. Although the Masters must have certainly been literate, due to their origin and education, they preached their Teachings by word of mouth, so that these became fixed in writing only later by their immediate disciples or the inheritors of the teaching tra-

dition. Because the editing process of the texts also continued after this, they acquired their final finished (canonical) form later still.

Buddhist base texts were recorded as late as the first century BC, the *Bhagavadgītā* possibly even later, most likely in the 2nd-3rd century AD.

There is evidence that of the numerous manuscripts of the *Lunyu*, only a few copies survived the anti-Confucian massacre towards the end of the 3rd century BC, and these served as the basis of the canonical text in the Han era.

The Gospels were probably recorded at the beginning of the 2nd century AD, but the process of editing lasted until the beginning of the 4th century AD, when the Church canonized the four gospels out of many.

A5. Despite all this, a certain authorial idiosyncrasy can be detected in all humanistic base texts, embracing both descriptions and the way the Teaching is presented. This and other characteristic features of the humanistic base texts have now and again given rise to opinions that the actual preachers of the Teaching are the nominal authors, or the latter are entirely unknown, and that the Master is altogether a fiction or a generalized literary figure.

Personally, I do not support the idea that the Masters of the humanistic base texts never really existed. But it is only natural that the descriptions of them in the base texts, as well as their teaching as presented there, are far from being complete. On the other hand, though, I do not consider it necessary in the present study to make efforts in order to find out what the 'real teaching' of the Masters was, because it was the texts themselves, and not the fantasies about the 'real' life and 'genuine original teaching' of the Masters, that have played an important role in history.

A6. The Master is depicted as an unusual person in some way, to whom extraordinary, supernatural and even divine qualities are ascribed.

The miracles ascribed to Jesus take up a major part of the Gospels, yet it is Kṛṣṇa that has been described as the most wondrous, as he reveals his Universal Form: "Of a thousand suns in the sky / If suddenly should burst forth / The light, it would be like / Unto the light of that exalted one..." (*Bhagavadgītā*, XI, 12).

The Buddha, too, sometimes displays his ability to perform miracles, as, for example, he defends himself against Devadatta's attacks. However, he does not make much of miracles, as a rule. All the same, he is described as an extraordinary man.

The same is true of Confucius, who deliberately avoided the supernatural: "Our Master cannot be attained to, just in the same way as the heavens cannot be gone up to by steps of stairs." (*Lunyu*, XIX, 25)

A7. Yet also the human features and even weaknesses of the Masters have been emphasized in the humanistic base texts. They all feel sad at times when they are not understood and they often doubt the expediency of their mission. They do not consider themselves to be unique and superior to other people. Instead, they think and expect that the others should follow them and become like them. This is particularly true of their relations with their disciples, among whom there are always some that are convinced that they surpass the Master so much that it even gives them the right of betrayal.

This in particular concerns Judas, a disciple of Jesus, and Devadatta, a disciple of the Buddha, whose stories of betrayal are generally known. Kṛṣṇa mentions more than once (*Bhagavadgītā*, VII, 15, 24–25) that he is not understood and his opinion of this could be regarded as quite human: the ones that do not understand him are malevolent, foolish and petty. Jesus was overcome by doubt several times, particularly before his arrest in Gethsemane. But Jesus also participates in the festivities of simple people. The descriptions of Confucius's behaviour in the 10th chapter of the *Lunyu* are especially interesting in this respect.

B1. The Teaching presented by any humanistic base text is formally, content-wise and also terminologically related to a certain cultural environment, within which it evolved. According to the Masters themselves, their doctrines are not entirely original, having also been preached earlier in one form or another.

Confucius, for example, repeatedly hints that his teaching is based on what he terms as *gŭ* – 'The Ancient'. For example, he says in the *Lunyu*, VII, 1: "I transmit but do not create. I believe and love the ancients."

Likewise, Jesus says that he has come to complete the work of prophets and not to create anything new: "Do not suppose that I have come to abolish the Law and the prophets; I did not come to abolish, but to complete." (Matthew, 5, 17)

The Buddha speaks on several occasions about the former Buddhas, and even Kṛṣṇa maintains that he has taught ancient sages in earlier times (*Bhagavadgītā*, IV, 1-3).

B2. Yet the novelty of the message of all humanistic texts was quite literally revolutionary, and not just because the Teachings that were proclaimed differed radically from the existing ones, but also partly due to the fact that the situation was right for their emergence.

As I mentioned earlier on, there were many other Masters in these areas at the time the humanistic base texts emerged, and certain similarities can be detected between their doctrines. Besides everything else, this demonstrates that we need not explain the emergence of the humanistic base texts by foreign influences (for instance, the view that Jesus had gone to study in India, or, that he received his teaching from his God the Father). Confucius speaks about Guan Zhong (Guan Zi) with great affection. Young Siddhārtha Gautama studied with several outstanding Masters of his day.

B3. As pointed out earlier, the most significant aspect of these Teachings is their humanism – their humanity and humanness. The main objective of humanistic teachings is to show to man the sense of his existence and what his possibilities and duties are, not only in the physical world, but also in the social and cultural situation at a given moment in a given place; to make man understand that he as a member of mankind and as a definite personality (but not as *ego*) is something unique in the world, which is why he can and even must act, bearing full responsibility.

B4. The uniqueness of man as a member of mankind is manifested in that gods and other supernatural creatures and phenomena are no longer unequivocally placed above man, but that they are considered equal to him in many ways and sometimes

even lower. A god may acquire human shape, appear as a human being, and man may become a god.

The Kṛṣṇa of the *Bhagavadgītā* is man, that is, he was born of man and reared as such. And yet he asserts that he is also a god, and not just a god, but the highest of all, the God of gods, the creator of all that exists, who, although in this world, is really outside it.

The Buddha proclaimed that only man is capable of attaining the highest state of mind – *nirvāṇa*, and that gods are not able to reach this.

Jesus constantly maintains in the Gospels that he is the Son of Man (*ho hyios tou anthrōpou*), who performs deeds that equal the ones accomplished by God, e.g. in Mark, 2, 6–12: "Now there were some lawyers sitting there and they thought to themselves, 'Why does the fellow talk like that? This is blasphemy! Who but God alone can forgive sins?' Jesus knew in his own mind that this was what they were thinking, and said to them: 'Why do you harbour thoughts like these? Is it easier to say to this paralysed man, "Your sins are forgiven", or to say, "Stand up, take your bed, and walk"? But to convince you that the Son of Man has the right on earth to forgive sins' – he turned to the paralysed man – 'I say to you, stand up, take your bed, and go home.' And he got up, took his stretcher at once, and went out in full view of them all."

Of Confucius it is said that he "never discussed strange phenomena, physical exploits, disorder, or spiritual beings." (*Lunyu*, VII, 20)

B5. The uniqueness of man as a personality is manifested above all in the emphasis of the fact that it is he as a definite person that has been chosen to carry out the Teaching.

For instance, Confucius claimed: "It is a man that can make the Way great, and not the Way that can make man great." (*Lunyu*, XV, 28)

According to the Gospels, Jesus was very good at making it clear to his disciples that it was they as definite human beings who were destined to become his disciples. As it is said in Matthew, 4, 21–22: "He went on, and saw another pair of brothers, James son of Zebedee and his brother John; they were in the boat with their father Zebedee, overhauling their nets. He called them, and at once they left the boat and their father, and followed him."

The Buddha's teachings are very often directed to definite people, and the same is true of Kṛṣṇa, whose teachings are addressed to his actual disciple Arjuna.

B6. This also means that man as an individual has an opportunity to improve himself, to change himself, to become new. Man is not destined to remain the same or to retain his former self. Instead, he has the freedom to choose between remaining the same and becoming new, as well as the freedom of choosing between the various possibilities and means or ways of becoming new.

For example, Jesus says: "Enter by the narrow gate. The gate is wide that leads to perdition, there is plenty of room on the road, and many go that way; but the gate that leads to life is small and the road is narrow, and those who find it are few." (Matthew, 7, 13–14)

Describing the way while allowing man the freedom of choice is also characteristic of Confucius and the Buddha.

The real ideal of Confucius, of course, is *shèngrén* (a sage), but he himself claims to lead the way only towards the ideal of *jūnzǐ* (this is rendered in different ways, e.g. 'a superior man', but in my opinion, 'a gentleman' would also be a very good translation).

Although Siddhārtha Gautama, or Śākyamuni, applied the term 'Buddha' to himself, in the base texts he teaches the way that leads to the level of Arhat. However, he applied this to himself as well. A lot is said about different ways and goals in the later Buddhist tradition but there are only a few references to such pluralism in the *Suttapiṭaka*.

B7. In all humanistic base texts, the emphasis has been placed on describing the way or the process of man's renewal. The interpretation of the way has been preceded by the analysis of the initial situation that man inevitably has to proceed from, as well as the more or less exact formulation of where man will end up.

Already in his first sermon the Buddha talks about suffering (*duḥkha, dukkha*), and the need to be freed of it. The *Suttapiṭaka* contains an opposition *'saṃsāra – nibbāṇa'* (*nirvāṇa*) as the initial and final levels of the way. It should be pointed out that just as in Buddhism in general, where there is a tendency to use as many different terms as possible to describe essential phenomena, these two levels have also been called in several ways. The way of Buddhist base texts is, of course, the *Noble Eightfold Way*.

In the *Lunyu* we could, with certain reservations, regard the level of 'inferior man' (*xiǎorén*, mean man, small man) as the initial level. Thus the way would be self-development by means of learning, following etiquette, and the like. Confucius describes his own development as follows: "At fifteen my mind was set on learning. At thirty my character had been formed. At forty I had no more perplexities. At fifty I knew the Mandate of Heaven. At sixty I was at ease with whatever I heard. At seventy I could follow my heart's desire without transgressing moral principles." (*Lunyu*, II, 4)

The teaching of Jesus as presented in the Gospels is likewise the way of common man to the Kingdom of God or Heaven, or, of "becoming his Father's son".

B8. In principle, everyone can renew themselves, and it does not depend on one's origin or status in the social hierarchy, but above all on how the Teaching or, to put it differently – how the new cultural paradigm – has been adopted.

According to Matthew (9, 10–13), Jesus is condemned for not recognizing class distinctions, and Buddha's disciples, too, come from all ranks.

Accordingly, Confucius says: "In education there should be no class distinction." (*Lunyu*, XV, 38)

Perhaps most eloquent of all is the statement of Kṛṣṇa in the *Bhagavadgītā*: "For if they take refuge in Me, son of Pṛthā, / Even those who may be of base origin, / Women, men of the artisan caste, and serfs too, / Even they go to the highest goal." (*Bhagavadgītā*, IX, 32)

B9. This means that man is culture-centered from the point of view of humanistic base texts: not only does he depend on the current state of culture, and recreates the culture, but he also possesses an ability to create and bring to culture utterly new phenomena, and even a completely new cultural whole, something that the Masters themselves have quite clearly accomplished.

Culture is naturally a concept that emerged in the European cultural area, and its meaning has been constantly changing. Most generally speaking, it could be defined as everything created by man, as contrasted to nature. There are terms in the humanistic base texts, the meaning of which partly overlaps with it. One of the most important terms in the *Lunyu* is *wén*,that above all denotes written culture. Several European and American sinologists have translated it as 'culture', accordingly. I find it quite reasonable, although the entire scope of this meaning can be attained by adding the concepts that were essential to Confucius, such as etiquette *lǐ*), music (*yuè*), education (*jiào*), learning (*xué*), etc. – one could even say, the entire positive conceptual whole of the *Lunyu*. There is no doubt that a synthesis of concepts like this was something extraordinarily new, although most of those terms had been used before. The fact that culture is contrasted to nature is proved by several quotations from the *Lunyu* (e.g. XII, 8).

The closest notion to culture in the *Bhagavadgītā* and *Suttapiṭaka* is *dhamma* (*dharma*), that emphasizes its relation to the spiritual and social values of man, and which is also contrasted to nature (*prakṛti*). It is not right to translate *dharma* simply as 'teaching', because it also involves such aspects as values, norms, assessments, and, more importantly, the conscious and psychic phenomena affected by culture. The Buddha opposed *buddhadharma* (Buddhist culture) to the hitherto prevalent *dharma* (culture) and this opposition sent out a definite message that an entirely new culture was about to emerge. As we know, due to the tensions that stemmed from this contrast during a long period of Indian history, an enormous amount of cultural riches has been created that has enriched world culture, and is still doing it today.

There was no notion like this in the Near East during the time of Jesus, but Jesus calls the new culture that he himself founded the Kingdom of God (*hē basileia tu theou*), or the kingdom of heaven (*hē basileia tōn ouranōn*), contrasting it with an ordinary state or kingdom (*basileia*). The fact that this is nothing mystical is eloquently proved by relevant parables in the Gospels, e.g.: "'What is the kingdom of God like?' he continued. 'What shall I compare it with? It is like a mustard-seed which a man took and sowed in his garden; and it grew to be a tree and the birds came to roost among its branches.'" (Luke, 13, 18–19).

B10. At the same time man has to understand that he himself is not the creator of culture, for the process of creation only takes place through him, that is, it is the culture that functions through him. Man must understand that the *ego* that thinks that it has its own thoughts and performs its own acts does not, in fact, exist, so that it has either to be done away with or at least subjected to something that in the given culture is regarded as greater or higher.

The Buddha has a simple solution: the *anātman* (*anatta*) doctrine excludes the existence of any *ego*.

Confucius taught the doctrine of putting one's personal ambitions to the service of the continuity of culture (*wén)* and the ideal of a great centralized state. As it is said in the *Lunyu*: "Confucius was completely free from four things: He had no arbitrariness of opinion, no dogmatism, no obstinancy, and no egotism."

Kṛṣṇa repeatedly admonishes Arjuna to give up egotism (*ahaṃkāra). Ego* will disappear when a person identifies himself with Brahma or Kṛṣṇa.

Jesus does the same: "If anyone wishes to be a follower of mine, he must leave self behind; he must take up his cross and come with me." (Matthew, 16, 24)

B11. The reason for the emergence of *ego* is the self-protective endeavour of the individual, caused by the fact that man originates from nature, or, in other words, from the animal world. The humanistic base texts accept this fact to a greater or lesser extent, while implying at the same time that the focus of human existence should be located somewhere else, on a cultural level, which also means that the natural nature should be replaced by the cultural one.

In the *Lunyu*, a 'gentleman' (*jūnzǐ) is described as the embodiment of the new cultural orientation, as an ego*-less person whose aims are located on a cultural level in opposition to 'inferior man' (*xiǎorén*), a person who is oriented to the fulfillment of egoistic and material objects. For example Confucius said: "The superior man does not seek fulfillment of his appetite nor comfort in his lodging. He is diligent in his duties and careful in his speech. He associates with men of moral principles and thereby realizes himself. Such a person may be said to love learning." (*Lunyu*, I, 14)

Jesus said: "Do not fear those who kill the body, but cannot kill the soul. Fear him rather who is able to destroy both soul and body in hell." (Matthew, 10, 28.)

Kṛṣṇa considers nature (*prakṛti*) an essential part of man that should not be overcome by violent means. One can overcome it only with a peaceful attitude.

B12. It follows from the above that the relations based on physical descent (i.e. genetic information) should not be as important as the culturally determined relations (i.e. cultural information).

B13. This in turn allows us to say that the transmission of cultural information is more important than that of genetic information. All humanistic base texts view the teacher-disciple relationship as more significant than the parent-child or kinship relations. Studying and passing on the teaching are considered more valuable than procreation and taking care of physical children.

This aspect is most radically presented by Jesus: "You must not think that I have come to bring peace to the earth; I have not come to bring peace, but a sword. I have come to set a man against his father, a daughter against her mother, a young wife against her mother-in-law; and a man will find his enemies under his own roof." "No man is worthy of me who cares more for father or mother than for me; no man is worthy of me who cares more for son or daughter." (Matthew, 10, 34–37)

Jesus said of his relatives: ""Who is my mother? Who are my brothers?"; and pointing to the disciples, he said, "Here are my mother and my brothers. Whoever does the will of my heavenly Father is my brother, my sister, my mother."" (Matthew, 12, 49-50)

We find equally radical statements in Buddhist base texts as well. For example, the *Dhammapada* contains a stanza (294) that is extremely harsh: "Having slain mother, father, two warrior kings, and destroyed a country together with its treasurer, ungrieving goes the holy man."

So far this has been regarded as just being figurative, where mother means craving, father *ego*-conceit, etc. But in my opinion it means that the main concepts of the old culture must be replaced by concepts of the new culture in which the new man will be living.

The teachings of the *Bhagavadgītā* are overshadowed by an incipient great war between close relatives. Kṛṣṇa maintains that according to *dharma* it is allowed to kill relatives in war.

Confucius, of course, is the most benign one. But even in the *Lunyu* we come across instances of placing teacher-disciple relationships above the relations between relatives. Confucius's own son was not his favourite disciple: "Chen Kang asked Boyu (i.e. the son of Confucius), saying: "Have you heard any lessons from your father different from what we have all heard?" Boyu replied: "No. He was standing alone once, when I passed below the hall with hasty steps, and said to me, "Have you learned the Odes?" On my replying "Not yet", he added, "If you do not learn the Odes, you will not be fit to converse with." I retired and studied the Odes. Another day, he was in the same way standing alone, when I passed by below the hall with hasty steps, and said to me, "Have you learned the rules of Propriety?" On my replying "Not yet", he added, "If you do not learn the rules of Propriety, your character cannot be established." I then retired, and learned the rules of Propriety. I have heard only these two things from him." Chen Kang retired, and, quite delighted, said, "I asked one thing, and I have got three things. I have heard about the Odes. I have heard about the rules of Propriety. I have also heard that the superior man maintains a distant reserve towards his son."'" (*Lunyu*, XVI, 13)

Elsewhere in the *Lunyu* the notion of brother has been reduced to one of culture: "Sima Niu, worrying, said, "All people have brothers but I have none." Zixia said, "I have heard [from Confucius] this saying: 'Life and death are the decree of Heaven; wealth and honor depend on Heaven. If a superior man is reverential without fail, and is respectful in dealing with others and follows the rules of propriety, then all within the four seas are brothers.' What does the superior man have to worry about having no brothers?" (*Lunyu*, XII, 5)

B14. At the same time, the humanistic base texts stress the need for man to remain humane, meaning that he must treat if not everything that is alive, then at least human beings, with compassion and love.

It is conspicuous that Confucius relates the notion of humanity (*rén*) with love (*ài*): "Fan Chi asked about humanity. Confucius said, "It is to love men."'" (*Lunyu*, XII, 22)

In Buddhist texts the terms *mettā* (*maitrī*) and *karuṇā* – 'friendliness' and 'compassion' – are basically used in a similar sense. Both Buddhism and the *Bhagavadgītā* make use of the word *ahiṃsā,* which became very famous in the 20th century thanks to Mahātmā Gāndhī.

The notion of love (*agapē*) has an important role in the Gospels as well. It is clearly this very aspect that allows us to classify the texts being examined in this article under the common denominator of 'humanistic base texts'.

B15. However, compassion and love are notions with many meanings that can and may be interpreted rather arbitrarily. Some intellectual effort is needed to grasp their truly humane significance and to know and employ them as such. Reason, mind, comprehension, understanding (i.e. intellectuality) – these are among the most essential concepts in humanistic base texts, the development of intellectual capacities being one of the principal means, as well as objectives, in the process of human renewal (or attaining a higher state of mind or repentance).

It is quite obvious that Confucius and the Buddha emphasized the significance of intellectual qualities. Such terms as *prajñā, jñāna, buddhi* in the Buddhist scriptures testify to this. The same terms occur in the *Bhagavadgītā* as well.

The *zhī* that Confucius uses also denotes high intellectuality.

Things are more complicated with the Gospels, especially because several Christian sects are known for their disapproval of intellect. (Actually, similar features can be found in Vishnuism as well, the *Bhagavadgītā* being one of its scriptures, and even in some Buddhist sects.) But Jesus has been presented in the Gospels as a wise man, successfully conducting dialogues with priests.

B16. Summarizing – the process of becoming a new man or humanization actually means becoming a cultural man. The ideal, however, is not one-sided (specialized) culturalization but a total cultural immersion or absolute culturalization, which from the point of view of humanistic base texts means that the natural animalistic or brutal human being has become a superman, saint, sage, gentleman, perfect, Buddha, bodhisattva, Son of God, God

etc. – the name depends on the specific character of the vocabulary of a definite cultural tradition.

C1. The dialogue between the base texts and background cultural environment already began at the first stage of their formation, at the time when the Master himself pronounced his Teachings, either as sermons or instructions meant for one or another specific person. Their impact was quite slight at first, becoming manifest mainly in the relatively limited circle of disciples. But their radical difference from the dominant or generally accepted ideology inevitably led to conflicts, which were often accompanied by severe repressions, the most radical of which was the crucifixion of Jesus. But other Masters, too, to a greater or lesser extent, had to put up with the counter-action by either rulers or representatives of the official ideology.

C2. As time passed, their impact gradually increased, reaching a truly explosive effect after the formation of canonical texts.

C3. Although one cannot detect a direct tendency in the humanistic base texts themselves, several religious, philosophical and other doctrines were formed on the basis of these, as well as certain institutions (churches, temples, monasteries, etc.) that often claimed the exclusive rights of interpreting these texts. If such institutions managed to attain a dominant position in society, the humanistic essence of the Teachings was considerably reduced in the accepted interpretations due to the dominant background system, either during the period of the formation of the text or the emergence of the given interpretation.

C4. At the same time we should not underestimate the role of these institutions in spreading both the humanistic base texts, as well as the humanistic ideas, due to which their impact has now reached global dimensions.

C5. By way of conclusion, let us maintain that even though throughout history, outright human-hating and *ego*-cult based teachings have been preached under the name of humanism – the latest of these is the implementation of the Leninist-Maoist

communism that emerged from Marxism – the direct and indirect impact of humanistic base texts has still been of cardinal importance in the ever-growing influence of humanistic ideas on the development of human society.

Before I conclude, I would once again like to stress the fact that humanistic base texts should not be identified with the institutions in which the same texts serve the function of scriptures. History offers us many terrible examples of the attempts of such institutions to forcefully spread their ideology, and this applies not just to Christianity.

Nevertheless, it was due to the same institutions that the humanistic base texts could exert their truly humanizing effect on the course of history, and to do this on a global scale. Let me provide some examples.

When, towards the end of the 17th century, the *Lunyu* was translated into Latin, it had an almost revelatory effect on the European Enlightenment movement throughout the entire following century. Voltaire, for instance, has provided excellent commentaries on the humanistic ideas of Confucius. It would not be an overstatement to assert that the positive impact of this is still with us today.

The publication of the *Bhagavadgītā* at the close of the 18th century was likewise a great event. The same is true of the Buddhist base texts. The ideas that they contained were first introduced and publicized by such great thinkers as Friedrich von Schlegel and Arthur Schopenhauer in Europe, and Walt Whitman and Henry David Thoreau in North America.

The great Russian writer and humanist Tolstoi disseminated the ideas of the humanistic base texts in Russia, referring both to Confucius, the Buddha, the *Bhagavadgītā*, and the *Sermon on the Mount* by Jesus. It is interesting to note that the above-mentioned thinkers, especially Tolstoi, caused a definite reaction in the countries where these texts originated. Mahātmā Gāndhī serves as a good example in this respect.

My personal experience allows me to say that humanistic base texts affected the liberalization process of the communist system in the Soviet Union to a considerable extent, leading to the collapse of this empire. This must have contributed, as one of the factors, to the disintegration of the colonial system in the whole world. Not to mention the spread of non-violence and peaceful solutions to an ever-increasing degree.

But the events that have taken place in the world during the last years indicate altogether different developments. This is why I'd like to conclude my paper with the following: at this very moment we must do everything we can to disseminate the humane ideas of the humanistic base texts everywhere. It is our task to demonstrate that these ideas are universal, inherent to the entire human race, not just one part of it. Perhaps this could be a contribution to the survival of mankind.

Linnart Mäll's Contribution to Oriental and Buddhist Studies in Estonia

Several world-famous scholars in Oriental studies of Baltic-German origin were born in Estonia, grew up here and studied at the University of Tartu, which was founded as early as the 17th century and was for a long time the only university in this area. Here we could mention Leopold von Schroeder (1851–1920), a famous scholar in Indian studies, Alexander Staël von Holstein (1877–1937), a brilliant researcher of Buddhist texts and philosopher Hermann Graf Keyserling (1880–1946).

Nevertheless, an academic school of Oriental studies was not established in Estonia until the late 1960s. Naturally, it was based at the University of Tartu, the most important intellectual and educational centre in the country, and from the very beginning it was associated with Linnart Mäll, the author of this book. The 1960s are known in Soviet domestic policy as "Khrushchev's thaw" when the free thought that had been relentlessly suppressed for decades found some opportunity for expression, particularly in the humanities (indeed, not for long, because the "thaw" was followed in the 1970s by Brezhnev's stagnation period, which lasted until Gorbachev's *perestroika* and the collapse of the Soviet Union).

Oriental Studies at the University of Tartu – the name under which Linnart Mäll's school is known in both Estonia and abroad - was born on the crest of this wave of free spirit when the grip of the totalitarian state was loosened slightly.

Although oriental studies were not officially taught in Tartu, it was possible to study some Eastern languages at a basic level from the so-called old school academics who had studied and worked here before the Second World War and who had survived the Soviet repressions. Linnart Mäll acquired his initial knowledge of Sanskrit, Hindi and classical Chinese from Villem Ernits (1891–1982) and Pent Nurmekund (1906–1996), the founders of the Estonian Oriental Society who had acquired fame in Estonia as linguists and polyglots.

Still, Linnart Mäll's development as a researcher and Buddhist scholar was to a greater extent affected by his post-graduate studies in Moscow and close contacts with leading Moscow orientalists as well as his participation in the Tartu-Moscow school of semiotics from the very start of its activities. On the one hand, Moscow as the capital of the Soviet empire was the centre of the communist superpower but on the other hand, it was a relatively open city where people met and new ideas spread, and where there was creative and active intellectual life in informal academic circles, free from party and KGB control and, of course, there was also criticism of the predominant political reality. It is no wonder that Moscow was also an important centre of Buddhist studies.

In fact, Linnart Mäll had been introduced to Buddhism by Uku Masing (1909–1985), an Estonian Christian theologian and cultural philosopher, writer and poet and a very original thinker who was out of favour during the Soviet period. A special place among Linnart Mäll's teachers belongs to Bidya Dandaron (1914–1974), the great Buryat lama and scholar who died in a Soviet prison camp. He was an inheritor of the Buddhist tradition as well as an innovator of Buddhism and a transmitter to the West.

An innovative interpretational model of Buddhism was developed under the influence of Buddhist teachings obtained from Dandaron and semiotic ideas. "A Possible Approach Towards Understanding *Śūnyavāda*" that was published in 1967 in Russian (and in next year in the journal *Tel Quel* in French) was a policy article that provided Buddhist studies with a new semiotic paradigm (which the author explains in the "Introductory Remarks" and in the article "Semiotics as a Possibility for the Study of Religious Texts Under Communist Dictatorship"). This article was published in Tartu in *Terminologia Indica* that although rather modest in appearance and volume it was very significant in terms of content. *Terminologia Indica* was also edited by Linnart Mäll and planned as a series, but the two subsequent volumes that were already being prepared were not published because of the pressure of a revived offensive by communist ideology.

In the early 1970s Linnart Mäll lost his job as a lecturer at the University of Tartu, which suspended his official academic career for more than ten years. The Communist leadership distrusted him. Still, he was allowed to work at the University, holding the neutral post of an engineer with no right of lecture. Nevertheless, he could continue publishing articles on the *Prajñāpāramitā* sūtras in Russian, editing the Oriental Studies series of the *Transactions of the University of Tartu* and actively cooperating with Moscow scholars.

It was during these years of "academic exile" that Linnart Mäll became a fruitful translator, publishing a book of translation almost every year. Paradoxically enough, the famous Indian and Chinese philosophical and religious works *Dhammapada*, *Diamond Sūtra*, *Bhagavadgītā*, *Bodhicaryāvatāra*, *Daodejing*, etc., were published in Estonian during the strictest stagnation period as commented editions with print runs of 20 000 or more, which certainly must be some kind of world record – not in terms of the absolute number of copies but the proportional size of the potential readership (the total number of ethnic Estonians then and now is barely one million). These books were extremely popular among students and intellectuals. They were sold out within days and even hours. Linnart Mäll also translated into Estonian the famous Ancient Indian story novels "Twenty-Five Tales of Vetāla" and "The Parrot Book" – *Śukasaptati*. A commented Estonian translation of the *Lunyu* by Confucius appeared some time later, in the late 1980s.

All the above-mentioned translations were first translations into Estonian. Thus, Linnart Mäll is the founder of the translation tradition of classical Oriental texts and of the appropriate methodology and terminology in Estonia. He translated Indian and Chinese religious base texts into Estonian knowingly and consistently, thereby bringing into the Estonian cultural space the ideas that have been extremely influential in the history of mankind and had earlier only been known here from secondary sources.

In the 1980s Linnart Mäll obtained the right to proceed with his studies as the leader of a research group and the head of a research laboratory, but still with no right to lecture at the University, let alone having his own chair. However, his charismatic personality always attracted young people and students. He developed his school of thought by teaching and lecturing in various formal and informal circles. The great humanistic ideas and teachings were disseminated by his students and translated books, and so influenced all of Estonian society.

The social and academic atmosphere changed dramatically after the collapse of the Soviet Union and the regaining of independence by Estonia in the late 1980s to early 1990s. Linnart Mäll participated in the restoration of Estonia's independence as a member of the Congress of Estonia, the representative body of Estonian citizens, and the Council of Estonia, the governing body of the Congress of Estonia, as one of the leaders of the Estonian National Independence Party and as a member of the Constitutional Assembly, thereby being one of the authors of the Estonian Constitution. As the founder and first Chairman of the Unrepresented Nations and Peoples Organization, Linnart Mäll became an international politician whose efforts in promoting the idea of the peaceful achievement of sovereignty according to the Estonian model, and initiating and developing the Universal Declaration of the Rights of Peoples are highly regarded amongst several national movements, particularly among the peoples of the former Soviet Union that have not yet become independent.

Linnart Mäll is also successfully proceeding with his academic career. The Centre for Oriental Studies at the University of Tartu, and a research group headed by him, is involved in the study of humanistic base texts and Mahāyāna sūtras.

Linnart Mäll's role as a scholar, translator and Buddhist teacher in Estonian culture and spiritual life has been paramount and has paved the way for further activities. If we look at the history of Buddhism, we could compare him with the famous 11th century Tibetan teacher Marpa the Translator, an inspired lonely scholar who also braved all hardships, obtained spiritual teachings in a faraway country, brought the holy texts to his homeland and translated them into his mother tongue.

As Linnart Mäll's student I am extremely happy that my teacher's works are now available in English.

Märt Läänemets

Notes and References

The Zero Way

1. I appreciate the assistance provided by Mr. M. P. Danilov.

A Possible Approach Towards Understanding *Śūnyavāda*

1. This is the viewpoint mostly represented in the works of the orientalists of the late 19th and early 20th centuries.

2. See number of works by S. Radhakrishnan, primarily his *Indian Philosophy,* vol. I–II, 1923; as well as the book by Th. Stcherbatsky, *The Conception of Buddhist Nirvāṇa,* Leningrad, 1925. M. Roy in his book *The History of Indian Philosophy* (in Russian: *История индийской философии.* Москва, 1958. ; the original was published in Bengali) considers the Buddha as the founder of dialectic materialism.

3. Agehananda Bharati suggests that we do not use 19th century terminology for Indian philosophy and replace it by the newest philosophical and philological terminology. See Bharati, A. *The Tantric Tradition.* London, 1965, p. 13. Works by Herbert V. Guenther are also interesting in this sense, see *The Jewel Ornament of Liberation of sGam.po.pa,* London, 1959 and *The Life And Teaching of Nāropa.* Oxford, 1963.

4. See the abovementioned works and Conze, E. *Buddhism.* Oxford, 1951; *Buddhist Thought in India.* London 1962; Lamotte, É. *Histoire du bouddhisme indien.* Louvain, 1958.

5. Nikolai Konrad (1891–1970), a prominent Russian sinologist and philosopher of history has written: "We apply in the evaluation of the philosophical ideas of the East terms that were evolved in philosophical science in Europe: for example, materialism, idealism, rationalism, intuitiveness, mysticism, criticism, monism, pluralism and all the rest, never pausing to consider seriously if these terms are applicable in general where we want to apply them. Would it not be better to make use of the terms and characterizations evolved by scientific thought in the East? Do not those terms correspond far more closely to the nature and content of the phenomena to which they have been applied?" Konrad, N. I. The Classical Oriental Studies and the New Problems. *West – East. Inseparable Twain. Selected articles.* Moscow, 1967, p 26.

6. "The greatest obstacle, however, to mutual understanding is the provincialism of Westerner himself. Beneath a popular façade of being the

world's classic example of an open society, Western people are tribally oriented in a grand but unconscious way." Jacobson, N. P. *Buddhism. The Religion of Analysis*. London, 1966, p. 15.

7. The term is derived from the Greek word λύσις, the meaning of which is equivalent to the Sanskrit word *mokṣa*. Λγσιολογία is thus the equivalent of *mokṣadharma*.

8. I realize that this viewpoint may cause strong objections. Still, it is not so easy for a European to become a *yogi*. It is much more convenient to discuss why such a weird phenomenon as *yoga* is possible.

9. The word *darśana* is usually translated as 'philosophy'.

10. *Aṣṭasāhasrikā Prajñāpāramitā*. Ed. by P. L. Vaidya. Darbhanga, 1960, p. 6.

11. M. Monier-Williams's *Sanskrit-English Dictionary,* gives the equivalents of *śūnyatā* on p. 1085: emptiness, loneliness, desolateness, absence of mind, distraction, vacancy (of gaze), nothingness, non-existence, non-reality, illusory nature (of all worldly phenomena); Pāli Text Society's *Pāli-English Dictionary* (p. 717): emptiness, "void", unsubstantiality, phenomenality; *The Cultural Heritage of India*. Vol. I, Calcutta, 1958, p. 506: non-existence; Stcherbatsky, Th. op. cit., p. 242: relativity.

12. "The doctrine of emptiness has baffled more than one enquirer. As a theoretical proposition it gives little sense, and seems to amount to a mere assertion of nihilism. The teaching of 'emptiness' does not, however, propound the view that only the Void exists. It is quite meaningless to state that 'everything is really emptiness'. It is even false, because the rules of this particular logic demand that also the emptiness must be denied as well as affirmed. /.../ The destruction of all opinions also includes the opinion which proclaims the emptiness of everything." Conze, E. *Buddhist Thought in India*, pp. 242–243.

13. See for example: Monier-Williams, M. *Sanskrit-English Dictionary*, p. 1085.

14. Heimann, B. *Facets of Indian Thought*. London 1964.

15. Ibid., p. 95.

16. Ibid., p. 110 ff., 128 ff.

17. Th Stcherbatsky, op. cit., p. 241. It is interesting to note that in common language the word *śūnya-madhya* was used instead of *śūnya* (see Betty Heimann, op. cit., p. 122) and that *mādhyamika* is a synonym of *śūnyavāda*.

18. Buddhists themselves consider silence to be the only sign of this.

19. *Vinaya-piṭaka*. Vol. I, London, 1964, p. 10.

20. *Udāna*. London, 1948, p. 80.

21. The eightfold way (*aṣṭāṅgika mārga*) should by no means be understood as an eight-stage path where each subsequent element is a higher degree of the previous.

22. Nāgārjuna. *Mūlamadhyamakakārikās*. XXV, p. 20.
23. *Aṣṭasāhasrikā Prajñāpāramitā*, p. 10.
24. Ibid., p. 12.
25. See Kristeva, J. Pour une sémiologie des paragrammes. – *Tel Quel*, 29, 1968, and the article "Zero Way" in this volume.
26. *Dharma* in the Indian tradition is a term that is difficult to translate adequately. In the semiotic model, *dharma* means a 'sign', or, rather, something that should be considered as a sign.
27. *Aṣṭasāhasrikā Prajñāpāramitā*, p. 3.
28. Ibid., p. 95-96.
29. Ibid., p. 8.
30. See J. Kristeva, op. cit., p. 58.
31. Conze, E. *Vajracchedikā Prajñāpāramitā*. Rome 1957, p. 49.
32. *Aṣṭasāhasrikā Prajñāpāramitā*, p. 8.
33. *Ratnakūṭa*, (quoted publication: Nāgārjuna, *Mūlamadhyamakakārikās*. Publiée par L. de la Vallée Poussin, *Bibliotheca Buddhica*. IV. St.-Pétersbourg 1913, p. 248).

Some Aspects of the Emergence of Mahāyāna

1.Suzuki, D. T. *Studies in the Laṅkāvatāra Sūtra*. London, 1931.
2. See Conze, E. *The Prajñāpāramitā Literature*. 's-Gravenhage, 1960, p. 9.
3. Ibid., p. 9 ff.
4. Lamotte, É. Sur la formation du Mahāyāna. – *Asiatica*. Leipzig, 1954, p. 386.
5. Murti, T. R. V. *The Central Philosophy of Buddhism*. London, 1955, p. 83.
6. Robinson, R. H. *Early Mādhyamika in India and China*. 1967, p. 63.
7. Conze, E. *Selected Sayings from the Perfection of Wisdom*. London, 1955, p. 16.
8. See the article "A Possible Approach Towards Understanding *Śūnyavāda*" in this volume.
9. See particularly chapter III of the *Aṣṭasāhasrikā* (*Aṣṭasāhasrikā Prajñāpāramitā*. Ed. by P. L. Vaidya. Darbhanga, 1960, p. 25–47; hereinafter *AP*).
10. *AP*, p. 29.
11. E.g.: I-Tsing. *A Record of the Buddhist Religion*. London, 1896.
12. *AP*, p. 29.
13. *AP*, p. 52.
14. *AP*, p. 36.
15. *AP*, p. 28-29 ff.

16. *AP*, p. 38 ff.
17. *AP*, p. 29.
18. *AP*, p. 48.

Studies in the *Aṣṭasāhasrikā Prajñāpāramitā*

1. See Guenther, H. V. *Philosophy and Psychology in the Abhidharma*. Lucknow, 1957; Govinda, A. *The Psychological Attitude of Early Buddhist Philosophy*. London, 1961; *Dharma*sena, C. B. *Aids to the Abhidharma Philosophy*. Kandy, 1963; Stcherbatsky, Th. *The Central Conception of Buddhism and the Meaning of the Word "Dharma"*. London, 1923.

2. "Two kinds of ideas can be distinguished in the *Aṣṭasāhasrikā*: The first set contrasts point by point with the Abhidharma, the second is newly created by the Mahāyāna." (Conze, E. *The Prajñāpāramitā Literature*. 's-Gravenhage, 1960, p. 12.)

3. The same idea but from a different viewpoint was suggested by the American scholar F. Streng: "The concern for analyzing phenomenal existence in both the Abhidharma and Prajñāpāramitā suggest that there was a common religious sensitivity. Both regarded the clear apprehension of reality as coincident with spiritual release. Both were born from the same matrix: the Buddhist struggle for release from the attachment to apparent reality." (Streng F. J. *Emptiness. A study in Religious Meaning*. Nashville–New York, 1967, p.33.)

4. The name "Leningrad school" was created by E. Conze. Although the city has restored its old name, St. Petersburg, I have kept the name "Leningrad" in this book as the articles were written when the city was called "Leningrad". (The footnote was written in 2003.)

5. About the significance of their works see, e.g.: Conze, E. Introduction. – In: Suzuki D. T. *Indian Mahāyāna Buddhism*. New York, 1968, p. 15.

6. The results of Pāli philologists' work are reported in the book: Geiger, M. und W. *Pāli Dharma vornehmlich in der kanonischen Literatur*. München, 1922. See also Rhys Davids, C. A. F. *Buddhism. A Study of the Buddhist Norm*. New York and London, s.a.

7. Suzuki, D. T. *Outlines of Mahāyāna Buddhism*. London, 1907, p. 221.

8. Розенберг, О. О. *Проблемы буддиской философии* , (*The Problems of Buddhist Philosophy*). Петроград (Petrograd), 1918, p. 83.

9. Ibid.

10. Ibid., p. 85. Suzuki's list does not include the second and third meaning of *dharma* suggested by Rosenberg.

11. Ibid., p. 106.

12. Stcherbatsky, Th. *The Central Conception of Buddhism and the Meaning of the Word "Dharma"*. London, 1923.

13. Ibid., p. 13.

14. Stcherbatsky, Th. The Doctrine of the Buddha. – *Bulletin of the School of Oriental Studies*. Vol. IV, London, 1931, pp. 873–874.

15. Stcherbatsky, Th. *The Central Conception*, p. 75.

16. Glasenapp, H. v. Zur Geschichte der buddhistischer Dharma-Theorie. – *Zeitschrift der Deutschen Morgenländischen Gesellsachaft*. Bd. 92, 1938, p. 383–420.

17. Liebenthal, W. Ding und Dharma. – *Asiatische Studien*. Bd. XIV, 1961, p. 3–25.

18. Ibid., p. 20.

19. *Aṣṭasāhasrikā Prajñāpāramitā*, III, p. 30.This paper is based on the following edition of the text: *Aṣṭasāhasrikā Prajñāpāramitā*. Ed. by P. L. Vaidya. Darbhanga, 1960 (hereinafter *AP*).

20. *AP*, XXVI, p. 216.

21. *AP*, X, p. 112.

22. *AP*, III, p. 37, X, p. 112.

23. *AP*, XI, pp. 120–121. When the *Aṣṭasāhasrikā* appeared the institute of guru - that spread in India in the Middle Ages and has maintained its significance today - had not yet developed. According to the *Aṣṭasāhasrikā*, the teacher only had to explain the text but the main function of a guru – an instructor who monitors and corrects the pupil's behaviour – was performed by the *Aṣṭasāhasrikā* itself with the help of such concepts as "shock", "*mārakarma*" and "*dṛṣṭadharmika guṇa*".

24. *Devaputra* (Tib. *lha'i bu*) – 'god's son' – is, in my opinion, an extremely mysterious term. Note that "devaputra" was also Kaniṣka's title and this can be explained by the literary translation from Chinese: son of heaven. (See Штейн, В. М. (Stein, V. M.) *Экономические и культурные связи между Китаем и Индией в древности*. (*Economic and Cultural Relations between China and India in Ancient Times*). Moscow, 1960, p. 152.)

25. *AP*, IX, p. 101.

26. *AP*, XXIV, p. 208.

27. See Bu-ston. *History of Buddhism*. Transl. By E. Obermiller. Heidelberg, 1931.

28. *AP*, I, p. 4.

29. This formula is used by Aśvaghoṣa. See Hakeda, Y. S. *Awakening of Faith. Attributed to Aśvaghosha*. New York and London, 1967, pp. 68–70. Regarding the meaning of this concept in late Buddhism see, in particular, the works of Suzuki (e.g. *Outlines of Mahāyāna Buddhism*, pp. 217–76).

30. *AP*, XXXI, p. 253. This opposition is also known in Theravāda. According to E. Conze's view, Chapter XXXI of the *Aṣṭasāhasrikā Prajñā-*

pāramitā belongs to the later strata of the *Aṣṭasāhasrikā Prajñāpāramitā*. (Conze, E. The Composition of the *Aṣṭasāhasrikā Prajñāpāramitā*. – *Thirty Years of Buddhist Studies*. Oxford, 1967, p. 252 ff.)

31. *AP*, IV, p. 50. E. Conze translates the word *rājapuruṣa* here as 'king', but it is the wrong translation, since the meaning of the comparison is lost. (Conze, *Aṣṭasāhasrikā Prajñāpāramitā*. Calcutta, 1957, p. 37).

32. *AP*, XXVII, p. 229.

33. *AP*, IV, p. 48.

34. About the cult of relics see Dutt, S. *The Buddha and Five After-Centuries*. London, 1957, p. 163 ff.

35. *AP*, IV, p. 48.

36. *AP*, III, p. 29.

37. *AP*, V, p. 52.

38. *AP*, III, pp. 28–29

39. *AP*, III, p. 30.

40. *AP*, XXVI, p. 216.

41. *AP*, III, p. 29.

42. Dutt, S. *The Buddha and Five After-Centuries*, p. 194.

43. Of course, Saṃgha can also be seen as a body in figurative thinking.

44. *AP*, VII, pp. 87, 89; IX, p. 101; X, p. 111; XXV, p. 210; XXVI, p. 217.

45. *AP*, XV, p. 150.

46. *AP*, XIII, p. 140.

47. *AP*, XIX, p. 178.

48. *AP*, XXII, p. 198.

49. *AP*, XV, p. 147.

50. *AP*, XIX, p. 173.

51. Lamotte, É. Histoire du Bouddhisme Indien, p. 658 ff. – *Encyclopaedia of Buddhism*. Ed. by G. P. Malalasekera. Vol. I, fasc. 1, Ceylon, 1961, pp. 46 ff.

52. *AP*, II, p. 18.

53. *AP*, VIII, p. 97.

54. Such lists are included not only in the *Aṣṭasāhasrikā* but also in other *Prajñāpāramitā* sūtras. E.g., using the material of the *Hṛdayasūtra*, we can reconstruct a list consisting of 65 *dharma*s which is very different from our list. (See Conze, E. *Buddhist Wisdom Books*. London, 1958, p. 89.) Of course, there are even more such lists in the *Aṣṭasāhasrikā*.

55. *AP*, XXII, p. 197.

56. *AP*, XVI, p. 157; VIII, p. 44; XIII, p. 139; X, p. 105 ff.

57. *AP*, VII, p. 88.

58. "What we call a body is just a combination of several parts of a stream; such a combination is also what we call our ego and what we call our world, our family or our things – all this together is just a complicated figure made of the elements that flow ceaselessly and that we can establish but that we do not have to explain." (Розенберг, О. О. (Rosenberg, O. O.) *О миросозерцании современного буддизма на Дальнем Востоке (About the Worldview of Modern Buddhism in the Far East)*. St-Petersburg, 1919, p.20–21).

59. We can see that this well-known *Abhidharma* truth is also accepted in the *Aṣṭasāhasrikā* from the quoted extensive lists. They include the following couples: eye – form, ear – sound, nose – smell, tongue – taste, body – touch, *manas* – *dharmas*. Therefore *dharmas* for the *manas* (the sixth sense organ) are the same as taste for the tongue, smell for the nose, etc., i.e. specific information for a special psychological organ.

60. E. Frauwallner translates *dharma* as 'reality' or 'something that is given' (*Gegebenheit*). (Frauwallner, E. *Die Philosophie des Buddhismus*. Berlin, 1956, p. 109.)

61. For example, the phrase that is frequent in the *Aṣṭasāhasrikā*: *iyam-eva prajñāpāramitā śrotavyā udgrahitavyā dhārayitavyā vācayitavyā paryavāptavyā pravartayitavyā.*

62. In other *Prajñāpāramitā* texts *udgṛhṇāti* has more meanings.

63. *AP*, VIII, p. 94; see also AP, IX, p. 101.

64. *AP*, XVII, p. 169.

65. *AP*, XIV, p. 144.

66. *AP*, XXII, p. 200.

67. *AP*, XIII, p. 140.

68. Stcherbatsky, Th. *Buddhist Logic*. Vol. I. Leningrad, 1932, p. 219.

69. Ibid., p. 555.

70. Such translations as 'false discrimination' (Edgerton, F. *Buddhist Hybrid Sanskrit Dictionary*. Vol. II. New Haven, 1953, p. 480) are totally unacceptable because in the original text these words are outside the dichotomy 'true–false'.

71. *AP*, I; p. 8.

72. See *AP*, X, p. 109.

73. *AP*, XVI, p. 153.

74. *AP*, XVI, p. 153.

75. *AP*, XX, p. 183.

76. *AP*, XIII, p. 157.

77. Conze E. *AP*, pp. 133, 146, 168, 180.

78. *AP*, XX, p. 183.

79. *AP*, XXVI, p. 218.

80. *AP*, XX, p. 183.
81. *AP*, XX, p. 184.
82. *AP*, XXVI, p. 218.
83. *AP*, XXVI, p. 220.
84. *AP*, XVII, p. 168.
85. *AP*, XX, p. 184.
86. Edgerton translated *bhūtakoṭi* as 'end', 'the true goal', 'real end', 'the true end' (Edgerton, *Buddhist Hybrid Sanskrit Dictionary*, II, p. 110); Conze – 'the reality-limit' (Conze, E. *AP*, p. 143 ff.); Lamotte – 'pointe du vrai'(Lamotte, É. *L'Enseignement de Vimalakīrti*. Louvain, 1962, p. 147.).
87. *AP*, XX, p. 185.
88. *AP*, XX, p. 184.
89. About the meanings, interpretations, etc., of the term *śūnyatā* see Streng, F. J. *Emptiness. A Study in Religious Meaning*. Nashville, 1967; Obermiller, E. A Study of the Twenty Aspects of *śūnyatā*. – *Indian Historical Quarterly*. Vol. 9, 1933, pp. 171–187; Obermiller, E. The Term *śūnyatā* and Its Different Interpretations. – *Journal of the Greater Indian Society*. Vol. I, 1934; May, J. La philosophie bouddhique de la vacuité. – *Studia Philosophia*. V. 18, 1959.
90. Stcherbatsky, Th. The Doctrine of the Buddha. – *Bulletin of the School of Orienatl Studies*. Vol. VI, p. 871.
91. Vallée Poussin, L. de la. *Mūlamādhyamakakārikās*. St.-Pétersbourg, 1903, p. 3.
92. Walleser, M. The Life of Nāgārjuna from Tibetan and Chinese Sources. – *Asia Major*. London, 1922, p. 421.
93. Murti, T. R. V. *The Central Philosophy of Buddhism*. London, 1955, p. 83.
94. Robinson, R. H. *Early Mādhyamika in India and China*. Madison, 1967, p. 63.
95. The term *śūnyatā* has central position only in the *Hṛdayasūtra*.
96. Suzuki, D. T. *On Indian Mahāyāna Buddhism*. Ed. by E. Conze. New York, 1968, p. 33.
97. Since we have not yet found the possible meaning of the term *śūnyatā* I had to describe the attitude of the Bodhisattva-Mahāsattva using the undefined word 'special'.
98. They are also used in Pāli texts (e.g. *Visuddhimagga*. London, 1921, p. 658.)
99. *AP*, IX, p. 102.
100. *AP*, XI, p. 112; XVI, p. 155; XX, p. 184
101. *AP*, XVI, p. 155.
102. *AP*, XVIII, p. 173.

103. *Aprameya* and *asaṃkhyeya* are defined in the *Aṣṭasāhasrikā* as follows (*AP*, XVIII, p. 172): "*Aprameya* is where all measures will disappear and *asaṃkhyeya* is where enumeration cannot be completed."

104. *AP*, VII, p. 89.

105. *AP*, XII, p. 136-137.

106. See also *AP*, X, p. 109.

107. It is absent in the Tibetan version of the text.

108. *AP*, XIII, p. 109: *acintya atulya iti vijñāna-gatasya-etad-dharmasya-adhivacanam* – 'unthinkable' and 'incomparable' mean *dharmas* belonging to the consciousness (*vijñāna*). About the meaning of *vijñāna* in Buddhism see Suzuki D. T. Reason and Intuition in Buddhist Philosophy. – *The Japanese Mind.* Ed. By Ch. A. Moore. Honolulu, 1967, p. 66 ff.

109. *AP*, XVIII, p. 173: *sarvadharmā-api subhūte anabhilāpyāḥ* ('All *dharmas*, O Subhuti, are inexpressible').

110. Ibid.

111. *AP*, VII, p. 95; XVIII, p. 170.

112. *AP*, VIII, p. 98.

113. *AP*, XXVI, p. 217.

114. *AP*, XI, p. 121.

115. See Conze, E. *The Prajñāpāramitā Literature*, p. 12.

116. *AP*, XI, p. 112.

117. Streng, F. J. *Emptiness,* p. 17 ff.

118. Stcherbatsky ,Th. *The Conception of Buddhist Nirvāṇa*. Leningrad, 1927, p. 232 ff.

119. Heimann, B. *Facets of Indian Thought*. London, 1964, p. 43.

120. *AP*, XI, p. 172.

121. *AP*, XVI, p. 156.

122. In the *Kāśyapaparivarta* the concept of *śūnyatā* is assessed as follows (translated by F. Weller): "Diejenigen aber, Kāśyapa, welche ihre Zuflucht in der Leerheit suchen durch die Wahrnehmung der Leerheit, nenne ich, Kāśyapa, hoffnungslos verloren für diese Lehre. " (Weller, Fr. *Zum Kāśyapaparivarta* H. II, p. 101.)

123. *AP*, XXVI, p. 217. This might be a reason why the word 'openness' is also suitable as a translation of *śūnyatā*.

124. *AP*, XXVI, p. 217.

125. E.g. in Har Dayal's monograph: Har Dayal. *The Bodhisattva Doctrine.* London, 1933. See also: *Cultural Heritage of India.* Vol. I. Calcutta, 1958, p. 510 ff.; Joshi, L. *Studies in the Buddhistic Culture of India.* Delhi, 1967, p. 121 ff.

126. See Suzuki, D. T. *On Indian Mahāyāna Buddhism.* p. 33.

127. *AP*, I, p. 9.

128. E.g. *AP,* XVI, p. 159.

129. The word *pṛthagjanayāna* has no sense and does not seem to be used anywhere in Buddhist literature.

130. *AP,* XVI, p. 159. The synonyms of these terms can be the following concepts: 'the person abiding on the vehicle of śrāvakas' (*śrāvakayānika pudgala,* Tib. *nyan thos kyi theg pa'i gang zag*), 'the person abiding on the vehicle of pratyekabuddhas' (*pratyekabuddhayānika pudgala,* Tib. *rang sangs rgyas kyi theg pa'i gang zag*), and 'the person abiding on the vehicle of bodhisattvas' (*bodhisattvayānika pudgala,* Tib. *byang chub sems dpa' kyi theg pa'i gang zag*).

131. *AP,* III, p. 30.

132. *AP,* XIV, p. 143.

133. *AP,* III, p. 30.

134. *AP,* XIV, p. 143.

135. *AP,* XIV, p. 143.

136. *AP,* XI, p. 116.

137. *AP*, XI, p. 116.

138. *AP,* V, p. 68.

139. This extremely interesting task probably cannot be solved using E. Conze's excessively simplified scheme, according to which, for example, Śāriputra is always described as a representative of the lower level of understanding. (See Conze, E. *The Prajñāpāramitā Literature.* 's-Gravenhage, 1960, p. 13.)

140. *AP,* XI, p. 115.

141. E.g. *AP,* XVI, p. 157.

142. E.g. Conze, E. *Buddhist Wisdom Books.* London, 1958, p.22: "the Bodhisattvas, the great beings".

143. *AP*, p. 282.

144. *AP*, I, p. 9.

145. *AP*, I, p. 9-10.

146. *AP*, I, p. 10.

147. E.g. Pali *diṭṭhi* in the *Dīghanikāya* (1, 31; 11, 13, 45), the *Majjhimanikāya* (1, 40), etc.

148. See the article "A Possible Approach Towards Understanding Śūnyavāda" in this volume.

149. *AP*, XXVII, p. 221-222.

150. E.g. *AP,* XV, p. 146, 149; XX, p. 185; XXVI, p. 218; XXVII, p. 220, etc.

151. We can translate *loka* as 'mankind' bearing in mind that it means 'mankind for this person', i.e. the number of people that can be embraced by the observer.

152. *AP*, I, p. 10.

153. *AP*, X, p. 114.

154. *AP,* XXI, p. 191.

155. Ibid.

156. *AP,* XXIV, p. 194.

157. Ibid.

158. *AP,* XXI, p. 194.

159. *AP,* XXI, p. 195.

160. E.g. *AP,* XXIV, p. 208.

161. *AP,* X, p. 106.

162. *AP,* VIII, p. 67.

163. *AP,* XIX, p. 182.

164. *AP,* XIX, p. 181.

165. *AP,* XVIII, p. 170.

166. See *AP,* XVI, p. 167.

167. *AP,* XVIII, p. 170.

168. *AP,* XVI, p. 167.

169. *AP*, XVII, p. 161.

170. *Na vikalendriya bhavati* (*AP,* XVII, p. 166).

171. *Puruṣavṛṣabha-indriya-samanvagataś-ca bhavati, na asatpuruṣaḥ.* E. Conze translated this as follows: "He possesses the organs of virile man, not those of an impotent man". (Conze, E. *Aṣṭasāhasrikā Prajñāpāramitā.* Calcutta, 1957, p. 126).

172. *AP,* XVII, p. 166.

173. *AP,* XVII, p. 166–167.

174. *AP,* XVII, p. 164.

175. *AP*, XIII, p. 141. On the term *nirvāṇa* see: Vallée Poussin, L. *Nirvāṇa*. Paris, 1925.

176. *AP*, I, p. 5.

177. *AP*, II, p. 20.

178. *AP*, III, p. 26.

179. Daniélou, A. *Hindu Polytheism*. London, 1963.

180. E.g., Suzuki, D. T. The Philosophy and Religion of the *Prajñāpāramitā. – Essays in Zen Buddhism.* London, 1953, p. 37: "*prajñā=saṃbodhi=sarvajñatā*".

181. Conze E. *Buddhism*, p. 124.

182. May, J. Kant et le Mādhyamika. – *Indo-Iranian Journal.* Vol. III, 1959, p. 109.

183. *AP*, VIII, p. 94.

184. See the following works by Suzuki: *The Philosophy and Religion of the Prajñāpāramitā*; *The Zen Doctrine of No Mind.* London, 1949; Reason and Intuition in Buddhist Philosophy. – *The Japanese Mind.* Honolulu,

1967. Apparently, Suzuki was influenced by medieval Chinese speculations where no distinction was made between these terms. (See Liebenthal W. *Chao Lun. The Treatises of Seng Chao.* Hong Kong, 1968, p. 23; Robinson, R. H. *Early Mādhyamika in India and China.* Madison, 1967, p. 124 ff.)

185. Walleser, M. *Prajñāpāramitā. Die Vollkommenheit des Erkenntnis.* Göttingen, 1913, S.1 ff; Stcherbatsky, Th. *The Conception of Buddhist Nirvāṇa*, p, 45.

186. See Conze, E. *Selected Sayings from Perfection of Wisdom.* London, 1955.

187. See Conze, E. *The Large Sūtra on Perfect Wisdom.* London, 1961.

188. The opposite replacement contradicts the logic of the development of Buddhism.

189. *AP*, XXV, p, 214.

190. *AP*, IV, p. 48.

191. *AP*, XII, p. 136.

192. The difference in the approaches of the authors of the *Prajñāpāramitā* sūtras and later commentators is conspicuous even in the first reading of the texts.

193. *AP*, XI, p. 118.

194. *AP*, X, p. 114.

195. *AP*, XI, p. 115.

196. *AP*, XI, p. 116.

197. *AP*, XXX, p. 238. See also *AP*, III, p. 36.

198. *AP*, XII, p. 125.

199. *AP*, XI, p. 123.

200. *AP*, V, p. 57.

201. *AP*, II, p. 35.

202. *AP*, XII, p. 136.

203. *AP*, III, p. 30.

204. *AP*, XXV, p. 213.

205. E.g. *AP*, VIII, pp. 94, 96, 97; X, p. 105; XV, p. 150; XVI, p. 156; XVIII, p. 170.

206. *AP*, IV, p. 51.

207. Ibid.

208. Ibid.

209. *AP*, V, p. 52.

210. Ibid.

211. Ibid..

212. Ibid.

213. Ibid.

214. *AP*, VIII, p. 96.
215. Ibid.
216. Ibid.
217. *AP*, IX, p. 100.
218. *AP*, X, p. 105.
219. Ibid.
220. Ibid.
221. *AP*, XXVI, p. 217.
222. Ibid.
223. E.g. *AP*, III, p. 36; IX, p. 100; X, p. 104.
224. *AP*, IX, p. 101; X, p. 110; XI, p. 123.
225. *AP*, III, p. 31.
226. Ibid.
227. *AP*, III, p. 31.
228. E.g. *AP*, V, p. 63; VIII, p. 98; XXIV, p. 206.
229. *AP*, XXV, p. 210 - 214.
230. See Monier-Williams, M. *A Sanskrit-English Dictionary*, p. 1070: *śikṣate* – 'to practice one's self in (loc.)'.
231. *AP*, XXV, p. 212.
232. *AP*, XXV, p. 210.
233. *antargatā* (*nang du 'das pa*) (*AP*, XXV, p. 213).
234. *AP*, XXV, p. 211.
235. *AP*, XXV, p. 211.
236. *AP*, XXV, p. 211.
237. A Bodhisattva-Mahāsattva who 'learns in *Prajñāpāramitā*' is opposed to them: he is free from all diseases and disabilities (*sarvākāraparipūrṇendriyo bhavati, svara-saṃpanno bhavati.*) – *AP*, XXV, p. 211.
238. *AP*, XXII, p. 201.
239. *AP*, XXVII, p. 220.
240. *AP*, XIX, p. 176.
241. E.g. *AP*, XVIII, p. 173; III, p. 40; IV, p. 51; XVI, p. 155; XIX, p. 178–179.
242. Lamotte, É. *L'Enseignement de Vimalakīrti*, pp. 114–115.
243. Honda, M. Annotated Translation of the Daśabhūmika-sūtra. *Studies in South, East and Central Asia.* New Delhi, 1968; Norman, K. C. *The Commentary on the Dhammapada.* Vol. I. London, 1906, p. 84.
244. Guenther, H. V. *The Jewel Ornament of Liberation of sGam.po.pa.* London, 1959, p. 148 ff. It is interesting that in the *Aṣṭasāhasrikā* the list of synonyms of *prajñāpāramitā* also includes *daśapāramitā* and *bala-pāramitā* (see p. 13).

245. Guenther, H. V. *The Jewel Ornament of Liberation*, p. 149 ff.

246. Tibetan authors call *pāramitāyāna* either the preparatory stage of Tantric practice or a way parallel to Vajrayāna. (See Guenther, H. V. *Treasures on the Tibetan Middle Way*. Leiden, 1968.)

247. Guenther, H. V. *The Jewel Ornament of Liberation*, p. 149 ff.

248. *AP*, III, p. 40; see also *AP*, IV, p. 51.

249. *AP*, XXV, p. 213.

250. *AP*, XXII, p. 198.

251. *AP*, VII, p. 87. see also *AP*, III, p. 40.

252. *AP*, XVIII, p. 171.

253. *AP*, XXII, p. 197.

254. Ibid.

255. For no apparent reason, Conze states that Omniscience is the only positive term of the New Wisdom School (i.e. *prajñāpāramitā-mādhyamika*) meaning 'salvation': "Salvation, as the New Wisdom School understands it, can be summed up in three negations – Non-attainment, Non-assertion, Non-relying – and one positive attribute – Omniscience. (Conze E. *Buddhism*, p. 135)

256. *AP*, XV, p. 151

257. *AP*, XV, p. 151

258. *AP*, XV, p. 151

259. Conze, E. *Buddhism*, p. 138.

260. Liebenthal, W. *Chao Lun. The Treatises of Seng Chao*. Hong Kong, 1968, p. 67.

261. *AP*, VII, p. 86.

262. *AP*, XXV, p. 212.

263. *AP*, III, p. 36; see also *AP*, III, p. 29, 40; XI, p. 123.

264. *AP*, XIII, p. 140; XIV, p. 143.

265. *AP*, XXIV, p. 208.

266. *AP*, XVIII, p. 170.

267. *AP*, I, p. 5.

268. *AP*, III, p. 29.

269. *AP*, IV, p. 49.

270. *AP*, XV, p. 148.

271. *AP*, XVII, p. 165.

272. *The Dīgha Nikāya*. Vol. II. London, 1903, p. 156.

273. E.g. Lessing, F. D., Wayman, A. *Mkhas-grub-rjes Fundamentals of the Buddhist Tantras*. The Hague, 1968.

274. *Encyclopaedia of Buddhism*. Vol. I, fasc. 1. Ceylon, 1961.

275. E.g. Suzuki, D. T. *Outlines of Mahayana Buddhism*, p. 82.

276. E.g. *AP*, III, p. 31; XVI, p. 157: *durabhisaṃbhavā hi anuttarā samyaksaṃbodhiḥ*.
277. *AP*, III, p. 31.
278. *AP*, XVI, p. 156.
279. *AP*, XVI, p. 157.
280. This is by no means a definition of *dharma*.
281. *AP*, XIX, p. 175.
282. *AP*, XIX; p. 178.
283. *AP*, XIX, p. 180.
284. *AP*, III, p. 31.
285. Hakeda, Y. S. *The Awakening of Faith, Attributed to Aśvaghosha*, pp. 23-24.
286. Karunatilleke, W. S. Aṣṭasāhasrikā-Prajñāpāramitā Sūtra. *Encyclopaedia of Buddhism*. Vol. II. Fasc. 2. Ceylon, 1967, p. 250.
287. Suzuki, D. T. *The Zen Doctrine of No Mind*. London, 1949, p. 59.
288. Nakamura, H. *Ways of Thinking of Eastern Peoples*. Honolulu, 1964, p. 147.
289. Takakusu, J. Buddhism as Philosophy of "Thusness". – *The Indian Mind*. Honolulu, 1967, p. 99.
290. *AP*, XII, p. 135.
291. *AP*, XVIII, p. 174.
292. *AP*, V, p. 67.
293. *AP*, XXV, pp. 212–213.
294. *AP*, XVI, p. 153.
295. *AP*, XVII, p. 161.
296. *AP*, XVI, p. 154.
297. *AP*, XVI, p. 154.
298. *AP*, I, p. 3.
299. *AP*, XXII, p. 201.
300. E.g. Fromm, E. *Zen Buddhism and Psychoanalysis*. London, 1960, p. 10 ff. D. Suzuki considered Zen Buddhism to be the direct continuation of the *Prajñāpāramitā* teaching. See Suzuki, D. T. The Philosophy and Religion of the Prajñāpāramitā. – *Essays in Zen Buddhism*. III Series. London, 1953, p. 239–331.
301. *AP*, I, p. 3, 4, 5.
302. *AP*, X, pp. 104, 112.
303. *AP*, I, pp. 9, 11; X, p. 106.
304. *AP*, XXII, p. 201.
305. *AP*, XVII, p. 163.
306. *AP*, XV, p. 150.
307. *AP*, XVI, p. 159.

308. *AP*, I, p. 15.

309. Walleser, M. *Prajñāpāramitā. Die Vollkommenheit der Erkenntnis*. Göttingen, 1913, SS. 35–36 (=*AP*, I, p. 3.)

310. Ibid., S. 37 (=*AP*, I, p. 4.)

311. Ibid., S. 39 (=*AP*, I, p. 5.)

312. Ibid., S. 44 (=*AP*, I, p. 9.)

313. Ibid., S. 46 (=AP, I, p. 11.)

314. Ibid., S. 89 (=*AP*, XXII, p. 201.)

315. Ibid., S. 93 (=*AP*, XV, p. 150.)

316. Ibid., S. 130 (=*AP*, XVI, p. 159.)

317. Ibid., S. 54 (=*AP*, I, p. 15.)

318. Conze, E. *Aṣṭasāhasrikā Prajñāpāramitā*. Calcutta, 1968, p. 2 (=*AP*, I, p. 3).

319. Ibid., p. 3 (=*AP*, I, p. 4.)

320. Ibid., p. 4 (=*AP*, I, p. 5.)

321. Ibid., p. 73 (=*AP*, X, p. 104.)

322. Ibid., p. 80 (=*AP*, X, p. 112.)

323. Ibid., p. 6 (=*AP*, I, p. 9.)

324. Ibid., p. 8 (=*AP*, I, p. 11.)

325. Ibid., p. 75 (=*AP*, X, p. 106.)

326. Ibid., p. 162 (=*AP*, XXII, p. 201.)

327. Ibid., p. 122 (=*AP*, XVII, p. 163.)

328. Ibid., p. 111 (=*AP*, XV, p. 150.)

329. Ibid., p. 119 (=*AP*, XVI, p. 159.)

330. Ibid., p. 13 (=*AP*, I, p. 15.)

331. Kumārajīva's translation is published in *Taisho Issaikyo*. Vol. 8. Tokyo, 1928.

332. The Tibetan translation is not very helpful here since trying to accurately convey the meaning of the original Sanskrit text left no room for free interpretation.

333. The words that mean fear can also be found in the *Aṣṭasāhasrikā* in the situations that are not directly related to the situations investigated here (See *AP*, XIX, p. 178-180).

334. *AP*, p. 289.

335. Ibid.

336. *AP*, p. 305.

337. Ibid.

338. There are many other *Prajñāpāramitā* sūtras apart from the *Aṣṭasāhasrikā*.

339. *AP*, XI, p. 123.

340. *AP*, XI, p. 115.

341. *AP,* XXI, p. 191.
342. *AP,* XI, p. 115.
343. *AP,* XI, p. 120 ff.
344. About this opposition in Buddhism see: Windisch, E. *Māra und Buddha.* Leipzig, 1895.
345. *AP,* XII, p. 125.
346. *AP,* XXIV, p. 206.
347. *AP,* III, p. 39.
348. E. Conze. *Aṣṭasāhasrikā Prajñāpāramitā,* p. 84.
349. Ibid., p. 87.
350. *AP*, XI, p. 123.
351. E. Conze has translated the term just that way: "Mara, the Evil One produces these deeds, which I have mentioned, and many others also." (Conze, *AP*, p. 91.)
352. E.g. Govinda, A. *Foundations of Tibetan Buddhism.* London, 1960; Naranjo, C. R., Ornstein, E. *On the Psychology of Meditation.* London, 1971.

Heart Sūtra of Transcending Awareness

1. Conze, E. *Thirty Years of Buddhist Studies. Selected Essays.* Oxford, 1967, p. 18.
2. Teemantsuutra. In: Parnov, J. *Pronksnaeratus.* Tallinn, 1975, pp. 243–261.

Dialogue in the *Bodhicaryāvatāra*

1. At the time this article was first published (1984), there were only four full translations of the *Bodhicaryāvatāra* into European languages: Finot's translation into French, Matics' translation into English, Steinkeller's translation into German and my translation into Estonian: *La marche à la lumière.* Paris, 1920; *Entering the Path of Enlightenment.* London, 1970; *Eintritt in das Leben zur Erleuchtung.* München, 1981; Šāntideva. *Bodhitšarjāvatāra.* Tallinn, 1982 (LR 3/4). There was also translation into English from the Tibetan version of the treatise: Batchelor, S. *A Guide to the Bodhisattva's Way of Life.* Dharamsala, 1979. Apart from the named translations, we can also refer to incomplete ones: Vallée Poussin, L. de la. *Bodhicaryāvatāra. Introduction à la pratique des futurs Bouddhas. Poème de Çāntideva.* Paris, 1907; Schmidt, R. *Der Eintritt in den Wandel in Erleuchtung von Śāntideva.* Paderborn, 1923; Tucci, G. *In cammino verso la luce, traduzione del Bodhicaryāvatāra di Śāntideva.* Turin, 1925. All quotations here are from Crosby's and Skilton's translation (Śāntideva. *The Bodhicaryāvatāra.* Translated, Introduction and Notes by Kate Crosby and

Andrew Skilton. With a General Introduction by Paul Williams. Oxford, New York: Oxford University Press, 1995).

2. It is also true regarding the present Tibetan commentators, e.g.: Geshe Kelsang Gyatso. *Meaningful to Behold.* Ulverston, 1980.

3. Only the *sāṃkhya* system mentioned in IX, 126 can be considered an exception.

4. The fact that *prajñā* is not intuition but highly developed intelligence, which is typologically similar to what is called scientific thinking in the European tradition, is confirmed by the whole text of the *Bodhicaryāvatāra*.

The Light Path and the Dark Path

1. Quotations from the *Bhagavadgītā* are from the English translation by Franklin Edgerton: *The Bhagavad Gītā.* New York, 1964. My own Estonian translation has been published twice: Bhagavadgītā. – *"Loomingu" Raamatukogu*, 40/41, Tallinn, 1980, and in a revised edition: *Bhagavadgītā.* Tartu: Biblio, 2000.

2. *The Bhagavad Gītā.* Transl. by. F. Edgerton, p. 96.

3. This opposition can certainly be presented on the basis of other Taoist texts.

4. The quotations from the *Daodejing* are given in my own translation on the basis of the translation of it into Estonian: Daodejing. Kulgemise väe raamat. Transl. by Linnart Mäll. – *"Loomingu" Raamatukogu*, 27, Tallinn, 1979. (Also see in this volume "The Course of the Translation".)

5. Conventionally because the word 'higher' directly contradicts what the *Daodejing* says about *dao*.

6. Chapters X and XI and some verses in several other chapters can be considered as descriptions of Kṛṣṇa.

7. The Chinese word *zhŭ 'Lord'* – is equivalent to *īśvara* in translations of Indian texts and to *κύριος* in translations of the Bible.

The Course of Translation

1. Спирин, В. С. *Построение древнекитайских текстов* (*The Structure of Ancient Chinese Texts*). Moscow, 1976.

2. ("One should practice inactivity, remain calm and taste what has no flavour." Ян Хин-шун. *Древнекитайский философ Лао-цзы и его учение* (Yang Hing-shung. *Ancient Chinese Philosopher Lao-zi and His Teaching*). Moscow, Leningrad, 1950, p. 150.

3. Waley, A. *The Way and Its Power. A Study of the Tao Te Ching and Its Place in Chinese Thought.* London, 1934, p. 219.

4. Wilhelm, R. *Laotse. Tao Te King. Das Buch des Alten von Sinn und Leben. Aus dem Chinesischen verdeutscht und erläutert von Richard Wilhelm*. Jena, 1921, p. 68.

5. Lau, D. C. *Lao Tzu. Tao Te Ching.* Translated with an Introduction by D. C. Lau. Harmondsworth, 1963.

6. Schwarz, E. *Laudse. Daudedsching.* Leipzig, 1970, p. 119.

7. *A Source Book in Chinese Philosophy.* Princeton, 1963, p. 108.

8. Feng, G. & English, J. *Lao Tzu. Tao Te Ching.* Translated by G. Feng & J. English. London, 1972, p. 63.

9. *The Sacred Books of the East. The Texts of Taoism.* Translated by James Legge. Part I. Oxford, 1891, p. 106.

10. Mäll, L. Lao-zi. Daodejing. Kulgemise väe raamat (Lao-zi. Daodejing. A Book of the Power of the Course. Translated from Chinese by Linnart Mäll). – *"Loomingu" Raamatukogu,* 27, Tallinn, 1979. Negation here is indicated by suffix *-ta.*

11. Конрад, Н. И. *Избранные труды. Синология* (*Selected Works. Sinology*). Moscow, 1977, p. 437.

12. *The Sacred Books of the East. The Texts of Taoism.* Translated by James Legge. Part I. Oxford, 1891, p. 12.

13. Ibid., p. 14.

14. Wilhelm, *op. cit.*, p. XV.

15. Maspero, H. *Le taoisme.* Paris, 1954, p. 81.

16. *The Chinese Mind.* Honolulu, 1967, p. 110.

17. *A Source Book in Chinese Philosophy*, p. 719.

18. *Философская энциклопедия* (*Encyclopaedia of Philosophy*). Vol. I. Moscow, 1960, p. 429.

19. Needham, J. *Science and Civilization in China.* Vol. I. 1956, p. 36.

20. Watts, A. *Tao. The Watercourse Way.* New York, 1975, p. 41.

21. Ibid., p. 49.

22. Ян Юн-го. *История древнекитайской идеологии* (Yang Yongguo. *A History of Ancient Chinese Ideology*). Moscow, 1957, p. 273.

23. Lau, D. C. *Lao Tzu. Tao Te Ching*, p. 89.

24. Ян Хин-шун, *op. cit.*, p. 132.

25. *Meng-zi*, V, 2, 2, 3.

26. Lau, D. C. *Lao Tzu. Tao Te Ching*, p. 102.

27. Confucius. *Analects*, XV, 29.

Buddhist Mythology

1. See the article "Once more about Yamāntaka" in this volume.

The Cultural Model of Tibet

1. The rivers Huanghe, Yangzi, Mekong, Salween, Brahmaputra, Indus, Sutlej (the biggest tributary of the Indus) and many tributaries of the Ganges

have their headwaters in areas inhabited by Tibetans. These rivers flow into the Yellow Sea, East China Sea, South China Sea, Andaman Sea and Arabian Sea and the Bay of Bengal.

2. Nevertheless, Tibet has never suffered from the famines that repeatedly ravaged medieval Europe.

3. He means the Tibetan legend about the country of Śambhala which is allegedly situated somewhere in the North. The legend says that at the highpoint of the moral degradation of mankind the army of Śambhala will challenge the forces of evil and assert the light of the true teaching everywhere so that mankind will experience a form of rebirth. Many mystically minded Europeans were inspired by this idea and decided that Śambhala actually exists either North of India or North of Tibet. In fact, the mythical image of Śambhala was only created for meditation, with the points of the compass having symbolic meaning.

4. One of the first studies based on such a judgment was the book: Waddell, L. A. *The Buddhism of Tibet or Lamaism*. London, 1895.

5. An innovative movement called 'rime' (*r̄is med*) – 'belonging to no school' emerged in the late 18th century. Its purpose was to create a synthetic Tibetan Buddhism on the basis of the doctrines of different traditions. Many representatives of rime thought that Tibet should become familiar with Western civilization.

6. Most chronicles are rather recent. For example, the famous *Blue Annals* (*Deb-ther sngon-po*) translated into English by George Roerich (*Blue Annals*, pts. 1–2. Calcutta, 1949–1953), were only written in the late 15th century.

7. "Unfortunately, almost none of the most ancient Tibetan historical works have survived. We can largely evaluate Tibetan historical literature on the basis of works written in the past five or six centuries, although this does not give us the full picture. We have a rather incomplete idea of earlier Tibetan historical literature."(Востриков, А. И. *Тибетская историческая литература* (*Tibetan Historical Literature*). Moscow, 1962, p. 19). Indeed, some important discoveries have been made in recent decades but the general picture of Tibet's past is still rather vague.

8. About his versatile activities see: Snellgrove, D., Richardson, H. A. *Cultural History of Tibet*. London, 1968, p. 27 ff.

9. Tibet might have had some relations with Byzantium (with its official name of Rome). This is confirmed by the fact that the main hero of the Tibetan epos is Gesar (derived from Caesar) and that he rules a country called Khrom (Rome). Of course, neither Khrom nor Gesar have anything to do with Byzantium and its Caesars apart from the names.

10. Chattopadhyaya, A. *Atisha and Tibet*. Calcutta, 1967, p. 198 ff.

11. Not all scholars agree with this since there is some evidence that writing existed earlier in Tibet.

12. The period of textual imitation basically ended in the early second millennium AD. Although translation continued even later, original works began to play a major role in the spiritual life of Tibet.

13. The latest Tibetan Buddhist sources say that Songtsen Gampo not only converted Tibetans to Buddhism but also built a number of monasteries in Tibet and introduced some laws that were in keeping with the "Ten rules of good behaviour" taught by the Buddha. In these sources Songtsen Gampo is called *dharmarāja* or the 'King of Dharma' and is considered to be a reincarnation of the bodhisattva Avalokiteśvara.

14. It is interesting to note that the successful spread of Buddhism in other Asian countries was only possible in the periods when the help of the ruler was guaranteed. See: Conze, E. Buddhism and Asian Society. – *Shambhala Review*. Vol. 5, Nos 1, 2, 1976, p. 15–19.

15. For the works of Śāntarakṣita and Śāntideva see: Joshi L. *Studies in the Buddhistic Culture of India*. Delhi, 1967, p. 222 ff and 245 ff.

16. Legend has it that the building of the Samye Monastery was started by the Indian scholar and philosopher Śāntarakṣita and completed by semilegendary Padmasambhava, a great teacher of Vajrayāna.

17. About this interesting dispute see: Demiéville, P. *Le Concile de Lhasa*. Paris, 1952; Tucci, G. *Minor Buddhist Texts*. Pt. 11. Roma, 1958 (*Serie Orientale Roma*, vol. IX, 2).

18. Tucci, G. *Religions of Tibet*. London, 1980.

19. See: Snellgrove, D., Richardson, H. *A Cultural History of Tibet*, p. 59.

20. For example, the translators of the *Bodhicaryāvatāra-pañjika*, the comment of Prajñākaramati to the poem *Bodhicaryāvatāra* by Śāntideva were the Indian Sumatikīrti and Tibetan Darmadag. The text was edited by the Tibetan Yönten Gyatso.

21. Relatively few Sanskrit Buddhist texts have survived. This can be explained by the fact that Buddhist centres in India have been destroyed by Muslim conquerors. Therefore Chinese and especially Tibetan translations are irreplaceable sources in the studying of Indian Buddhism.

22. Therefore there are very few original works written in the natural style similar to colloquial language. These include "Songs of Milarepa", some works of the Nyingma school, the verses of the sixth Dalai Lama and some others.

23. Lotsawas (*lo tswa ba*) were translators of Buddhist texts. This is the common name for Tibetan monks who spent a long time in India studying Sanskrit and Buddhist texts and specialized as translators.

24. Nālanda, Vikramaśilā and other Indian monasteries had thousands of monks and students arriving from many Asian countries. The library of Nālanda had almost all the Buddhist texts existing at the time, and copies of them could be ordered. Later on, Tibetan monasteries were modelled on Indian monasteries.

25. Vajrayāna is also called Tantrayāna (the 'Vehicle of Tantras' or special texts meant for the practice of contemplation). Therefore in European tradition Vajrayāna is often called Tantrism. But we should not forget that there is also Hindu Tantrism and its teaching is quite different from Buddhist.

26. In Mahāyāna logical philosophy and mythology form an integral whole. For more detail see the article "Buddhist Mythology" in this volume.

27. Buddhism states that there is an infinite number of worlds. Each world has its own Buddhas and bodhisattvas. The world of the Supreme Healer, for example, is in the East and separated from our world by a great number of other worlds as numerous as sand grains in ten Ganges rivers.

28. Vajrayāna is opposed to another tradition within Mahāyāna – Pāramitāyāna (the 'Vehicle of Pāramitās), the main mechanisms of which are so-called 'transcending actions': generosity, morality, patience, energy, contemplation and awareness. About these two traditions see in more detail in the book: Guenther H.V. *Treasures of the Tibetan Middle Way*. Leiden, 1969, p. 52–73.

29. The concept of a 'guru' was apparently borrowed from Hinduism in the middle of the first millennium AD (before that Buddhist teachers were called *kalyāṇamitras* – 'benevolent friends'). Nevertheless, the concept of a guru in Buddhism is different from its interpretation in Hinduism. In Buddhism relations between a student and a teacher are relatively free. A student can go to another teacher, etc. The equivalent of guru in Tibetan is the word 'lama' (*bla ma*).

30. Gugé was then the strongest of the three Tibetan Himalayan states (the other two were called Purang and Maryul). About Gugé's past grandeur see the first chapters of the book: Govinda, A. *The Way of the White Clouds*. London, 1972.

31. Avalokiteśvara is the central figure in many Mahāyāna texts (for example, the "Lotus Sūtra"). Avalokiteśvara can assume different forms in order to save those who suffer. He is depicted either similar to an Indian prince (Siṃhanāda Avalokiteśvara) or holding a lotus flower (Padmapāni Avalokiteśvara) or four-handed (Ṣaḍakṣarī Avalokiteśvara) or with 11 faces and 1000 hands (Ekadaśamukha Avalokiteśvara). Dalai Lama and the head of the Karma Kagyu school – Karmapa – are considered to be reincarnations of Avalokiteśvara.

32. The Geluk school founded by Tsong Khapa is sometimes called the New Kadam.

33. The main historical work by Putön was translated into English by the famous Russian scholar E. Obermiller (Obermiller, E. *History of Buddhism by Bu-ston.* Pts. I–II. Heidelberg, 1931–1932).

34. About these two outstanding Indian Buddhist yogis see: Guenther H. V. *The Life and Teaching of Nāropa.* Oxford, 1963.

35. See Evans-Wents, W. Y. *Tibet's Great Yogi Milarepa.* Oxford, 1928.

36. These poems or, rather, songs were collected in *The Hundred Thousand Songs of Milarepa.* Transl. by Garma C. C. Chang. Vols. I–II, New York, 1962.

37. About Gampopa see: Guenther, H. V. *The Jewel Ornament of the Liberation by sGam.po.pa.* London, 1959.

38. According to Buddhism, all sentient beings are reborn after death in one of the six worlds of *saṃsāra* depending on their *karma.* Rebirth in the world of men is considered to be the happiest since one can only attain *nirvāṇa* in a human body. Even celestial beings cannot do it. The idea that took root in Tibet in the 12th century was that a spiritually advanced person who has liberated himself from the influence of the law of *karma* could choose the place of his rebirth in any of the worlds of *saṃsāra* and turn into any inhabitant of this world in order to propagate the teaching. Tibetan spiritual hierarchs preferred to reincarnate in Tibet giving before their death some vague hints about the place of their next rebirth. Reincarnations were found with the help of an oracle and from a very young age prepared for the role their predecessors played. Thus, the institution of reincarnations constituted the spiritual elite of the Tibetan theocratic state.

39. About the consequences of Muslim invasions in North India see in the travel notes of Dharmasvāmin, a Tibetan pilgrim from the middle of the 13th century, translated by G. Roerich (Рерих, Ю. Н. *Избранные труды* (*Selected Works*). Moscow, 1967, p. 453–572).

40. Many scholars doubt that Padmasambhava actually existed. His biography looks more like a collection of legends. See: *The Life and Liberation of Padmasambhava. As Recorded by Yeshe Tsogyal.* Pts. I–II. Emeryville, 1978. However, we should bear in mind that Tibetans generally tended to mythologize the biographies of famous persons.

41. There is some interesting material in a work about the history of Buddhism in India and Tibet: Tarthang Tulku. A History of the Buddhist Dharma. – *Crystal Mirror*, vol. 5, p. 127–330.

42. "The Book of the Dead", or, more precisely, "Liberation by Hearing on the After Death Plane" describes the experiences of the mind after death before the next rebirth. The book was first translated into English by

Evans-Wentz (Evans-Wentz, W. Y. *The Tibetan Book of the Dead.* Oxford, 1927). A new excellent translation was published in 1975: *The Tibetan Book of the Dead.* A New Translation by Ch. Trungpa and F. Freemantle. London, 1975). See also: Lauf, D. I. *Secret Doctrines of the Tibetan Book of the Dead.* London, 1977.

43. The Karma Kagyu school is, in turn, divided into eight sub-schools. See: Douglas, N., White, M. *Karmapa: The Black Hat Lama of Tibet.* London, 1976.

44. Many outstanding researchers emphasize the closeness of Tibetan Buddhism to Indian. See: Conze, E. *Thirty Years of Buddhist Studies.* Oxford, 1967, p. 21.

45. For example, there were 7700 monks in Drepung, 5500 in Sera, 3300 in Ganden and 3000 in Labrang in the mid-twentieth century. (*Buddhists in New China.* Peking, 1956, p. 108 ff).

46. Book-printing must have begun in Tibet in the 14th century. Books were printed using the xylographic method. The text was carved on wooden blocks. This art came from China. Tibetan books were also printed in China: even *Kangyur* was first printed in Beijing (1411).

47. Tsong Khapa's works are still relatively little known in Europe. Some chapters of Lamrim, his main work, were published in the 1970–80s (*Calming the Mind and Discerning the Real.* Transl. by A. Wayman. New York, 1978). See also: Tsong-ka-pa. *Tantra in Tibet. The Great Exposition of Secret Mantra.* Pts. I–II. London, 1977–1980.

48. The term "Yellow hats" was borrowed by Europeans from the Chinese. The term is not used in Tibet.

49. 'Dalai' means 'ocean' in Mongolian. Tibetans rarely use this term. For them the Dalai Lama is Gyalwa Rinpoche – the 'Jewel of Victory'.

50. This concerns primarily the Nyingma school whose biggest monastery was founded in 1685.

51. Not only the fifth but almost all Dalai Lamas were authors of a number of works.

52. Tsangyang Gyatso died in 1706 at the age of 23.

53. This article was published as the introduction for the Russian translation of the "Atlas of Tibetan Medicine" (Атлас тибетской медицины. Moscow, 1994) which was compiled at the end of 17th century. Therefore, my article also does not go beyond that time.

Once More about Yamāntaka

1. A person brought up in traditional Buddhist culture may see the very asking of this kind of question as nonsense, let alone the different answers.

2. 'God' or 'deity' are not always appropriate equivalents for the Sanskrit words *deva* and *devatā* or Tibetan *lha*, particularly in the cases where

these terms are used to describe the special contemplative practice *bhāvanā* which is very well translated by H. V. Guenther as 'creative imagination'.

3. Here the term 'god' ('deity') is in the right context since it is a mythological figure.

4. European science might have first learnt about this legend from the book of E. Pander, *Das Pantheon des Tschangtscha Hutuktu*. Berlin, 1890, S. 61.

5. Гумильев, Л. Н. и Кузнецов, Б. И. Опыт разбора тибетской пиктографии. – *Декоративное искусство в СССР*. (The Experience of the Deciphering of Tibetan Pictography. – *Decorative Art in the USSR*). 1972, No 5,'p. 26–34. See also Гумильев, Л. Н. *Старобурятская живопись. (Ancient Buryatian Painting.)* Moscow, 1975, p. 26–34.

6. Гумильев, Л. Н. и Кузнецов Б. И., ibid., p. 26: "The images of Yama and Yamāntaka are based on the following myth. Once there was a hermit..."

7. Ibid., p. 27.

8. Ibid.

9. Yamāntaka – *gshin rje gshed*, Kṛṣṇayamāri – *gshin rje gshed nag po*, Raktayamāri – *gshin rje gshed dmar po*.

10. The Indian origin of Yamāntaka is also confirmed by the fact that one of its Chinese equivalents is the phonetic transcription (*Yan man de jia*).

11. *Sādhanamāla*. Ed. by B. Bhattacharya. Vols. I–II, Baroda, 1925–8.

12. Ibid., Vol. II, pp. 555–558.

13. Ibid., Vol. II, pp. 542–554.

14. Ibid., Vol. II, pp. 528–541.

15. Ibid., Vol. I, pp. 107, 109, 137, 255, etc.

16. Ibid., Vol. II, p. 598.

17. *Mañjuśrīmūlakalpa*. Ed. by P. L. Vaidya. Darbhanga, 1964. – *Buddhist Sanskrit Texts*, Vol. 18. Previously the *Mañjuśrīmūlakalpa* was published in 1920–1925 in *Trivandrum Sanskrit Series*. Opinions about the date of creation of the *Mañjuśrīmūlakalpa* vary. According to Warder it was the early 8th century (Warder, A. K. *Indian Buddhism*. Delhi, 1970, p. 525). On the other hand, *The Cultural Heritage of India* places it as early as the 3rd century (see Vol. I, Calcutta, 1958, p. 525).

18. Chapters 49, 50 and 51.

19. *bhagavato mañjuśrīyasya mahākrodharājā yamāntako*... (*Mañjuśrīmūlakalpa*, p. 15). Vajrabhairava is also mentioned in the *Mañjuśrīmūlakalpa* at least once (Ibid., p. 10).

20. *Guhyasamājatantra*. Ed. by Bhattacharya. Baroda, 1931. This tantra must have emerged in the 3rd or 4th century (See Wayman, A. *The Buddhist Tantras*, London, 1974, p. 19).

21. Ibid., p. 65, 70, 74, 76.

22. Yamāntaka is also an anthropomorphic symbol in the main tantras related to Yamāntāka such as the *Kṛṣṇayamāritantra* and the *Vajrabhairavatantra*, the Sanskrit versions of which have been found in India and Tibet (see Bhattacharya, D. Ch. *Tantric Buddhist Iconographic Sources*. Delhi, 1974, pp. 49–51).

23. 'Creative imagination' (a kind of meditative thinking, in Sanskrit *bhāvanā*) can hardly be seen as mythological thinking since the latter implies the actual existence of so-called mythological images that can affect the course of events in the external world. On the other hand, in meditation it is accepted that anthropomorphic symbols do not actually exist, although they may have quite a tangible effect on the mind of the contemplating person.

Bibliographical Data

The Zero Way, written in 1964.

First published in Russian: Нулевой путь. – Sign System Studies. Vol. 2. – *Acta et Commentationes Universitatis Tartuensis*. Issue No. 181. Tartu, 1965, pp. 189–191. Re-published in: *Буддизм России* / Buddhism of Russia. No. 34, 2001, pp. 80–81. In Estonian: Nulltee. – Linnart Mäll. *Nulli ja lõpmatuse kohal* (*Above the Zero and Infinity*). Tartu: Ilmamaa, 1998, pp. 299–301.

A Possible Approach Towards Understanding *Śūnyavāda*, written in 1967.

First published in Russian: Об одном возможном подходе к пониманию *śūnyavāda*. – Terminologia Indica. Vol. 1. Tartu, 1967, pp. 13–24. Re-published in: *Буддизм России* / Buddhism of Russia. No. 35, 2002, pp. 80–84. In French: Une approche possible du *śūnyavāda*. – *Tel Quel*. No. 32, 1968, pp. 54–62. In Estonian: Ühest võimalikust lähenemisest *śūnyavāda* mõistmisele. – *Nulli ja lõpmatuse kohal*, pp. 302–311.

Some Aspects of the Emergence of Mahāyāna, written in 1968 for a report held in the international conference on the History, Archeology and Culture of Central Asia in the Kushan Period. Dushanbe, September 27th – October 6th, 1968.

First published in Russian: Некоторые проблемы возникновения махаяны. – *Центральная Азия в кушанскую эпоху* (*Central Asia in the Kushan Period*). Vol. 2. Moscow, 1975, pp. 219–222. In Estonian: Mahajaana tekke mõnigaid aspekte. – *Nulli ja lõpmatuse kohal*, pp. 234–238.

Studies in the *Aṣṭasāhasrikā Prajñāpāramitā*, written in 1969–71.

First time the complete work is published in this volume. Parts of it are formerly published in Russian and Estonian in several issues under different titles.

К буддийской персонологии (бодхисаттва в "Аштасахасрике Праджняпарамите") (On the Buddhist Personology (Bodhisattva in the *Aṣṭasāhasrikā Prajñāpāramitā*)). – Sign System Studies. Vol. 5. – *Acta et Commentationes Universitatis Tartuensis*. Issue No. 284. Tartu, 1971, pp. 124–132. The same in Estonian: Budistlikust personoloogiast. – *Nulli ja lõpmatuse kohal*, pp. 277–287. Четыре термина праджняпарамитской психологии (Four Terms of the Prajñāpāramitā Psychology). Part 1. – Oriental Studies. Vol. 2₁. – *Acta et Commentationes Universitatis Tartuensis*. Issue No. 309. Tartu, 1973, pp. 202–213. Part 2. – Oriental Studies. Vol. 3. – *Acta et Commentationes Universitatis Tartuensis*. Issue No. 392. Tartu, 1976, pp. 93–124. The same in Estonian: *Prajñāpāramitā psühholoogia neli terminit*. – *Nulli ja lõpmatuse kohal*, pp. 239–276. Использование текста как средства психического воздействия (по материалам "Аштасахасрики Праджняпарамиты"). (The Use of the Text as the Mean of Psychological Intervention (On the Sources of *Aṣṭasāhasrikā Prajñāpāramitā*)) – Sign System Studies. Vol. 20. – *Acta et Commentationes Universitatis Tartuensis*. Issue No. 746. Tartu, 1987, pp. 30–38. The same in Estonian: Teksti kasutamine psüühika mõjutamise vahendina. – *Nulli ja lõpmatuse kohal*, pp. 288–296. Дхарма – текст и текстопорождающий механизм. (Dharma as Text and the Text-generating Mechanism) – Sign System Studies. Vol. 21. – *Acta et Commentationes Universitatis Tartuensis*. Issue No. 754. Tartu, 1987, pp. 22–25. The same in Estonian: Dharma kui tekst ja tekstiloome mehhanism. – *Nulli ja lõpmatuse kohal*, pp. 312–315. Шуньята в семиотической модели дхармы. (Śūnyatā in the Semiotical Model of Dharma) – Sign System Studies. Vol. 22. – *Acta et Commentationes Universitatis Tartuensis*. Issue No. 831. Tartu, 1988, pp. 52–58.

Heart Sūtra of Transcending Awareness, written in 1989.
First published in Estonian as the introduction to the Estonian translation of the *Prajñāpāramitāhṛdayasūtra*: Ületava mõistmise südasuutra. Sissejuhatavad märkused. – Ex Oriente. – *"Loomingu" Raamatukogu*. No. 16/17, 1989, pp. 8–12. Re-published in: *Nulli ja lõpmatuse kohal*, pp. 225–232.

Dialogue in the *Bodhicaryāvatāra*, written in 1984.
First published in Russian: Диалог в "Бодхичарьяватаре". – Sign System Studies. Vol. 17. – *Acta et Commentationes Uni-*

versitatis Tartuensis. Issue No. 641. Tartu, 1984, pp. 45–47. In Estonian: Dialoog "Bodhitšarjāvatāras". – *Nulli ja lõpmatuse kohal*, pp. 52–54.

The Light Path and the Dark Path, written in 1983.

First published in Russian: Светлый и тёмный путь. – Sign System Studies. Vol. 16. – *Acta et Commentationes Universitatis Tartuensis*. Issue No.635. Tartu, 1983, pp. 106–114. In Latvian: Gaišais un tumšais cels. – *Karogs*. No. 6, 1990, pp. 126–132. In Estonian: Hele tee ja tume tee. – *Nulli ja lõpmatuse kohal*, pp. 78–89.

The Course of Translation, written in 1981–85.

First published in Russian (shorter version): К пониманию "Дао-дэ-цзина". (Towards the Understanding of the *Daodejing*) – Oriental Studies. Vol. 6. – *Acta et Commentationes Universitatis Tartuensis*. Issue No. 558. Tartu, 1981, pp. 115–126. Full version was published in Estonian: Tõlkekulg. – Poeetilise teksti tüpoloogia, tõlke ja retseptsiooni probleeme. (On the Problems of Translation and Reception of the Poetical Texts) – *Acta et Commentationes Universitatis Tartuensis*. Issue No. 709. Tartu, 1985, pp. 43–60. Re-published in: *Nulli ja lõpmatuse kohal*, pp. 90–107.

Buddhist Mythology, written in 1975.

First published in Russian: Буддийская мифология. – *Мифы народов мира. Энциклопедия*. (*Encyclopaedia of the Myths*) Vol. 1. Moscow, 1980 (re-printed 1991), pp. 190–195. The same in Hungarian: Buddhista mitológia. – *Mitológiai enciklopédia.* Vol. 1. Budapest: Gondolat, 1988, pp. 383–408. In Estonian: Budistlik mütoloogia. – *Nulli ja lõpmatuse kohal*, pp. 175–188.

The Cultural Model of Tibet, written in 1984.

First published in Russian: Культурная модель Тибета. – *Атлас тибетской медицины*. (*Atlas of Tibetan Medicine*) Moskva: Galart, 1994 (re-printed 1998), pp. 5–14. In Estonian: Tiibeti kultuurimudel. – *Nulli ja lõpmatuse kohal*, pp. 153–168.

Once More about Yamāntaka, written in 1977.

First published in Russian: Ещё раз о Ямантаке. – Oriental Studies. Vol. 4. – *Acta et Commentationes Universitatis Tartuensis*.

Issue No. 455. Tartu, 1978, pp. 43–46. In Estonian: Veelkord Jamāntakast. – *Nulli ja lõpmatuse kohal*, pp. 169–171.

1, ∞ and 0 as Text Generators and States of Mind, written in 1988.

First published in Russian: 1, ∞ и 0 как генераторы текстов и как состояния сознания. – Sign System Studies. Vol. 23. – *Acta et Commentationes Universitatis Tartuensis*. Issue No. 855. Tartu, 1989, pp. 151–152. In Estonian: 1, ∞ ja 0 kui tekstigeneraatorid ja teadvuse seisundid. – *Nulli ja lõpmatuse kohal*, pp. 316–318.

Semiotics as a Possibility for the Study of Religious Texts Under Communist Dictatorship, written in 1999 for the report held in the international conference "The Academic Study of Religion During the Cold War. East and West", Brno, August, 1999.

First published in: The Academic Study of Religion During the Cold War. East and West. – *Toronto Studies in Religion*. Vol. 27. 2001, pp. 163–170.

The Concept of Humanistic Base Texts, written in 2000–2002.

Shorter version was first published in Estonian as a part of introductory essay of the new translation of the *Bhagavadgītā* into Estonian: "Gītā" kui humanistlik baastekst. ("Gītā" as a Humanistic Base Text) – *Bhagavadgītā*. Tartu: Biblio, 2000, pp. 5–16. Shorter version was published in English in: *Sign System Sudies*. Vol. 28, pp. 290–298. The present longer version was prepared for the lecture held in the Institute of Chinese Literature, Academia Sinica, Taiwan, in the February 2002. It was also presented in the international symposium "The Meaning of Religion for the Societies in the Past and Present Time", Tartu, November 2–3, 2001, and published in: *Forschungen zur Anthropologie und Religionsgeschichte*. B. 36. Münster: Ugarit-Verlag, 2003, pp. 137–153.

Index of Terms

Index of Names

Index of Titles